8.50

85-121

Reading and Writing Poetry:

Successful Approaches for the Student and Teacher

Reading and Writing Poetry:

Successful Approaches for the Student and Teacher

Edited by Charles R. Duke and Sally A. Jacobsen

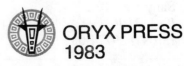
ORYX PRESS
1983

The rare Arabian Oryx is believed to have inspired the myth of the unicorn. This desert antelope became virtually extinct in the early 1960s. At that time several groups of international conservationists arranged to have 9 animals sent to the Phoenix Zoo to be the nucleus of a captive breeding herd. Today the Oryx population is nearing 300 and herds have been returned to reserves in Israel, Jordan, and Oman.

Copyright © 1983 by The Oryx Press
2214 North Central at Encanto
Phoenix, AZ 85004

Published simultaneously in Canada

Printed and Bound in the United States of America

Library of Congress Cataloging in Publication Data
Main entry under title:

Reading and writing poetry.

   Includes index.
   1. Poetry—Study and teaching (Secondary)—Addresses, essays, lectures. I. Duke, Charles R.   II. Jacobsen, Sally A.
PN1101.R38   808'.1'07'1273   82-12629
ISBN 0-89774-031-9

Table of Contents

RESOURCES   187

Index   261

Preface

Once, in a time best forgotten, many people thought that poetry could be found only in the graveyard, in the diary, or in the classroom. Since students seldom went to graveyards—certainly not to read epitaphs—and since the majority would not admit to keeping diaries, young people's main perceptions of poetry were shaped by experiences in the classroom. This could have been a good thing because, traditionally, English teachers probably read more poetry than any other form of literature in their training. Yet, aside from having poetry read to them in the early grades, and having an opportunity now and then to write some of their own rhymed verse, most students have spent little time considering with their teachers what poetry might be or could become.

For too long, far too many students have considered poetry as some kind of mysterious artifact, meant to be observed at a distance always, under the eye of a critical curator. But this distancing is contrary to all we now know about how readers develop a liking for various types of literature. Growth comes from direct engagement, not from any distancing of reader and text. We believe, therefore, that the teaching of poetry needs an expanded view which emphasizes student interaction with the text, as well as creation of new texts. In fact, we can say with assurance that there are no official entrances to or exits from the reading of, responding to, or writing of poetry; therefore, as teachers, we would do well to explore as many options as possible for promoting students' direct engagement with poetry if we want to make poetry a part of their lives.

Because we believe a need for broader perspectives on the teaching of poetry exists, we have put together this collection of essays from poets, teacher-poets, and regular classroom teachers to demonstrate the rich resources available for making poetry a more pleasant and meaningful experience for young readers.

The collection focuses on the needs of the young adult reader, because it is at this level that the resources seem to be most lacking. At the elementary school level, there often seems to be a rich environment for promoting active involvement with poetry. Oral reading of poems, acting out of poems, building poetry collections, talking with poets, and listening

...*try* and music—all happen on a regular basis. As a result, elementary p...ils tend to view poetry as a very natural part of their classroom experiences. Yet when the transitions to high school and college occur, students' pleasure and interest in poetry noticeably decline.

Current research on the reader's response to literature suggests one reason for this decline. Many times the reading of a text is oversimplified. For example, in *Literature and the Reader: Research in Response to Literature, Reading Interests and the Teaching of Literature* (Urbana, IL: National Council of Teachers of English, 1972), Alan Purves and Richard Beach show that readers are not only moved by what they read but also are changed, not just intellectually but in their attitudes as well. Purves and Beach believe that understanding and liking are associated and that readers tend to be more interested in content than form. Louise Rosenblatt in *Literature as Exploration* (New York: Noble and Noble, 1968) contends that a special transaction occurs between an individual and a text and that only through this transaction is the poem "produced"; the result of the transaction is dominated as much by the process of reading as by the text on the page. Norman Holland in *Poems as Persons* (New York: W.W. Norton, 1973) believes that poetry in particular depends heavily on what the reader brings subjectively to the reading process. These views suggest that responding to a poem is a multifaceted experience which calls for more exploration in the classroom.

As a guiding principle, then, for the selection of essays, we looked for ideas that stressed active response on the part of students and that demonstrated that engagement with poetry in the classroom can be a varied, pleasurable, intellectual experience. We have divided the collection into three sections to highlight the varied approaches and resources through which this active response and broadened perspective may be developed.

First, we have attempted to provide some perspectives on what poetry is and how it comes into existence. Such knowledge is imperative if we are to comprehend fully how poems begin and how poets view their work. To obtain such perspectives, we went to practicing poets and asked them to share some of their thoughts and feelings about poetry and the writing of it. We believe that this may be one of the first attempts to put teachers directly in touch with some of the leading poets of our time. The pieces in this section offer insights into the creative process which can be shared with students, helping to underscore how totally absorbed in the activity of making, of writing, are poets. Teachers also will find in these poets' accounts of their work ample reinforcement for stressing the value of poetry to their students.

But this is not simply a collection of poets talking about their craft. Although such conversations are useful as a starting point, there also has to be an emphasis upon classroom approaches which make poetry accessible to students. For this information, we went to classroom teachers who have been successful in engaging students directly with poetry, both as readers and as writers. The result is a potpourri of techniques and approaches: introducing language play to students; unlocking the meaning of poems; comprehending the significance of meter, rhythm, tone, voice and mood; and ways of creating poems.

Finally, we include a section on resources that go beyond the conventional materials usually found in the classroom: popular music; ethnic poetry; connections among art, film, and poetry; methods for publishing student poetry; and sources of poetry beyond the traditional literature anthology.

The ideas and approaches in all of these three sections are practical and classroom-oriented. Readers will quickly perceive that no single approach to the teaching of poetry is being advanced, only the idea that engagement with poetry should be an active, not passive, experience and that helping students to reach that goal should be the objective of all literature teachers. We hope only that *Reading and Writing Poetry: Successful Approaches for the Student and Teacher* will prove a useful resource and possibly even an inspiration that will lead its readers to approach the teaching of poetry with renewed interest, confidence, and enthusiasm.

Contributors

Robert A. Armour is a professor of English at Virginia Commonwealth University, Richmond, Virginia. He is the author of two books on film: *Fritz Lang* (Twayne, 1978) and *Film: A Resource Guide* (Greenwood Press, 1980). His essay for this collection was written while he was a Fulbright professor in Cairo, Egypt.

R.L. Barth teaches at Cincinnati Country Day School, Cincinnati, Ohio and has taught at St. Henry High School in Kentucky and at the University of Cincinnati and Northern Kentucky University. He has spent a year as Kentucky Poet in the Rural Libraries. Since starting his own small press in 1981, he has published *Looking for Peace* (1981), poems growing out of his Viet Nam experience; *To Be Plain* (1981), Raymond Oliver's translations of Greek, Latin, French, and German poetry; and Suzanne Doyle's *Sweeter for the Dark* (1982).

Marvin Bell teaches at the University of Iowa, Iowa City, Iowa, in the Writers' Workshop. He has published five books of poems with Atheneum: *A Probable Volume of Dreams* (1969), *The Escape into You* (1971), *Residue of Song* (1974), *Stars Which See, Stars Which Do Not See* (1979), and *These Green-Going-to-Yellow* (1981). Two books will appear in 1983: *Segues: A Correspondence in Poetry* (David R. Godine), a book of poems written back-and-forth by William Stafford and Marvin Bell; and *Old Snow Just Melting: Essays and Interviews* (University of Michigan Press, "Poets on Poetry" Series). He has received the Lamont Poetry Award. "To You Readers and Teachers of Poetry" appears by permission of the author. Copyright © 1981 by Marvin Bell.

Philip Billings teaches modern literature, composition, and creative writing at Lebanon Valley College, Annville, Pennsylvania. His poems have appeared in the magazines *Stone Country* and *The Windless Orchard*, and in the bibliography *Literature and Medicine* by Joanne Trautmann and Carol Pollard (Society for Health and Human Values, 1975). On a sabbatical in England in 1977, he wrote the first draft of a short novel, *Uncertain*

Harvest, for which he is now seeking a publisher. He enjoys visiting the Annville, Pennsylvania public schools to teach poetry writing.

Warren Carrier is Chancellor of the University of Wisconsin at Platteville, Wisconsin. He has held administrative posts at the University of Bridgeport, San Diego State and Rutgers Universities and has taught at the University of Montana and Portland State University. He is an editor of *Reading Modern Poetry: A Critical Anthology* (revised edition, Scott, Foresman, 1968) and the *NCTE Guide to World Literature* (National Council of Teachers of English, 1980) and (with Bonnie Neumann) of *Literature From the World* (Scribner's, 1981). His books of poems are *Toward Montebello* (Harper and Row, 1966), *Leave Your Sugar for the Cold Morning* (St. Andrews, 1977), and the just-completed *Visions and Losses* (not yet published). New Directions will publish his translations of Claudio Solar's poems, *The City Stopped in Time*.

Michael Cohen is Associate Professor of English at Murray State University, Murray, Kentucky. His interests, in addition to the pedagogy of poetry and composition, include relationships between poetry and painting, and topics in eighteenth century English literature. He is coauthor, with Robert E. Bourdette, Jr., of the forthcoming *The Poem in Question* (Harcourt Brace Jovanovich, Inc.).

Madeline DeFrees is Director of the Writing Program at the University of Massachusetts, Amherst, Massachusetts. Two books of poems published in 1978 are *When the Sky Lets Go* (G. Braziller) and a chapbook, *Imaginary Ancestors* (Smokeroot Press). She has taught at the University of Victoria, British Columbia, the Universities of Montana and Washington, Seattle University, and Holy Names College. For 30 years she was known as Sister Mary Gilbert and published under that name; titles from this period include *From the Dark Room* (Bobbs-Merrill, 1964) and two autobiographical accounts of convent life and work for the order: *Springs of Silence* (Prentice-Hall, 1953) and *Later Thoughts from the Springs of Silence* (Bobbs-Merrill, 1962). She spent 1981–1982 on a Guggenheim Fellowship, writing poetry in Cannon Beach, Oregon.

Thomas G. Devine is a professor in the Reading and Language Center at the University of Lowell, Lowell, Massachusetts. He has taught poetry at all grade levels, from middle grades through graduate school. He has edited three secondary school literature anthologies and written two college textbooks on the teaching of reading and more than 60 articles on teaching language and literature. His most recent book is *Teaching Study Skills: A Guide for Teachers* (Allyn and Bacon, 1981). "Poetry in the English Class" is reprinted here from *Connecticut English Journal* (Spring 1979) by the author's permission.

Suzanne J. Doyle has had a volume of her poems, *Sweeter for the Dark* (R.L. Barth Publisher, 1982), published and has had poems and reviews appear in *The Southern Review, Greensboro Review, The Compass,* and *Gramercy Review*. She has been a participant in the Bread Loaf Writers' Conference and a member of its administrative staff. She has taught English at the secondary level in California and is presently employed there as a technical writer for a microcomputer firm.

Charles R. Duke is Professor of English and Director of Freshman Composition and Lower Division Studies at Murray State University, Murray, Kentucky. Formerly a high school English teacher and department chairperson, he teaches undergraduate and graduate English methods courses in writing and adolescent literature. He is the author of three books on the teaching of English—*Creative Dramatics and English Teaching* (NCTE, 1973), *Teaching Fundamental English Today* (J. Weston Walch, 1976), and *Teaching Literature Today* (J. Weston Walch, 1979)—and over 50 articles on the teaching of literature and writing. He has worked closely with student poets in various schools, is an active supporter of the poets-in-the-schools programs, and has edited collections of student poetry. "Language Play and the Teaching of Poetry" is reprinted here from *Indiana English* (November 1979) by the author's permission, and an edited version of "Selecting Poetry: Resources," which originally appeared in the *Connecticut English Journal* (Spring 1979), is included by the author's permission.

Rose M. Feinberg is a former Director of Language Arts and Reading for the Lunenberg, Massachusetts Public School System. She has presented poetry theater at various professional conferences. She has written a number of articles relating to dramatics and writing and has produced materials in all areas of language arts.

Jim Heynen is Distinguished Writer in Residence at the University of Idaho, Moscow, Idaho. His most recent collection of poetry is *A Suitable Church* (Copper Canyon Press, 1981); earlier volumes are *How the Snow Became a Goddess* (Confluence Press, 1977) and *Notes from Custer* (Bear Claw Press, 1976), which grew out of his translations of Sioux songs (he was born in Sioux Center, Iowa). His poems have appeared in such anthologies as *A Geography of Poets* (Bantam, 1979). A collection of his tales is *A Man Who Kept Cigars in His Cap* (Graywolf Press, 1979). In the mid-1970s, he coordinated the Idaho Artists-in-the-Schools program.

Patricia Holler is a teacher of English at Lone Oak High School, Paducah, Kentucky. She has had numerous poems and short stories published in the magazine *Square Pegs and Round Holes*. An avid music listener, she has also composed a number of song lyrics.

Jeffrey F. Huntsman teaches Native American Literature and English at Indiana University, Bloomington, Indiana. He has published widely on the teaching of Native American literature, most recently an article in the Native American issue of *Shantih* (1980) and an introduction to *New Native American Drama: Three Plays by Hanay Geiogamah* (University of Oklahoma Press, 1980). His "Caveat Editor: Chaucer and Medieval English Dictionaries" appeared in *Modern Philology* (vol. 73); his is currently editing the forthcoming *Dictionary of Native American Literature* (Greenwood Press). "Teaching Native American Poetry" appears by permission of the author. Copyright © 1981 by Jeffrey F. Huntsman.

Sally A. Jacobsen teaches English at Northern Kentucky University, Highland Heights, Kentucky and has taught at the University of Massachusetts at Boston, MIT, and the University of Wisconsin at Platteville and in the public schools in Monon, Indiana and Beaverton, Oregon. Her poetry reviews have appeared in the Corvallis, Oregon *Gazette-Times* from 1971–1973; and she has published articles in *Insofarforth: Functions of Discourse in Science and Literature* (Michigan State University Honors College, 1979) and in the New England Association of Teachers of English *Newsletter*. She began teaching Black poetry in 1975 to preparatory writing classes at Portland State University.

X. J. Kennedy is the editor of the widely used anthologies *An Introduction to Poetry* and *Literature: An Introduction to Fiction, Poetry, and Drama* (both Little-Brown, 1978 and 1979). Collections of his own poems include *Breaking and Entering* (Oxford, 1971), which contains, besides newer poems, several from *Growing Into Love* (Doubleday, 1969), the long poem *Bulsh* (Burning Deck, 1970), and poems from *Nude Descending a Staircase* (Doubleday, 1961), which won the Lamont Poetry Award. Poetry books for children are *The Phantom Ice Cream Man* (Atheneum, 1979) and *One Winter's Night in August* (Atheneum, 1975).

Philip Levine won the American Book and National Book Critics' Circle awards for *7 Years From Somewhere* and *Ashes: Poems Old and New* (both Atheneum, 1979). His latest book of poems is *One for the Rose* (Atheneum, 1982); a book of interviews is *Don't Ask* (University of Michigan Press, 1981). He teaches at Tufts University, Medford, Massachusetts and has taught at Columbia University and California State University at Fresno. He spent 1965–66 and 1968–69 writing in Spain; *Not This Pig* (Wesleyan University, 1968) and *The Names of the Lost* (Windhover, 1976) include Spanish Civil War themes. *They Feed They Lion* (Atheneum, 1972) portrays his solidarity with the oppressed.

Tom Liner is a poet and teacher with 16 years of experience in public schools. He is presently teaching at the Model Lab School at Eastern Kentucky University, Richmond, Kentucky; he edits *The Moonshine Review* and is the coauthor with Dan Kirby of *Inside Out: Developmental Strategies for Teaching Writing* (Boynton/Cook, 1981).

Harry MacCormack teaches playwriting at Oregon State University, Corvallis, Oregon. *The Revolving Door* (Pegastian Press, 1969) reflects his S.D.S. background and *Kachina* (Joint House Publishers, 1971), family themes. *The Displaced Warrior* cycle was produced in quadrasonic sound in 1973 (KPFA, Los Angeles). For 10 years he has experimented with dairying at Sunbow Farm, Corvallis and has written *The Soy Dairy, A Way to Save the Small Farm* (Sunbow Publishing, 1982). Current poems, *In the Absence of Blood/12 Moons,* will be published in German (Ogham Verlag, 1983); an English translation will be forthcoming. Judy Felt has recorded two of his songs. He plans in the future to incorporate rhythmic electronic techniques in ritual theater pieces.

Ron McFarland has taught seventeenth century and modern poetry and poetry writing at the University of Idaho, Moscow, Idaho since 1970; he serves as editor of *Snapdragon* and as general editor of *The Slackwater Review*. Among his publications are a chapbook of poems, *Certain Women* (Confluence Press, 1977), and an edited anthology, *Eight Idaho Poets* (University Press of Idaho, 1979).

James S. Mullican is a professor of English and the Director of English Education at Indiana State University, Terre Haute, Indiana. He taught high school English for nine years and has been a university supervisor of student teachers for 15 years. He is a former editor of the *Indiana English Journal* and is the author of more than 40 reviews and articles, including essays on poetry and the teaching of poetry.

Donald M. Murray is the winner of a Pulitzer prize for journalism. He is presently a professor of English at the University of New Hampshire, Durham, New Hampshire, where he teaches courses in creative writing. He is the author of *A Writer Teaches Writing* (Houghton-Mifflin, 1968), as well as numerous articles for professional journals on the teaching of writing; he has also published poetry in various publications. "Listening to Writing" is reprinted here from *Composition and Teaching* (December 1980) by permission.

Marie Wilson Nelson teaches at George Mason University, Fairfax, Virginia and conducts research into how writers teach writing. A poet who sees herself as a teacher, her poetry has appeared in *The Moonshine Review* and her articles in *English Journal, Research in Composition Newsletter,* and *Georgia English Counselor*.

Marge Piercy lives in Wellfleet, Massachusetts on Cape Cod, an experience reflected in poems in *Living in the Open* (Knopf, 1976) and *Twelve-Spoked Wheel Flashing* (Knopf, 1978). *The Moon Is Always Female* (Knopf, 1980), like these, includes poems about love and writing and reflects her work for the women's movement, as does *To Be of Use* (Doubleday, 1973). *Selected Poems: Circles on the Water* (Knopf) and *Parti-Colored Blocks for a Quilt* (in the University of Michigan's "Poets on Poetry" series) appeared in 1982. She has published three other books of poems, a play, and seven novels, most recently *Vida* and *Braided Lives* (both Summit, 1980 and 1982). "Inviting the Muse" appears by permission of the author. Copyright © 1981 by Marge Piercy.

Joseph E. Price teaches courses such as Literature and Medicine and Language and Culture at Northern Kentucky University, Highland Heights, Kentucky, where he has also held various offices in the central administration. He is completing a book on the influence of prosody on the structure of the grammar of *Beowulf*. He is interested in computer-assisted instruction and assists faculty in using computer programs for text editing.

Raymond J. Rodrigues is a former teacher of creative writing in high schools in Nevada and New Mexico. His poetry has been published in *Poet Lore* and *Anthologist*. He has been an author/editor of seven high school anthologies and author of a literature methods book, *A Guidebook for Teaching Literature* (Allyn and Bacon, 1978). He has taught literature and writing methods courses at the university level and occasionally teaches poetry workshops for elementary and junior high school students.

David C. Schiller teaches courses in literature and writing at Princeton High School, Cincinnati, Ohio. "Testing an Understanding of Poetry" is reprinted here from *Exercise Exchange* (Fall 1979) by permission. Copyright © 1979 by *Exercise Exchange*.

Diane P. Shugert teaches English at Central Connecticut State College, New Britain, Connecticut. She is the author of articles on adolescent literature and has served as coordinator of a poets-in-the-schools program funded by the Connecticut Commission on the Arts and the National Endowment for the Arts. She has also presented poetry workshops for professional organizations. "Poetry Readers: Publishing Student Writing" is reprinted here from *Connecticut English Journal* (Spring 1979) by the author's permission.

R. Baird Shuman is Professor of English, Director of the Rhetoric Program, and Director of English Education at the University of Illinois, Urbana, Illinois. He has frequently served as a poet-in-the-schools and is himself a poet. Among the 14 books he has written or edited are *Nine Black Poets* (Moore Publishing Company, 1968) and *A Galaxy of Black Writing* (Moore Publishing Company, 1970). He also serves as executive editor of *The Clearing House* and is a consulting editor for *Poet Lore, The Journal of Aesthetic Education,* and *Cygnus*.

Anna Lee Stensland is a professor of English at the University of Minnesota, Duluth, Minnesota. She teaches courses in English methods, adolescent literature, images of women in literature, and teaching reading in the junior and senior high school. She is the author of *Literature by and about the American Indian: An Annotated Bibliography* (National Council of Teachers of English, 1979). She has written numerous articles on Native American Literature and the teaching of it and did her doctoral research on the teaching of poetry.

David Sudol teaches English at Lincoln High School, Des Moines, Iowa, where he is responsible for upper-level expository writing classes and a sophomore English survey that includes a three-week poetry unit. He has contributed articles to professional journals and has written a collection of children's verse entitled *To an Ocean in Iowa Went a Whale on Vacation* (Featherstone Press, n.d.). "On Teaching Narrative Poetry: My Collective Ballad Bard" is reprinted here from *English Journal* (October 1980) by permission of the author and The National Council of Teachers of English. Copyright © 1980 by the National Council of Teachers of English.

Helen J. Throckmorton serves as Professor of English and English Education Coordinator at Wichita State University, Wichita, Kansas, where she teaches beginning and advanced courses in writing and English methods and supervises student teachers. Her current interest in poetry lies in teaching what poetry is, what poets do, how, and with what effect. She is the coauthor with Nancy C. Millett of *How to Read a Poem* (Ginn, 1966). "Language Can Do What We Want It To Do" is reprinted here from *Exercise Exchange* (Fall 1980) by permission. Copyright © 1980 by *Exercise Exchange*.

Diane Wakoski has published 31 books of poems, recently *Cap of Darkness* (Black Sparrow, 1980), *Trophies* (Black Sparrow, 1979), *The Man Who Shook Hands* (Doubleday, 1978), *Waiting for the King of Spain* (Black Sparrow, 1976), and *Virtuoso Literature for Two and Four Hands* (Doubleday, 1975). *Smudging* (Black Sparrow), often reprinted, appeared in 1972, *Motorcycle Betrayal Poems* (Simon & Schuster) in 1971, and *Inside the Blood Factory* (Doubleday) in 1968. Earlier work is collected in *Trilogy* (Doubleday, 1974). Her critical prose is collected in *Toward a New Poetry* (University of Michigan Press, "Poets on Poetry" Series, 1979). She teaches at Michigan State University in East Lansing, Michigan. "Color Is a Poet's Tool" appears by permission of the author. Copyright © 1981 by Diane Wakoski.

Ingrid Wendt received an M.F.A. in writing from the University of Oregon, Eugene, Oregon, where she was managing editor of the *Northwest Review* and received the Neuberger Award for poetry. Over 50 of her poems have appeared in journals such as *Greenfield Review, Feminist Studies,* and in anthologies, including *No More Masks* (Doubleday, 1973). A collection of her poems, *Moving the House,* with a foreword by William Stafford, was published by BOA Editions, 1980, and she is the coauthor of *In Her Own Image: Women Working in the Arts* (McGraw-Hill and The Feminist Press, 1980). Currently she is a writer-in-residence in 30 Eugene, Oregon elementary schools, under the sponsorship of the Oregon Arts Foundation's Poets-in-the-Schools program.

Denny T. Wolfe, Jr. has been a high school English teacher, a state director of English and foreign language instruction in North Carolina, and a university teacher and administrator at Old Dominion University, Norfolk, Virginia. He has contributed more than 50 articles to professional journals and books. He teaches a methods course in poetry for classroom teachers and serves as the director of the Tidewater Virginia Writing Project, a part of the National Writing Project.

Reading and Writing Poetry:

Successful Approaches for the Student and Teacher

PERSPECTIVES

Introduction

The poem on the page—where did it come from? How did it begin? Students and teachers approaching the reading, writing, and studying of poetry often fail to comprehend what lies behind the words that suggest a poem on the printed page. It is what happens between the creation and product that needs to be grasped if what is read is to be appreciated. We need a clearer understanding of the process that leads to the expression of an idea or feeling in a poem. As X. J. Kennedy says,

> Students need to take a longer view of life, need to perceive there is common sense in preparing themselves for the unexpected. To cope with a switch of careers, or to accept an unforeseen opportunity, they need general and basic language skills. Far more useful than acquiring a corpus of technical information is building a sensitivity to words. Here is where poetry offers rewards.

The poets in this section mention a variety of sources and feelings for their poetry. Not surprisingly, each agrees that poems tend to grow from one's experiences and the perspectives that one develops about those experiences. A poem actually may start anywhere; for Marge Piercy, it might begin in the middle of reading *Natural History* magazine or the *Farmer's Almanac;* for Marvin Bell, a poem may be started by a visit to a certain place, such as the home of Emily Dickinson. Madeline DeFrees finds herself influenced by the rhythms of nature, especially those of the ocean. Diane Wakoski often finds her stimulus through color; Warren Carrier discovers a poem in a photograph. The sources of poetry are infinite.

But not everyone seems able to take advantage always of the rich source material that exists. Marge Piercy suggests that the poet has to learn "how to flow, how to push oneself, how to reach that cone of concentration . . . when the voices in the head are one voice." And Marvin Bell indicates that "writing poetry is not a way of saying only what one already has the words for, but a way of saying what one didn't know one knew." Madeline DeFrees' comparison of her own tumultuous writing process with that of a controlled "inland" poet typifies the juggling act often performed by poets as they try to bring experience and feeling together.

How does one actually write a poem? There is some similarity among the poets in this section on their perspectives toward the act of writing, although the particular rituals to get through "hard places" and the specific strategies for shaping ideas may vary. Some poems come quickly, a rush of words and emotion leading to expression; others seem to incubate for varying periods of time, sometimes becoming partially expressed only to stop short until some idea or incident triggers a return to the draft and completion.

It is understandable, therefore, that most poems do not come out the first time in a clear, organized fashion. Frequently the poet is on a voyage of discovery and does not know until near the end of the voyage what form the final version will take. Often a poem may start out in one direction or form and finish in a completely different form and location. In between, a considerable amount of shifting of words, of phrases, of whole sections may occur, suggesting that poets often engage in as much revision as many prose writers do.

But what are the implications for teaching that may be drawn from these poets' perspectives on poetry? Aside from endorsing the obvious— students should read as much poetry as possible—all the poets believe strongly in the benefits of having students and teachers attempt to write poetry. The writing may not always be successful. Philip Levine, for example, says, "I'm never brutal with people who don't have talent. It seems to me utterly pointless. You are brutal only with people who need it. I don't encourage or discourage them, but I am tough on people who can bear it. The better they are, the tougher you are." Still, Donald M. Murray, for one, believes strongly that students need to engage in the writing process to help destroy many of the myths that surround poetry. He suggests that

> Too often when we teach writing, we give our students the misconception we plan writing, that we intend what will appear on the page. They are frustrated when they are not able to visualize before the first draft what will appear on their page. The students think they are dumb. We must be honest and let them know how much writing is unconscious or accidental. You do not think writing; you write writing.

Successful writing takes serious commitment. To demonstrate that commitment, Marie Wilson Nelson shares drafts of her poetry with students, showing them how a poem grows through multiple drafts, and suggesting that students, too, will need to pursue their ideas in a similar way. Philip Billings suggests that beginning poets need to "have the courage of their obsessions. They will want to write about their convictions, instead. They'll want to say Uncle Ray was sweet; don't let them. Get them to tell you about the pungent odor from some kind of plant that always makes them remember Uncle Ray's backyard.''

The goal is not necessarily to produce superior poets; in fact, often the results of students' first attempts will be anything but superior poetry. However, the experience of having wrestled with some of the same problems as these poets have will tend to make students more appreciative readers of poetry and more sensitive to what good poets can accomplish.

The Usefulness of Poetry

by X. J. Kennedy

Of what practical use is the study of poetry? Students will rarely come right out and ask you, but they'll want to know. The question is worth raising in class, and in the following notes I should like to suggest two ways to answer it.

Students are aware—overly aware, maybe—that their studies are supposed to lead to career goals. In the minds of many, a young person puts in time, like a coin in a slot, and eventually receives a gold-edged degree or diploma, exchangeable for a safe and happy future in some career. It is well to throw a little cold sleet on this assumption. Ellen Goodman, one of my favorite newspaper columnists, lately provided some in a piece called "Steering Clear of the One True Course." Goodman's point was that students don't *know* for sure the course of their future lives and seldom end up in the professions to which they first aspire. The U.S. Department of Labor has estimated that the average person, in the course of a working life, changes jobs or professions at least four times. Lately, at the University of Vermont, I heard a guidance man report a survey of the school's English majors of 20 years ago. Few were doing what might have been expected of them. Some, to be sure, had entered the professions of words—as writers and teachers. But one former student of Milton had turned out to be an airline pilot. Another was now the proprietor of a pet shop, while still another had ended up as a vice-president of the Chase Bank. Had they known that they would reach these startling destinations, the students would have been wise, I suspect, to study English anyway.

Students need to take a longer view of life, need to perceive that there is common sense in preparing themselves for the unexpected. To cope with a switch of careers, or to accept an unforeseen opportunity, they need general and basic language skills. Far more useful than acquiring a corpus of technical information is building a sensitivity to words. Here is where poetry offers rewards.

It would be folly to estimate the value of poetry in dollar signs, but in truth, there are quite tangible benefits that poetry imparts. People, one crusty old IBM executive once remarked, don't usually fail in business because they don't know their jobs; they fail or have to be dismissed because they can't understand other people. Unable to imagine themselves inside the skin of a co-worker or a customer, they make bad decisions and arouse resentment. Poetry helps us travel beyond ourselves. Poems can help Whites glimpse what it is like to be Black, and the other way around. For any White venturing forth into the world at large, I should think a familiarity with the poems of Langston Hughes, Amiri Baraka, Gwendolyn Brooks, and Sterling A. Brown indispensable. Poems show a man how a woman thinks, and vice versa. While not sure I understand women completely, I thank the poems of Adrienne Rich, Anne Sexton, and Emily Dickinson for helping me to glimmers of comprehension. For the city dweller, poetry affords insight into the mind of someone from the country or a small town. It enables the young to see through the eyes of the old. In "Sailing to Byzantium," Yeats conveys his sense of being an aged scarecrow, with flesh and faculties falling away, and a fierce desire in his heart for immortality. Poems of such caliber expand both our minds and our sympathies.

In another obvious way, poems have practical usefulness. As Mark Twain said, the difference between the right word and the almost right word is like the difference between the lightning and the lightning bug. And that is what poems make us sense: the choice of words that will make our explanations and our arguments memorable. The ability to write and speak is perhaps the most valuable of safety nets in the student's future tightrope-walk through life. To read a few poems and to learn them by heart will do more, I suspect, than many hours of workbook drill and vocabulary memorization.

Inviting the Muse*

by Marge Piercy

Here is Henry Thoreau from his journal for October 26, 1853, although he is talking about spring. "That afternoon the dream of the toads rang through the elms by Little River and affected the thoughts of men, though they were not conscious that they heard it. How watchful we must be to keep the crystal well that we are made, clear!"

Writing poems can be divided crudely into three kinds of labor: beginning and getting well and hard into it; pushing through inner barriers and finding the correct form; drawing back and judging what you have done and what is still to be done or redone. This essay is about the first stage, learning how to flow, how to push yourself, how to reach that cone of concentration I experience at its best as a tower of light, when all the voices in the head are one voice.

I do not know how to teach that, although concentration can be learned and worked on the same as flattening stomach muscles or swimming farther. You could perhaps set someone to studying a rock or a leaf or a bird—perhaps a warbler. Nothing requires more concentration than trying to observe a warbler up in the leafy maze of a summer tree. If I were really and truly teaching poetry, I would probably drive everybody crazy by sending them off to notice the shades of sand on a beach.

Of course observation isn't concentration, but learning to do one brings on the ability to do the other. My mother taught me to observe. A woman who had not been allowed to finish the tenth grade, she had some extraordinary ideas about how to raise very young children. Later when I was grown out of dependency and highly imperfect, she had trouble with me and could not endure my puberty. However, when I was little enough to fit comfortably into her arms and lap, we played unusual games. She had contempt for people who did not observe, who did not notice, and she would require me to remember the houses we passed going to the store or play mental hide and seek in other people's houses that we had visited. We would give each other three random objects or words to make stories around. We would try to guess the stories of people we saw on the bus and would argue to prove or disprove each other's theories.

I suppose such training might have produced what she wanted, a sharply observant person like herself, a reporter's mentality, a little Sherlock Holmes in Shirley Temple guise. What it produced in me was observation suffused with imagination, since our life was on the whole skimpy, hard, surrounded by violence outdoors and containing familial violence within, a typical patriarchal working-class family in inner-city Detroit. Blacks and whites fought; the Polish and Blacks who lived across Tireman (a street) fought the Irish who went to parochial school. The neighborhood offered the kind of stable family life that writers like Christopher Lasch, beating the dolly of the new narcissism, love to harken back to. Although husbands sometimes took off and not infrequently had girlfriends on the side, women almost never walked out of their homes. Wife beating was common, child beating just as common; drunkenness, drug abuse, rape, and molestation of children occurred on every block, but families went on from generation to generation. In such a neighborhood where the whites comprised Polish, Irish, a few Italian and German Catholics, some remaining WASPS and some newly arrived Appalachian families (I divide the Appalachian Wasps from the others because they were often Celts, and because they were looked down on by everybody as hillbillies and provided some of my closest friends), being a Jew was walking around with a kick-me sign. I'd say the level of tolerance for lesbians was higher than that for Jews. You learn to observe street action and people's muscular tensions and involuntary tics rather closely.

Detroit sprawls there, willfully ugly mile after flat smoggy mile; yet what saves it are trees. Every abandoned vacant lot becomes a jungle in a couple of years. Our tiny backyard was rampant with tomatoes, beans, herbs, lettuce, onions, swiss chard. One of the earliest poems I wrote and still like is subtly about sex and overtly about peonies. Pansies, iris, mock orange, wisteria, hollyhocks along the alley fence, black-eyed susans, golden-glow whose stems were red with spider mites, golden chrysanthemums, a lilac bush by the compost pile. Nothing to me will ever be more beautiful than the flowers in that yard, except my mother when I was young.

You learn to sink roots into your childhood and feed on it, twist it, wring it, use it again and again. Sometimes one daub of childhood mud can set a whole poem right or save a character. It's not always a matter of writing about your family, although at times we will do that. You use your childhood again and again in poems about totally other things. For one thing, you learn how to use that rush of energy and how to make sure your use transcends the often trivial and ludicrous associations you are touching and drawing power from.

Some poets get going, get the flow by reading other poets. You learn whose writing moves you to your own, whether it's Whitman or the King James version of the Bible or Rukeyser or Neruda in Spanish or in translation. Actually I've never met anyone who got themselves going by reading poetry in any other language than the one they were working in, but I'm curious if anybody does. On the other hand, I have met a number of poets who use work in translation to prime themselves. It is a priming act we're talking about. You get the words and rhythms going through you and you begin to align yourself. It has disadvantages, of course; if you are the least impressionable you may produce involuntary pastiche. You may find yourself churning out imagery that is bookishly exotic, imagery culled from others and bearing the imprint of being on loan like clothes that fit badly. Some poets intentionally use poetry of another time to prime themselves, to minimize the unintentional fertilization.

This priming can happen by accident. Often times I am reading poetry and suddenly a poem starts, that change in the brain, maybe words, maybe an image, maybe an idea. It need not even be poetry. That quotation from Thoreau that begins this essay instigated a poem called "Toad dreams." I remember starting a poem in the middle of reading a *Natural History* magazine or the *Farmer's Almanac*.

I think of that instigation as having a peculiar radiance; that is, the idea, the image, the rhythm, the phrase—radiates. I find myself wanting to attend to it. I may not know at once; often I may not find out for several drafts, what that meaning, that implication, that web of associations and train of utterances will be or even in what direction it is leading me. Sometimes the original moment radiates in many directions and my problem is sorting out the direction to pursue first or exclusively.

At that point, if concentration is not forthcoming, the whole possibility may be blown. If you can lose a novel by talking it out, you can easily destroy a poem by not paying attention. I have lost many poems that way; I must lose one a week because I can't get to a typewriter or even to a piece of paper fast enough—sometimes can't break through to silence, to solitude, to a closed door. I am not good at working at the cafe tables, as Sartre was supposed to do, although I have written on planes often enough. Even then I work only when I have a bit of space—never while wedged in the middle seat. I need at least seat between me and any other person to work on a plane. At home, I need a closed door.

Poems can be aborted by answering the phone at the wrong moment. They can be aborted when an alien rhythm forces itself in or the wrong other words are juxtaposed. I cannot work with a radio on loud enough to hear the words, or a television, or music with words playing. I have trouble working at all with music on, for the rhythms are much too insistent. I know other writers who work to music, but I cannot do so. Rhythm is extremely important to me in building the line and the poem; any other insistent rhythm interferes. Irregular rhythms—hammering on a construction site nearby—have little effect.

I had a friend in Brooklyn who used to work with wax plugs in her ears, but I find that difficult. I talk my poems aloud and my voice roaring in my head gives me a headache. However, I pass on this method as it may do the trick for you. I know another writer who uses a white noise machine— usually purchased to help you sleep. I used to run an air conditioner to screen the noises from outside the apartment, when it seemed to me that every window opening onto the center of our block in Adelphi had a radio or a TV or both turned to top decibel.

Often I begin a poem simply by paying attention to myself, by finding what is stirring in there. I need a quiet moment. I try to use the routine of waking to bring me to work, whether into a novel I am working on or into poetry. I work best in the morning, although I started out believing myself to be a night person. I changed over during the 60s when the one quiet time I was assured of was before the rest of the anti-war movement in New York was awake. I learned to get out of bed and to use waking to move toward work.

Without the pressure on me now to work before friends are stirring, I get up more leisurely but I use the time. I always do some exercises in the morning and I take a morning bath. All of that routine I use to become thoroughly awake but retain some of the connectedness, some of the rich associativeness, of dreaming sleep. I don't want to shed that dark energy of dreams, not lose that concentration and involvement in the clutter of the day. I don't think of it quite as self-involvement. I remember when a relationship that had been part of my life for 17 years was breaking up, I would wake very early after three or four hours sleep and lie in anxiety and pain. Nonetheless by the time I rose through my morning schedule, when I came to the typewriter, I was clear of my immediate anguish and fussing and ready to turn them into work or to write about something entirely different.

I am not saying every writer should get up, eat a good breakfast, take a hot bath and do exercises without talking much to anyone, and then she will write richly. I am trying to say that you must learn how to prepare in a daily way for the combination of concentration and receptivity, a clearing which is also going down into yourself and also putting antennae out. One thing I can not do and work well is worry about something in my life. If I sit at the typewriter fussing about where the money to pay the real estate taxes is coming from or whether my lover loves me more or less today, whether I am spending too much money on oil this winter, whether the decision taken at the MORAL meeting was correct, I will not find my concentration. I can carry emotions to my typewriter but I must be ready to use and transmute them. They must already be a little apart. It is not exactly "emotion recollected in tranquility" I mean, although for 25 years I have contemplated that phrase with increasing respect. I often feel the emotion but with less ego, less anxiety than in ordinary life. The emotion is becoming energy, the pain, the regret, the anger, the pleasure. I suppose whenever I find my life too much more fascinating than work, I work less and less well. I certainly write fiction poorly in these stretches. I produce some poems, often decent ones, but my output is down.

Such periods are not frequent because I love to write more than almost anything—not essays, to be honest, but poems and novels. I am still writing in letters to friends this week that I am immensely relieved that I have finally shipped off my novel *Braided Lives* in its last draft to my publisher. I do, in fact, feel as if an elephant had risen daintily from its perch on my chest and ambled away. Free, free at last, oh free! Of course it will return soon enough all pencilled over with the comments of some copy editor enamored of commas and semicolons. Comes back again as galleys. But essentially it is gone, finished.

Then yesterday afternoon Woody and I were chatting about the next novel I am planning to start when I finish the next volume of poetry. Say, December? It is June now. He made a suggestion as I was mulling over something about the novel and I fell on it immediately and began chewing it, worrying it. It was just right. In the evening in the car on the way to see a movie two towns away, we began chatting again about my next novel until I shrieked that we must stop it, because I can not get to it before December.

I try to put on with other writers how much I suffer at this excruciating martyrdom and all that posing we are expected to do, but the simple truth is I love to write and I think it an enormous con that I actually get paid for doing it. After all, I did it for 10 years without pay.

Find out when you work best and arrange the days that you have to write or the hours you have, to channel yourself into full concentration. If like Sylvia Plath you have only from four a.m. till the babies wake, if you have only from six a.m. till nine a.m. as I did in New York, if you have only weekends or only Sundays or only afternoons from three-thirty to five-thirty, you have to figure out the funnel that works for you: the set of habitual acts that shuts out distractions and ego noise, shuts out your household, your family, and brings you quickly to the state of prime concentration.

Whatever habits you develop as a writer, your ability to work can not depend on them. I went from writing late afternoons and evenings to writing mornings because that was the only time I could be sure of. I used to smoke all the time I wrote. I imagined I could not write without the smoke from a cigarette curling around me. Then my lungs gave out. I had to die or learn to live without smoking. Given that choice I abandoned smoking rather fast. I can't say my productivity was amazing the couple of years afterwards, but that was mostly because I had chronic bronchitis and it was a while before I was not sick at least 50 percent of the time with too high a fever to work. I have had to give up alcohol at times and to give up coffee, my keenest addiction of all, for periods, and work goes on whatever I am giving up, so long as I have enough strength to make it to the typewriter and sit there.

You can permit yourself any indulgence to get going, so long as you can have it—Cuban cigars, a toke of the best weed, Grandma Hogfat's Pismire Tea, a smelly old jacket—but you have to be able to figure out just what is ritual and what is necessity. I really need silence and to be let alone during the first draft. I like having a typewriter but can produce a first draft of poetry without it; I cannot write prose without a typewriter as I write too slowly by hand. My handwriting is barely legible to me. All the other props are ritual. I have my sacred rocks, my window of tree, my edge-notched card memory annex, my bird fetish necklace hanging over the typewriter, my Olympia standard powered by hand, my reference works on near-by shelves, my cats coming and going, my good coffee downstairs where I am forced to go and straighten my back on the hour as I should. But I have written in vastly less comfort and doubtless will do so again. Don't talk yourself into needing a cork-lined room, although if someone gives it to you, fine. Do ask the price.

For many years I felt an intense and negotiable gratitude to my second husband because, while I had supported myself from age 18 and was doing part-time jobs, at a certain point he offered me five years without having to work at shit jobs, to establish myself as a writer. I took the offer and by the end of five years was making a decent income—decent by my standards, compared to what I earned as part-time secretary, artist's model, telephone operator, store clerk and so on.

Not until I was looking at my own output over the years since I began writing poetry seriously and began my first (dreadful) novel at 15, did I ever realize that I was less productive during those years of being supported than before or since. Women have to be very cautious with gift horses. We feel guilty. Traditional roles press us back and down. When I stayed home I was a writer in my eyes but a housewife in the world's and largely in my husband's view. Why wasn't the floor polished? What had I been doing all day?

I began to write at a decent clip again not during two years of traditional wifehood in Brookline but in New York when I was passionately involved in the anti-war movement and working as an organizer at least six hours a day and sometimes twelve.

I am not saying we work best if we use up a lot of our lives doing other work. Some poets do; few prose writers do. It depends on the type of other work in part; I think the less that other work has to do with writing, with writers, with words, the better. I understand the temptation young writers have to take jobs associated with writing. Sometimes it's the only affirmation available to you that you are a writer in the often many years before publication certifies you to the people around you. I don't think I could have resisted writer's residencies if they had been available when I was un- or underpublished. In an ideal world for writers, we would be paid while apprenticing at some minimum wage and then be encouraged to do something entirely different, in work parties digging sewers or putting in gardens or taking care of the dying, at a reasonable wage.

What I am saying is that the choice may be offered to a woman to stay home (where it is much, much nicer than going out to a lousy job) and write because the amount she can earn as a part-time female worker is negligible from the viewpoint of a professional or skilled male wage earner. The offer can help but it also can hinder. You may find yourself doing a full-time job instead without pay and writing in the interstices—just as before except that you may have even less time that is really yours, and you have lost your independent base of income.

Similarly a job teaching can be wonderful because it answers the question, what do you do? If you get hired as a writer after you have published, say, five short stories, you have sudden legitimacy. If you started in workshops and got an MFA, you have more legitimacy. You have items to add to your resume. Of course once you have taken the teaching job, you may have little time to write, especially given the way the academic marketplace is a buyer's market and teaching loads are getting heavier. You're certified a writer, you deal professionally with literature and words, you make better money and are more respectable in middle class society, but you have less time and energy to put into your own writing than you would if you worked as a waiter or secretary.

Actually sitting and writing novel after novel before one gets accepted at last, the way fiction writers usually must do, actually working and working on poems till they're right when hardly anybody publishes them and when they do you're read by two librarians, three editors and six other poets, gives you little to put in your resumé. We all make it as we can, and I do a lot of gigs. Unless writers are of draftable age, we are seldom offered money to do something overtly bad like kill somebody or blow up hospitals or burn villages, seldom paid to invent nerve gases or program databases for the CIA. The jobs available to us range from the therapeutic to the mildly helpful to the pure bullshit to the menial and tedious; all of them sometimes prevent us from writing and sometimes enable us to write. Jobs that have nothing to do with writing often provide more stimulation to the gnome inside who starts poems than jobs that involve teaching writing or writing copy.

When I am trying to get going and find myself empty, often the problem is that I desire to write a poem rather than one specific poem. That is the case sometimes when I have been working eight hours a day finishing up a novel and have not had the time to write poems or the mental space that allows them to begin forming. That is when the writer's notebook or whatever equivalent you use (my own memory annex is on edge-notched cards) can, if it is well organized, disgorge those tidbits put in it. I think of those jottings as matches, the images, the poem ideas, the lines that wait resurrection. Often lines that were cut from other poems will in time serve as the instigation for their own proper home. For me the absolute best way to get going is to resort to my memory annex. That summons the Muse, my own muse for sure.

The notion of a muse is less archaic than a lot of vintage mythology because most poets have probably experienced being picked up by the nape of the neck, shaken, and dumped again miles from where their daily life or ordinary preoccupations could have been expected to bring them. *Duende*, Lorca called that possession. Poems that come down like Moses from the mountaintop, that bore their way through my mind, are not better or worse than poems I labor on for two days, two months, or 15 years. Nonetheless I always remember which ones arrived that way. Sometimes in writing I experience myself as other. Not in the sense of the "I" as social artifact, the other that strangers or intimates see, the mask the camera catches off guard. When we see ourselves videotaped, often we experience a sense of naked-ness and say, "so that is what I am really like," as if the exterior because we cannot see it is therefore the truth of our lives. Nor do I mean the artifact we construct, the "I" writers, perhaps more than most people, make up out of parts of themselves and parts of their books as camouflage and adver-tisement.

What I mean is simply that, in writing, the poet sometimes transcends the daily self into something clearer. I have often had the experience of looking up from the typewriter, the page, and feeling complete blankness about who I am—the minutia of my daily life, where I am, why. I have for a moment no sex, no history, no character. Past a certain point I will not hear the phone. I respect that self, that artisan who feels empty of personal concern even when dealing with the stuff of my intimate life. I guess the only times I ever am free of the buzz of self-concern and the sometimes interesting, often boring, reflection of consciousness on itself is during moments when I am writing and moments when I am making love. I overvalue both activities because of the refreshment of quieting the skull to pure attention.

That to me is ecstasy, rapture—being seized as if by a raptor, the eagle in "The Rose and the Eagle"—the loss of the buzz of ego in the intense and joyous contemplation of something, whether a lover, a sensation, the energy, the image, the artifact. The ability to move into the state I called concentration is a needful preliminary to, in the first and commonest case, the work that you gradually build or, in the second and rarer case, the visit from necessity, the poems that fall through you entire and burning like a meteorite.

In a society that values the ability to see visions, such as some of the Plains Indians did, many people will manage to crank out a few visions at least at critical moments in their lives; very few people will not manage a vision at least once. Some will become virtuosos of vision.

In a society where seeing visions is usually punished by imprisonment, torture with electroshock, heavy drugging that destroys coordination and shortens life expectancy, very few people will see visions. Some of those who do so occasionally will learn early on to keep their mouths shut, respect the visions, use them but keep quiet about seeing or hearing what other people say is not there. A few of my poems are founded in specific visions: "Curse of the earth magician on a metal land," which also was the seed of *Dance the Eagle to Sleep*; "The sun" from the tarot card sequence in "Laying down the tower," which was the seed of *Woman on the Edge of Time*.

That a poem is visionary in inception does not mean it comes entire. Actually writing a poem or any other artifact out of a vision is often a great deal of work. The hinge poem, for the month of Beth in "The Lunar Cycle," called "At the well," was a case in point. I first wrote a version of that experience in 1959 when it happened. Here I am finally being able to bring off the poem that is faithful to it in 1979.

To me, no particular value attaches to the genesis of a poem. I am not embarrassed by the sense I have at times of being a conduit through which a poem forces itself and I am not embarrassed by working as long as it takes to build a poem—in the case I just mentioned, 20 years. I write poems for specific occasions, viewing myself as a useful artisan. I have written poems for anti-war rallies, for women's day rallies, for rallies centering on the rights and abuses of mental institution inmates. I have written poems to raise money for the legal defense of political prisoners, for Inez Garcia who shot the man who raped her, for Shoshana Rihm-Pat Swinton who was for many years a political fugitive and finally acquitted of all charges. I wrote a poem for a poster to raise money for Transition House (a shelter for battered women) along with a beautiful graphic by Betsy Warrior, a warrior for women indeed. I wrote a poem to be presented to the Vietnamese delegation at Montreal during meetings with anti-war activists.

Some of those occasional poems (as some of the category that arrive like a fast train) are among my best poems; some are mediocre. Frequently I find the necessity to write a poem for a specific purpose or when an occasion focuses me; perhaps coalesces is a better verb. A charged rod enters the colloidal substance of my consciousness and particles begin to adhere. ''For Shoshana-Pat Swinton'' is a meditation on feeling oneself active in history that I consider a very strong poem, for instance. I was, of course, to deal with the figure of the political fugitive as a paradigm of certain women's experiences as well as a touchstone for our recent political history in *Vida*; that swirl of ideas and images was obviously rich for me. What doesn't touch you, you can't make poems of.

One last thing I have learned about starting a poem is that if you manage to write down a certain amount when you begin, and failing that, to memorize enough, you will not lose it. If you cannot memorize or scribble that essential sufficient fragment, the poem will dissolve. Sometimes a couple of lines are ample to preserve the impulse till you can give it your full attention. Often it is a started first draft, maybe what will become eventually the first third of the poem, that I carry to my typewriter. But if I can't memorize and record that seed, that match, the instigating factor, then I have lost that particular poem.

Good work habits are nothing more than habits that let you work, that encourage you to pay attention. Focus is most of it: to be fierce and pointed, so that everything else momentarily sloughs away.

To You Readers and Teachers of Poetry*

by Marvin Bell

Poetry is an emotional approach to thinking, a means to saying what one didn't know one knew, a trust in process. I write by maneuvering toward the sense I make. I begin with something that occurs to me (it may be an image or the start of a story, a scene, a piece of rhetoric attached to a scene, or something else; it may be a phrase or a sentence, one or two or three lines), something that intrigues or moves me and which does not yet make sense or seems partial. In other words, I write toward my ignorance, beginning with whatever surfaces and trusting my interest. I am intuitive while writing first drafts, analytical in revision. I don't plan as much as I recognize, follow, and connect. I think by increments. And I write when moved to: inspiration? need?

THE MYSTERY OF EMILY DICKINSON†

Sometimes the weather goes on for days
but you were different. You were divine.
While the others wrote more and longer,
you wrote much more and much shorter.
I held your white dress once: 12 buttons.
In the cupola, the wasps struck glass
as hard to escape as you hit your sound
again and again asking Welcome. No one.

Except for you, it were a trifle:
This morning, not much after dawn,
in level country, not New England's,
through leftovers of summer rain I

went out rag-tag to the curb, only
a sleepy householder at his routine
bending to trash, when a young girl
in a white dress your size passed,

so softly!, carrying her shoes. It must be
she surprised me—her barefoot quick-step
and the earliness of the hour, your dress—
or surely I'd have spoken of it sooner.
I should have called to her, but a neighbor
wore that look you see against happiness.
I won't say anything would have happened
unless there was time, and eternity's plenty.

About "The Mystery of Emily Dickinson"

Anyone who has seen a photo of Emily Dickinson (1830–1886), or read her poems, knows how easy it might have been to fall in love with her. She was a great and original American poet who wrote almost 1,800 poems—all of them short, most of them very short—but published only seven during her lifetime. She was delicate and private. As the years went by, she grew more and more reclusive and took to wearing only white.

Once, I wangled a private tour of the Dickinson home in Amherst, Massachusetts. There, I did what there was to do: I looked through the house, went up the front staircase and down the back one, climbed to the cupola where wasps were hitting the windows in the heat, and visited her bedroom (which was also her writing room). Suddenly, my host reached into the closet and brought forth one of the white dresses she had worn, which he let me hold. I sized her up. One way to measure was to count the buttons. Afterwards, there were family photo albums to view, and I picked a violet from the lawn before leaving.

Of course it's somewhat silly! *Of course* I was probably out to make the experience Important, though that is not usually my approach. *Of course* I hoped to manage a poem set at Emily's home.

(When the Emily Dickinson postage stamps appeared, perhaps four or five years earlier, I bought 100. I had thought to write 100 poems to her, each using one of her lines, and of course I would put a stamp on each. But I managed only one, an 18-line poem titled "Never Say Die," which appeared in a book titled *Residue of Song*.)

Home again in Iowa City, I wrote the first stanza of "The Mystery of Emily Dickinson." It took me a line and a half to get to E. D. It was an Iowa summer—hot for days. In contrast to the boring oppression of the heat, and the sameness of a routine life, I placed Emily Dickinson. I can't say that I thought this out and then wrote it. Rather, one of two things happened. The first possibility is that I wrote what engaged me (the endless weather, the sameness, the little joke in line one) and then sought to bend it to events (her life, my visit to her home). The other possibility is that I looked aside from what I most wanted to write about (the visit) so that I could sneak up on it with a viewpoint.

The first eight lines tell what I did there in her house and a few things about her. Having written them, I was stuck. There really wasn't any more to say about the visit. That one stanza sat around with other drafts of poems, odd lines and miscellaneous stanzas for months.

It was still summer, though, when I woke one morning at sun-up. It must have been about 5:30 a.m. My wife and two sons were visiting her parents on a farm in southern Illinois, and it was garbage day. I couldn't go back to sleep and decided to take the garbage cans to the curb. I put them out on a sidewalk still drying from a light rain, in that cool, crisp air one feels and smells at such times, not fully awake in it, when suddenly there appeared a young girl in a white dress, carrying her shoes, padding quickly past, hardly disturbing the air. I turned and went back inside, but I was not through with her.

Later that day, looking again at my one stanza about Emily Dickinson, to which there was nothing to add about Emily Dickinson, I knew I would have to go elsewhere in the poem to extend it. There was also, now, the sudden vision of the girl at an odd hour in an odd manner, and I connected the two. I knew that one was like the other, that my feelings toward one were based on my feelings toward the other. Surely, the white dress might have been the same dress!

From there on, it was easy. I was working with material I could apprehend in the presence of a clear emotion. The poem went down the page, describing the time and terrain, myself and the girl, my reticence and desire—whatever occurred to me with clarity, in order.

The final sentence in the poem employs one of Emily Dickinson's favorite words, "eternity." And of course the sentence is ambiguous. Does "eternity's plenty" mean "the plenty of eternity" or "eternity is plenty?" The former reading suggests that nothing could have happened except in an endless amount of time. But the latter reading suggests that there is always eternity and it will be plenty. I think Emily would have liked that ending and thought it doubly true.

I could play with many small discoveries that took up residence in this poem. E. D.'s "asking Welcome" in stanza one is answered by no one, while in stanza three I fail to call to the girl. I don't even speak of it right away. I am, like Emily, bent by public opinion and proper behavior, silent in public, expressive in private. Who is that young girl? What is Emily to me except she reappear?

Sometimes, poetry affords the poet permission. "The Mystery of Emily Dickinson" afforded me permission to feel something for that girl who carried her shoes past me on the wet sidewalk at dawn. The poem afforded me permission to take her seriously—as seriously as I take Emily Dickinson. It afforded me permission to counter the distance between us with song and idea. It afforded me the *freedom* to do all of this and more. In the end, poetry is rooted in freedom: the freedom to say anything and then to be responsible to it. What has one confessed? The answer is always there in the poem.

TO AN ADOLESCENT WEEPING WILLOW‡

I don't know what you think you're doing,
sweeping the ground. You
do it so easily, backhanded, forehanded.
You hardly bend. Really, you sway.
What can it mean
when a thing is so easy?

I threw dirt on my father's floor.
Not dirt, but a chopped green
dirt which picked up dirt.

I pushed the pushbroom.
I oiled the wooden floor of the store.

He bent over and lifted the coal
into the coalstove. With the back of the shovel
he came down on the rat just topping the bin
and into the fire.

What do you think? —Did he sway?
Did he kiss a rock for luck?
Did he soak up water
and climb into light and turn and turn?

Did he weep and weep in the yard?

Yes, I think he did. Yes,
now I think he did.

---

‡From *These Green-Going-to-Yellow*, by Marvin Bell, Atheneum Publishers, Copyright © 1981 by Marvin Bell.

So, Willow, you come sweep my floor.
I have no store.
I have a yard. A big yard.

I have a song to weep.
I have a cry.
You who rose up from the dirt,
because I put you there
and like to walk my head in under
your earliest feathery branches—
what can it mean
when a thing is so easy?

It means you are a boy.

About "To an Adolescent Weeping Willow"

My father was an immigrant from the Ukraine who supported us by means of a small five-and-ten in a small town on the south shore of eastern Long Island. At first, the store was heated by coal, and its basement inhabited by rats. I often swept up at closing time. I would scatter a green "something" on the wooden floor to help pick up dirt. Then I would push a wide broom down the aisles, trying not to sweep up customers. Afterwards, I would sprinkle the floor with linseed oil to keep it from drying out.

My father died while I was in my first year of graduate school. I had yet to begin to write poetry seriously. I had married young and would soon have a son. When the marriage ended, I would keep the baby.

Marrying changes your life a little, but having a child changes your life a lot and for good. You become conscious of the difference between the parent and the one who is dependent.

Over the years, I also became "the tree poet"—a title awarded to me by a radio interviewer who noticed that the five poems used during our conversation contained four trees: a mulberry, an elm, a gingko, and a pine. (I have also written about a wild cherry tree and, more recently, a downtown banyan tree in Honolulu. Of course, the trees serve subjects besides themselves.)

Poets are always looking into nature to see if it is a mirror. My poems have often made a distinction between what nature is and the uses we make of it. In "To an Adolescent Weeping Willow," I talk to a young willow in my backyard in Iowa. Like any weeping willow, it is graceful and sweeps the ground. I'm unwilling to let it go at that, and I ask it what it thinks it's doing and what it means when a thing is so easy.

When the question is first posed, there is no answer. If I had known the answer, there would have been no need for the poem. Instead, I associate the sweeping motions of the willow and the dirt in which it grows with my sweeping up in the store and the green "dirt" which was a part of it.

Having said that much, a difference arises. Poetry often develops out of a need (willingness?) to question what one has just said. My first sense of changing direction comes with a mention of my father's tasks—harder than my own.

Then I continue to challenge the willow. What do you think, I ask it, Did my father live like you? Did he do what you do? Yes, now I think he did. Now that I am myself his age and a parent, I more fully comprehend his life.

But what *does* it mean when a thing is so easy? It means you are a boy. It means you are only a boy. By means of my challenge to the willow, and the necessity in poetry to pay attention and to connect, I come to say— almost to blurt out—the truth: that an adolescent, for all the pleasure he provides the parent, does not know the parent's life.

To You Teachers of Poetry

Most students are probably reassured to be told a few things right at the start. One of these is that writing poetry is not a way of saying only what one already has the words for, but a way of saying what one didn't know one knew. This is true of everything about poetry, including meter and rhyme. While meter and rhyme create specific effects of expression, they are there in the poem because the poet wanted to be led, somewhat, by the language into saying things previously unexpressed, at least by him or her. We do this all the time in lively conversation, and it might be argued (I'll argue it!) that good essays are written the same way.

Students are also reassured to see that contemporary poems are written in the language of their time. Indeed, it could be argued that the history of poetry (and perhaps of any art) is in large measure the history of poets finding ways (daring) to put into their poems both content and styles formerly thought "unpoetic." Poets are often seemingly crude, vulgar, casual, personal, emotional, or critical, and this presents a problem in teaching poetry where offense might be taken. This is a shame because the very essence of much first-rate poetry is its ability to think twice, to qualify the conventional wisdom, to say, "Yes, but . . . ." or "Why not?"—skills basic to education.

Finally, students ought to be told that neither a semester nor a year is enough to encompass the astonishing variety in American poetry, let alone in poetry from other languages and cultures.

Why study poetry at all? It doesn't have to be because the student is specifically interested in poetry. Rather, one might study poetry simply to learn to read: not simply to cover the words but to understand deeply. Poetry is perfect for learning to read well and to think clearly (the same thing?) because it insists on slow reading and sustained attention, because in it the words themselves are presumed to matter beyond the information they carry in common with "synonyms," because it offers great variety in language and organization in short forms, because it engages the imagination and heart as well as the lungs and brain, and because there are no rules in art except those the work of art establishes as it goes. Beyond that, the best poetry is a synthesis of form and content that articulates the truth of our lives—what it feels like and all the things we think at once.

Writing is not as much a matter of intention as a matter of effect. Often we say, "What did the poet mean by this or that?" The question might be better phrased, "What is the effect of this or that?" Because writing is a great adventure, in which we are free to be only what we are and everything that we are, the poet is not just a formulator, but a discoverer. In poetry, all the discoveries are brought back and exhibited there in the poem. The willing reader can make them too, again and again.

The Sea as Cement Mixer: Re-Directing the Negative Roar

by Madeline DeFrees

Like human consciousness, for which it serves as the great natural ana-
logue, the sea is a cement mixer. At any given moment, we recognize only a
small part of the flotsam and jetsam lifted to light, carried ashore, and then
swept back into the secret deep. Repetitive and violent in its rhythms—
destructive, even—the sea contains the energy to dismantle, to erode, to
fuse and reassemble.

If recent history suggests that the sea, too, may be a nonrenewable
resource, the figure of the cement mixer is still valid for our purpose. The
volume and variety of material cast up each day is so overwhelming that the
machine sometimes threatens to break down. The disproportion between
the cargo and the carrier recalls St. Augustine trying to fathom the mystery
of the Trinity. It took an apparition to persuade him how impossible that
was, a child with a sand bucket, trying to move the ocean from one place to
another. In "Slow-Motion Elegy for Kathy King," I allude to that incident.

> . . . No child
> wearing a halo
> ladles the ocean into this hole at my feet. A tourist
> stalking elegant cuisine
> appears to me . . .

In those five lines I have, so to speak, established the polarities on
which the discussion of my own creative process will turn. I'll be using a
tidy, if somewhat arbitrary, division of poets into two groups, roughly
corresponding to the old division between Classical and Romantic. For
Classical, substitute Inland, and for Romantic, Coastal. In the Geography
of the Imagination, let these serve for the way perception, memory, and
imagination work, regardless of one's place of origin or residence. There

are, of course, no such neat dualisms, but a whole series of gradations and variations. Even so, it may be helpful to establish the boundaries.

The Inland Poets, then, tend to be more focused, more coherent, safer, and more concentrated. They live in the middle. Coastal Poets are more open, more fluid, more inclusive, and extreme. They live on the edge. It is not so simple a matter as the images employed—corn, say, versus sea gulls—but a question of how much is attempted and how high the degree of personal risk.

In the lines quoted earlier, the speaker recognizes the disproportion between death and elegy, but that does not silence the poet. Instead, the disparity itself is caught up in the motion of the cement mixer, where the violence of the feeling can be fused with a whole complex of intellectual and emotional responses, including a nod to the Inland Poet, whose "apparition" remains well within the margins of the possible: a "*tourist/ stalking elegant cuisine.*" Like Dylan Thomas making his elegy out of a refusal to mourn, like John Crowe Ransom's character making a snare of evasion, like Wallace Stevens reducing a Great Disorder to an order in "The Connoisseur of Chaos," Coastal Poets devour everything encountered on the way: the original observation(s), the memories and associations clinging to them, the anticipated resistance, the process itself, and the hand that feeds them into the hopper. No wonder they sometimes feel that the sheer centripetal force will destroy them.

The problem is that everything interests the Coastal Poet and everything seems connected. The points of juncture are so numerous that the only way to choose among them is to apply some external pressure to balance the pressure from within. Deadlines may help. Distractions are sometimes useful—what Arthur Koestler in *The Act of Creation* calls "turning aside." My own recourse is to strenuous physical activity such as splitting wood, moving the wood pile onto the porch, or running. I am beginning to believe what John Berryman told us: that the poet considers every impulse towards a new poem a temptation and resists it for years. If destruction is the obverse of creation, as Maritain argues in *Art and Poetry,* and if we intend to moor our craft beside those twin seas, we would be well advised to batten down the hatches.

I once heard a woman on the bus lament her time spent at a West Coast convention. "It was terrible," the woman said. "I nearly died of boredom. No department stores or theatres, no supermarkets or cable TV. Nothing to look at from morning to night but all that water!" The woman may be distantly related to the Inland Poet, able to exclude on sight any force too powerful to contain. The Coastal Poet must learn to live with the sense of being flooded out, just as Inland Poets must study to survive the long drought of their exclusions.

It isn't easy. All kinds of things appear and disappear. I am like an epileptic, asked to thread a needle while having a seizure. If I am running, as I often am, I try to memorize what I can, to "swallow the whole ocean at one look," moving the not-so-Pacific into the cavities of my skull where the tides wear away the unpolished edges. Because running is a way of traveling light, it helps. By the time I get home, I go straight for paper and pencil to make the notes that will help me to retrieve the diverse materials from a single hour. The burden shifts from my head to my living quarters, which takes on the semblance of rooms hit by a tidal wave. The task now is to arrange what I have gathered. I start by typing each item on a separate piece of copy paper. Then I deal them into piles of notes that seem to me related.

When I have exhausted myself and the time, I turn to reading or housework, shopping or recreation. The cement mixer goes right on turning. My favorite tempo is one of alternating writing with physical activity. This is an old habit retained from convent days when I had little time to concentrate on poems.

Living with all this unfinished business can be difficult, but it has two advantages: (1) it prevents me from imposing a false resolution; and (2) it gives me distance on my work. By the time I return from Project 7, I can be more realistic in assessing Project 1.

If you have followed my argument thus far—an argument that has evolved from the very process I am describing—you will understand that, next to writer's block, what I am most afraid of is the St. Vitus's Dance of ungovernable creation. I seldom know where I'm going when I start out, and this process demands a great deal of faith. I usually know whether I am writing prose or verse, but I often can't tell whether the prose is auto-biography or fiction. What I work towards is a feeling, almost physical, like that of a car motor turning over. Once I feel that, I can usually continue to believe in what I'm doing, although the goal is unclear and the way there, devious and unpaved—even with good intentions. It *is* a kind of hell because I often feel that the center will *not* hold, and at such times, it's always a mistake for me to try to dissipate the force of feeling by showing my work to an Inland Poet, who will tell me that it lacks focus or straddles the line between essay and story.

When I am most at sea, I try to follow my ear, to forget for the moment where I am going or might go. Over and over, I repeat the words that attract me, saying them aloud like a mantra until other words follow. Researchers have learned that "ear" is less a matter of musical aptitude than of the habit of listening. Speech therapists may score as high in the Seashore and similar tests as trained musicians. This brings me to the question of what we hear and how we interpret it.

Although my hearing is not especially acute, I am skittish about unexpected or unfamiliar noise, a legacy from those years of convent silence, including what we called ''silence of action.'' So when I move to a strange house, I often wake at odd hours trying to identify a sound I haven't yet assimilated. By the time my alarm goes off in the morning, I am tense and irritable from anxiety and loss of sleep.

When I moved to Cannon Beach last summer, I'd wake up thinking, ''Why is the furnace on in July?'' Or, ''How can the motor of a late-model Frigidaire work so hard?'' My ear was not yet attuned to the roar of ocean and the Magnavox of the house; I was uneasy about the building's dialogue with the elements. Appliances wheezed and whomped, manic as my typewriter. The housewife's helpers had their distinctive rhythms, and the house was their acoustic shell. One load, and I swore off the dishwasher forever.

My own negative voices are less easily silenced. After 50 years of writing, I still have to work at that every day. At the beach, I discovered running. Forty minutes into the day's distance, I begin to think that I can do anything. I try to stay tuned to that voice as long as I am working.

Now I call my process creative chaos, a sleight-of-hand performance that makes the disorder a bit more livable. The cement mixer asks only for raw material, a very large capacity, a durable enclosure, and perpetual motion. So what if the dispersal of my energies is a little like being commissioned to knit socks for a centipede. One stitch at a time. I don't have to count or measure them, much less publish them for all the world to see. The one thing that matters is to keep on doing it: writing my poems, my stories, my unclassifiable expressions. No one else can do it, and if I work every day at keeping the motor turning over, no one can stop me.

Color Is a Poet's Tool*

by Diane Wakoski

In a poem called "What you should know to be a poet," Gary Snyder says that, basically, poets have to know everything, but he starts with this catalogue:

> all you can about animals as persons.
> the names of trees and flowers and weeds.
> names of stars, and the movements of the planets
> and the moon.
>
> your own six senses, with a watchful and elegant mind.
>
> at least one kind of traditional magic:
> divination, astrology, the *book of changes*, the tarot;†

As a young writer I agreed with Snyder that poets had to know everything, but I didn't quite understand how one conveyed that knowledge in poems. I loved the wisdom of Shakespeare on the subjects of love and aging and beauty in his sonnets, but when I tried to write that way, I simply sounded pompous or corny. And his images never made me see pictures. They were abstractions which gave me ideas, but when I tried with similar images of the moon or sun or stars or trees, sketched as they are in Shakespeare, I simply was trite, banal, more clichéd even than I was in ordinary talk.

What I needed, then, was some system for presenting this material in poems. And it was a combination of poets and poetry which assaulted me during my first two years of college, teaching me about images, surrealism, big metaphors, incantation. And it was reading poems and imitating them which finally led to my own prosody and craft.

A poem that inspired me deeply and continues to move me is Lorca's "Somnambule Ballad." Of course I read this in translation. In fact it was because a student friend of mine, Michael Rossman, was passionately and diligently translating Lorca's gypsy poems that I was introduced to this work. The poem offered me so much that was exciting. And more, so much that was new to me at the time. I don't think repetition or incantation were part of my tradition. And the poetry I had read and most enjoyed was not ecstatic poetry, so the use of the intensely lyrical repetition, "Green, how much I want you green./ Green wind. Green branches." thrilled me. And the use of repetition as an organizing device, as well as a means of conveying passionate feeling, excited my desire to try the same.

Because I am a visually oriented person, poems that used vivid imagistic description appealed enormously to me. But I had not, at that time, read a great deal of poetry that did this. Heavy in our curriculum were poems of narrative or lyric poems which barely touched the visual world, or did so as Shakespeare's sonnets did, with the mind rather than the painterly eye. I am sure the use of color as an organizing device was one of the aspects of this poem which implanted in me so firmly and which gave me permission to continue to use color for the rest of my life, not as decoration, but as a device for organizing a poem.

In the "Somnambule Ballad," Lorca uses the folk tradition of the gypsy world along with twentieth century surrealist images, and they come together surprisingly well. The simplification of images. and symbolic speech, which is in all folk poetry and painting ("Your white shirt bears/ three hundred dark roses." or "eyes of cold silver," or "I want to change/ my horse for your house,/ my saddle for your mirror,/ my knife for your blanket."), meshes well with the surreal images such as calling the girl "green flesh, hair of green," or referring to "the fish of darkness/ that opens the road of dawn," or referring to the stars as "a thousand crystal tambourines" which were "piercing the dawn."‡

Taking this poem into my heart entirely, and accepting the gift of its structures, I wrote a whole group of college poems in which I tried to make the world respond to my visions of color. The most successful of these was a poem using blue. In it, my love of the music of Debussy, of early Chinese poems which I had just begun to read, of this Lorca poem, all combined with my own desperately unhappy adolescent life. My longing for love I could not seem to find. My desire for lovers who did not desire me. And a wish for a world of the past, more structured, more orderly, and perhaps more royal or elegant. The poem was a dramatic monologue in which I spoke as the "blue jester' whose lady is royal and throws him out at dawn because he isn't good enough for the world to know that he's her lover. Speaking in the voice of the man rejected by the woman, I think I felt freer than if I had tried to speak in my own desperate adolescent girl's voice then. But I knew well the theme of lost love, as every 20-year-old does, and the lost love of the "Somnambule Ballad" glittering through its images, repeated by its refrain, embodied by the color green, inspired me to use those devices to talk about my own life through the story of the blue jester.

About five years later I was again to use color to organize another of my best poems. Probably each year of my life, since I discovered this Lorca poem I have written at least one poem in which color has been the primary organizing structure. Often I have tried different techniques, but always the color domination has worked best when I am attempting a theme of lost love, as was presented in my early model. A poem that I must have discovered at about the same time in my undergraduate life that I began to read Lorca was/is Wallace Stevens' "Domination of Black." This poem uses the image of blackness to present a dramatic feeling about death or closure. Perhaps in my mind this reinforced the power of color being associated with pain or with loss or grief. For I think it is almost always true that the most successful color poems I write are explorations of those themes.

In the following poem, I was again attempting to talk about lost love.

THE PINK DRESS§

I could not wear that pink dress tonight.
The velvet one
lace tinting the cuffs with all
the coffee
of longing. My bare shoulder
slipping whiter
than foam
out of the night to remind me
of my own
vulnerability.

I could not wear that pink dress tonight
because it is a dress
that slips memories like
the hands
of obscene strangers
all over my body.
And in my fatigue I could not fight away the images
and their mean touching.

§From *The Motorcycle Betrayal Poems*, Simon and Schuster, 1971.

I couldn't wear that pink dress,
the velvet one you had made for me,
all year, you know.

I thought I would tonight because
once again
you have let me enter your house
and look at myself
some mornings
in your mirrors.
                    But
I could not wear that pink dress tonight
because it reminded me
of everything
that hurts.
It reminded me of a whole year
during which
I wandered,
a gypsy,
and could not come into your house.
It reminded me of the picture of a blond girl
you took with you to Vermont
and shared your woods with.
The pretty face you left over your bed to stare
at me
and remind me
each night
that you preferred her face to mine,
and which you left there to stare at me
even when you saw how it
broke me,
my calm,
like a stick smashing across my own
plain lonesome face,
and a face which you only
took down
from your wall
after I had mutilated it
and pushed pins into it to get those smug
smiling eyes off my cold
winter
body.

I couldn't wear that pink dress tonight
because it reminded me
of the girl who made it,
whom you slept with,
last year while I was sitting in hotel rooms

wondering why I had to live
with a face
so stony no man could love it.

I could not wear that pink dress
because it reminded me
of how I camp on your doorstep now,
still a gypsy,
still a colorful imaginative beggar
in my pink dress,
building a fire in the landowner's
woods, and my own fierceness
that deserts me
when a man
no, when you,
show a little care and concern
for my presence.

I could not wear that pink dress tonight.
It betrayed all that was strong in me.
The leather boots I wear to stomp through the world
and remind everyone
of the silver and gold and diamonds
from fairy tales
glittering in their lives.
And of the heavy responsibility
we all must bear
just being so joyfully alive
just letting the blood take its own course
in intact vessels
in veins.
That pink dress betrayed my one favorite image
          —the motorcyclist riding along the highway
              independent
              alone
              exhilarated with movement
              a blackbird
              more beautiful than any white ones.

But I went off
not wearing the pink dress,
thinking how much I love you
and how if a woman loves a man who does not love her,
it is, as some good poet said,
a pain in the ass.
For both of them.

I went off thinking about all the girls
you preferred to me.

Leaving behind that dress,
remembering one of the colors
of pain
Remembering that my needs
affront you,
my face is not beautiful to you;
you would not share your woods with me.

And the irony
of my images.
That you are the motorcycle rider.
Not I.
I am perhaps,
at best,
the pink dress
thrown against the back
of the chair.
The dress I could not wear
tonight.

In this poem, the obvious narration of lost love is implemented through the image of the pink dress. To me, the idea that women are symbolized by pink has always been hateful. Perhaps because pink is a pastel color, an off shade, a dilution of the primary and powerful color red. Red, of course, is the color of blood and is often used to represent anger. In my poem, the pink dress becomes that dilution of person that a woman is to a man in our culture. Since red would be the color of blood, there is something of the stain of blood, death, and pain about this dream which is the diluted color of blood. And the diluted color of anger.

In "The Pink Dress" I wanted the idea of the color to represent again the emotions I was experiencing, this time not through a verbal pun, but through the symbols of the color itself. In fact, the whole poem works with symbol. The dress itself is a symbol for woman as she is seen by most men, a decorative object, and as she chooses to present herself through her clothes. She is no more than the dress. So both the dress itself and its color, pink, are working as symbols throughout the poem.

Symbol and image are two of the major tools of figurative language. They are a vivid and real part of anyone's life and can be used most powerfully, I think, when they come naturally out of the matrix of one's life. I knew this, theoretically, when I was young and first starting to write, but I did not know how to apply what I knew until I began to discover how to talk personally about my own life in ways that were not obscure or embarrassingly intimate. It was the wonderful examples of poets who also had a painterly, visual vision of the world, like Garcia Lorca and Wallace

Stevens, who led me away from cliché, banal language, and trite phrases, permitting me to talk somewhat originally about the clichéd, banal, and trite subject of lost love and the pain of rejection which was to become a major theme in my work. Perhaps "The Pink Dress" can be used by students as a model for writing poems that use organizational devices that they might not have thought of previously, in particular, color.

From Picture to Poem: How "John Frederick Alfrey" Got Written

by Warren Carrier

JOHN FREDERICK ALFREY*

He sits on the porch in his suspenders
His gaze reaches across a field that bends from
Indiana to Arkansas
and back.

A field in Wisconsin rolls with mown hay
after a hot day.
I stop to gaze and meet my grandfather.

In the morning a crow rises slowly
from the cornfield beyond U.S. 151.
Clouds stored in Canada begin their usual ride south.

In his sandbox my son makes noises
like a tractor.
An imaginary field is turning gold under his eye.

—Warren Carrier

The poem begins with an actual snapshot and a memory fixed in my mind like a photograph. It's an old man sitting on the front porch of his farmhouse in Indiana. The first thing you notice is his suspenders. The man is my mother's father, John Frederick Alfrey.

The first thing I want to do is capture that picture in the poem, because poems are basically images that come to mean something more than they

---

*"John Frederick Alfrey" appeared originally in the *Ocooch Mountain News*. Printed with permission of Warrien Carrier and the *Ocooch Mountain News*.

seem to in the beginning. But the image has to be realized first. So I put it down as simply and straightforwardly as I can:

> He sits on the porch in his suspenders.

"Suspenders" is the detail that fixes the image sharply in the mind's eye. Now I ask myself what is he looking at. I remember that he worked as a logger in Arkansas for many years of his life. His brother bought forests and my grandfather cut them down. (The logging was to make another poem about Grandfather.) Now I take liberty with the literal and make the field "bend"; that is, I make his eyes see both the field beyond the porch and the Arkansas of his memory, for I remember his absentmindedness the day that picture was taken.

> His gaze reaches across a field that bends from
> Indiana to Arkansas and back.

My grandfather died not too long after that photograph was taken, and I remember him on the day I write the poem. I am in Wisconsin, also farm country, on another hot day. I jump to the present place and try to say it simply again:

> A field in Wisconsin rolls with mown hay
> after a hot day.

Jumps keep a poem alive. If I just go on with one image or one time or idea, the poem becomes something all too expected and nothing new. (The poet Ezra Pound borrowed a Chinese phrase and applied it to writing poems. He said: "Make it new.") By juxtaposing one image against another and one time against another, I can see or feel something freshly as though it were new. Now, like my grandfather, I gaze beyond the field and see him gazing across a field and in remembering him, I have a kind of "meeting" with my grandfather:

> I stop to gaze and meet my grandfather.

Then I want more in the scene, exact things, present events succinctly given that make me realize more about place and time and that set up what should follow:

> In the morning a crow rises slowly
> from the cornfield beyond U.S. 151.
> Clouds stored in Canada begin their usual ride south.

These images are, I hope, sharpened, made new by certain details or a new way of using words. ''Suspenders'' fixes the eyes in the first image; ''bends,'' not usually used to characterize fields, provides a different way of seeing them; ''meet'' for ''remember'' makes memory more immediate and goes beyond simple reality to enhance it; ''stored'' about clouds visualizes clouds banked up (an old image) in a fresh way. These uses of language intend to make the images ''new.''

Now I have this much: My grandfather gazing across a field and into memory, caught there as in a photograph, and myself gazing across a field and into that caught memory of my grandfather in a present time. What now? I still haven't discovered where the poem is going. I need a jump to something else that will be different yet that links with what I have, and that will make the poem mean the something it is headed for. I see my younger son playing in his sandbox, and that's it.

> In his sandbox my son makes noises
> like a tractor.

It seems to be simply another thing—though unexpected, a jump—in the landscape. But it is more than that. It is the next generation. What does he see? My grandfather saw a field and his memory. I saw a field and a memory. What does my son in his own scene observe that aligns him with us? He does not look back, for he is very young. In his play he projects into his imagination the future time and place of tractors (and the tractor and the sand are projections, miniatures of the real which is as yet beyond him), the autumn when hay and corn and—though he doesn't know it yet—memories are gathered. It is a real time that he, in his time, will come to. But not yet. What was autumnal and is now gone for his grandfather, what is autumnal and now present for me, he anticipates in his mind in play.

> An imaginary field is turning gold under his eye.

Against each other I have juxtaposed my grandfather, myself, and my son in three similar scenes, different in time. Yet we are all tied together. We ''meet'' in the identity of our lives. We are gathered in our generations. The poem is discovered. It is an old theme, but I hope that the ''jumps,'' the unexpected images succinctly realized as in a haiku, have ''made it new.''

Philip Levine on Teaching Poetry: An Interview

by Sally A. Jacobsen

Sally Jacobsen: How would you get young people interested in poetry?

Philip Levine: My experience is with high school kids and college kids, but I really don't see any difference between the people I deal with and anybody else. So I suppose the answer is simply to present them with the wealth of poetry, trying to use relevant poetry as much as I can. I try to read it just as well as I can, to show them how it works without being too much of a pedant, suggest they write it—showing their work alongside a professional poem—and see what happens. I think some people will take to it and some won't. Poetry is not for everybody. It's been my experience that nothing seems to be for everybody, nothing worth having; people are different.

Jacobsen: What does the poet say to a teacher of poetry who *doesn't* write? How do you overcome the gulf of ignorance between you and people who haven't had that experience?

Levine: I suppose what the poet says to a teacher of poetry who doesn't write is "good luck." I think that most people who love poetry, who live with it, try to write it. I don't think that the experience of writing mediocre poetry is all that different from writing good poetry or bad poetry. It seems to me that I am just as ignorant as any other passionate reader of poetry when the two of us sit down to read Ben Jonson or James Wright—that there is a "gulf of ignorance." There is the experience and confidence of writing, so there is a sense sometimes of certain strategies, of certain methods, but I think that only works with poetry in the same cast as the kind I write. It seems to me that when I sit down and read a poem by Rilke or Stevens, who don't work the way I do, except for the narrative structure, relation of imagery, the way the lines and structure are arranged, written strategies, I don't have much advantage over anyone else.

Jacobsen: T. S. Eliot recommended 16 or 17 as the optimum age for students to read Shelley. Which poems of yours would you like to be read by students of that age and why?

Levine: It would seem to me that all of my poems would be accessible to a bright person of 16 or 17, given that the opportunity is presented for that person to know the essentials. If the poem is about a particular event, they have to know the event; if the poem is about certain kinds of conditions in the 30s that I happen to be writing about, they have to know what those conditions are; or if the poem makes a reference to people living in Spain in the 30s, they have to know about the Civil War. Anybody could present that to them. I hope my poems are available to bright 17-year-olds.

Jacobsen: My 15-year-old daughter enjoyed *Not This Pig*. She liked ''Animals Are Passing from Our Lives,'' ''To a Child Trapped in a Barber Shop,'' and 'The Cemetery at Academy, California''—especially the idealistic, in-tune-with-nature ending.

But is there an optimum age for which one should wait before challenging students with ambiguity, so as to avoid their feeling ''dumb'' when the poem stumps them? Didn't you have some students susceptible to that feeling when you were first at Columbia? Or at Fresno State? Or should one begin as early as possible teaching that poems are puzzles to which the reader contributes some of the meaning?

Levine: I don't think poems are puzzles. I do think readers contribute a great deal of meaning. Of course I had students at Columbia, at Fresno, and now at Tufts who did feel ''dumb'' and will continue to feel dumb, because they *are* dumb in the face of the poem. Other people are dumb in the face of something else—the season, their sexuality, growing corn, driving an automobile. I am not sure that there is an optimum age for which one should wait. I wouldn't teach Wallace Stevens to a 10-year-old; it would just be a waste of time. I don't know how old students have to be to read Shakespeare. They have to be old enough to be familiar with the kind of sentence structure, that kind of syntax—if you have to be constantly breaking a sentence down into little components the students can deal with, they are not going to get the poetry. In other words, students must have a capability of the English language that matches the difficulty or lack of difficulty of poems.

Jacobsen: You say [in your book, *Don't Ask*] that schools should educate people to make meaningful choices about how they live—and that you dislike teaching where a school isn't committed to that. Should poetry do that, too—be relevant in that way?

Levine: Of course it should, if it chooses to be. There are plenty of us who choose that.

Jacobsen: You recommend reading Keats' letters as well as his poems for students, because the letters show that the poetry grew out of an experience of "life as tough as it is." What other poets do you recommend for students who want to write, to widen their horizons?

Levine: I think a much overlooked poet in America is Kenneth Patchen—a very powerful political poet, a beautiful poet of love, and a poet who wrote about ecology before the word existed. I certainly would introduce Rilke's letters; unfortunately in translation they seem to be very formal—they probably were, from one middle European to another. I would present the political poetry of Latin America and Spain by Garcia Lorca, Miguel Hernandez, Rafael Alberti. The poetry of Allen Lewis, the political poetry of Jon Silkin in our time, as well as other poetry. I teach James Wright to young people; I teach Ginsberg. Students find him dated. I teach William Carlos Williams, Thomas Wyatt, Edward Thomas, Dylan Thomas; D. H. Lawrence is one of my favorites; Denise Levertov, Emily Dickinson, Walt Whitman.

Jacobsen: You once said [in *Don't Ask*] you would like to have been able to believe you "stopped the war with your little poems"—that you "turned this country right around." What political poets and poems now, 10 years later, do you think students should read?

Levine: I think there are very few good poems that aren't political. A poem which is about the beauty of love, after all, is political. We exist in a time where sexual love has been dragged into such things as the presidency, the right to enjoy sexual love, the right to have air that is uncorrupted—all political questions. So when poetry deals with any kind of atmosphere, internal or external, we are entering into a very political sphere; we don't have to say, "Don't go to war, don't fight, don't kill." There are the more obviously political poets—Rexroth, Kenneth Patchen, Jim Wright, myself. It seems to me all of us who are writing well are to a degree political poets.

Jacobsen: The "little stories" in your poems, capturing the places you like and the people, are very important. You speak of being obsessed with the universality of that, of what "we all make up together, . . . the thing that comes into being because we touch each other's lives and become part of each other"—that you can be "still a young man in Detroit, a woman in California, a guy wandering the roads of Alabama"—that you're many people, living and dead. Do you ever give students the exercise of writing a poem from another specific point of view, and do you think that's a good idea for teenage students?

Levine: Yes, I do. I rarely give assignments, actually, but sometimes, to beginning students, I do—students who need it, really. Once a student writes awhile, she or he perhaps doesn't need it. But without experience they tend to write, "I fell in love, I was lonesome, I'm miserable," etc., etc., and I think it a very good exercise to get them out of that concern and the vocabulary that accompanies it. I think it would be just as good for teenagers. Of course, some of my students are teenagers.

Jacobsen: Are you "brutal with mediocre poems"?

Levine: I'm never brutal with people who don't have talent. It seems to me utterly pointless. You are only brutal with people who need it. I don't encourage them or discourage them, but I am tough on people who can bear it. The better they are, the tougher you are.

Jacobsen: How could one make demands on even younger students without their feeling the teacher was brutal?

Levine: I don't know—that is very tricky. It seems to me that the younger kids are—not so much younger, but the less experienced they are—the more I encourage them. I don't know what's there, so I have to do a lot of encouraging. I won't talk about a problem unless I have something good to say.

Jacobsen: How does one get students to make greater demands of themselves?

Levine: They begin to read their poems with an eye to an audience, and at the same time they begin to see poems by other students in new ways. They see their vices and they see their virtues. I also introduce to them "real poems" by mature poets, and I think that does a great deal to raise their standards.

Jacobsen: What practical tips for becoming established would you offer unknown poets convinced of the value of their work—or teachers who recognize such talent?

Levine: I'm not in the business of giving tips. But my advice to most people is, "Stay out of the market place as long as you can. There is a time when you should try to publish—if you don't, you become embittered." I could imagine I would have become embittered if I'd had to wait another 10 years. At 40 I published a "real" book. It did me a lot of good not to be published too early.

Jacobsen: Could you talk a little about "writing as an act of discovery"?— Writing through a conventional "you" to the point where you "break into something fresh, and start from there and throw the rest away?" It seems that would be a very useful idea to teach student writers. How do you get them to recognize that point?

Levine: I would say largely that you don't. I am not sure that happens very often to student writers. I don't think that breaking into something fresh and throwing the rest away happens without discipline. However I think you can talk to young poets and young writers about the level of the "trite" in their work, how often the characters and situations, the dramas, are just loose borrowing from the popular arts, from junk, from television, from bad popular songs. They don't really believe in this stuff and know perfectly well that the stuff they are seeing on television is unreal; that is, it does not involve people they care about, the people they really know. It really does not involve anybody except the kind of celebrity who is in *People* magazine. I think they go for these things like I go for similar junk, for release, and for the pure foolish entertainment that we all seem to need and love. When their work involves that sort of thing you can say, "Hey, you don't believe in that junk. What are you putting it in your poetry for?"

From that sense I think you can get them to throw a lot away. You can get young kids, as they go through emotions about love, to turn to themselves rather than to require *you* to suddenly enter the room of their imagination. I really believe that.

As for myself, when you talk about writing as an act of discovery, it's hard for me to talk about; it happens in a kind of a flash. Frequently I begin writing in a sort of mechanical, I might even say, stupefied way. I sit down in the usual place with the usual pen and pad of paper, and I start making scratchings. I may even start writing lines—none of it is particularly awe-inspiring—a poem, or what I think is a poem. It seems that, when I write at my best, a point comes at which I take something I put on that page, or something that passes through my mind because of this sort of wasted effort (which is, in fact, not wasted), which triggers a deeper layer of awareness or emotion, and then I just turn away from everything and proceed toward whatever direction that new thing is taking. Sometimes I'll write a whole draft of a poem and it may sit around for a few days; I'll look at it and then I'll see that there is a life, vitality, integrity, intensity in some passage, and I'll just banish the rest and pursue the implications of that unfulfilled portion that is so much livelier, so much more intense, more imaginative.

I think that took me a long time to learn to do, so I wouldn't bring something like that up to young writers. I do bring up to students in my class the need to follow the hints of their imaginations and to become, as quickly as possible, dissatisfied with the kinds of conscious aims that one sits down to write with. They tend to write the poem of ideas, of social service, the right poem with the right attitudes, the most boring thing imaginable, when the real self is somewhere gasping for breath or calling for a voice of his or her own. So, very quickly, I say to them, "Hey, this is why this is dead. Why don't you follow this?"

"Yeah, but my intention is to write a poem of this kind."

I say, "Well, forget that intention. Listen to the poem you are writing, don't listen to that conscious voice, that obligatory 'daddy' that says, 'No, thou must not do this.' Listen to what your imagination is really doing."

Jacobsen: You mentioned once in an interview that it is important to avoid being seduced by one's own writing, and elsewhere you have indicated that writers tend to fall back with a "sigh of fulfillment as if writing something were a big meal they'd just finished." How do you keep the young from being mesmerized by their own writing?

Levine: It's much easier to keep the young from being mesmerized by their writing, and I wish that, when I was young, I'd had friends who had been capable of it. By and large, when I was in my 20s, most of the people I showed my work to said, "Oh, it's so awesomely gorgeous," and it wasn't. It took me years to see, "Hey, my friends don't know enough and they're not tough enough." They weren't sure of themselves and they didn't know as much about writing as I do. Later on I made friends who had more confidence, friends who knew more about poetry; they were tougher on me.

So I think that function that my friends performed I can perform for students. They respect me; they know I know a lot; they may not even *like* me all the time; they get angry at me—that's not the problem. My problem is not to be their friend. I'm not in a classroom to make loving friends; I'm not there to seduce the girls or have the boys admire me; I'm there to help them with their writing and, in order to do that, sometimes I have to risk being disliked by them. When I get a gifted person who repeats him or herself over and over, I say, "Hey look, we know you can do this, and while you think it's extraordinary, I think it's just okey-dokey." I have to put next to it what I think *is* extraordinary and say, "Hey, wake up." There are some people who can't take it; they shouldn't be in classrooms and after a while they aren't. They get upset, they create scenes, and sometimes people who know the truth resist it most fiercely—those are the difficult ones. But I've been in a teaching situation with some awfully good people who got very angry and wound up in the long run being awfully good writers. They struggled, they fought, but in the long run they really did take the criticism. So it can be a painful process. I've been told I was a son-of-a-bitch; I didn't feel that bad about it. I didn't start teaching till I was in my 30s, so I had the advantage of knowing that these kids could behave in infantile ways. I could too. So they didn't love me that day.

Jacobsen: How do you prod yourself?

Levine: The problem of doing it for myself is much harder. I think if I have had any success the secret is that I have been writing—I've had poems. I was talking to a boy the other day whose manuscript I looked at—it was perhaps 60 pages long; he's perhaps thirty. He writes seriously; he's a slow worker; he got a late start; and here he is, thirty years old, and he's got 60 pages of poems. I suggested the 60 ought to be cut down to about 30, because there were about 30 rather interesting pages and 30 very conventional or badly written pages. He was a little upset. Something got him to go back to my criticism, and the second time around he found more value in it and began to throw out. Also, the fact that he was writing new work and could add eight or ten pages meant he could take eight or ten pages out. Then he took more out. He finally ended up cutting as much as I had suggested to him—maybe even more. One of the reasons he was able to do this was that he did have new work that he could bank his hopes on. I think that, since I have written almost continuously all these years, I've been able to throw a lot of stuff away because I *had* a lot of stuff. I think if you write a poem every two months, it's awfully tough to throw it away. If you are writing constantly and trying, and the work is coming, you have some faith that the lines you wrote yesterday will not be the last—that since you wrote yesterday and you wrote Tuesday and Friday, it's likely that you'll get some more. You're going to be able to be tougher and harder on what you did.

However, there is always that deep, unkillable desire to love what you've done. "No memory of having starred/Atones for later disregard,/Or keeps the end from being hard," says Frost in a wonderful poem. All those early successes that you have as a writer don't matter that much if you're not having recent successes. And sometimes you seduce yourself into believing that what you are doing is the best you can do when it isn't. Sometimes your writing is not as good as it could be because you *need* it too badly. One of the advantages of being a poet, and living by and large as poets do, not off their poetry but off something else they do, is that they don't need it to make a living; so at least it doesn't suffer that. You can throw it away because you aren't going to starve, because it never made the difference between your eating and starving anyway. I still try hard to prod myself, and I still find that a lot of what I write is not going to get in any published pages. I dismiss a great many of my poems. Whitman says, "Dismiss whatever insults your own soul." Well, I don't think I have the courage to do that in terms, say, of the institutions I teach in—to most of them I should say, "School dismissed," but at least I think I am able to do it quite often with my own writing. I say, "You're dismissed."

Listening to Writing*

by Donald M. Murray

In trying to write an essay which would speculate about how the writer discovers the draft which marks the watershed between prewriting and rewriting, I heard a poem. And in hearing the poem I found this essay which made me newly aware of the importance of listening to writing—both as a writer and a teacher of writing.

A poem was unexpected. As much as I welcome the surprises which are central to the writing process, I felt a bit guilty. Poetry was not on the agenda. I had just finished a draft of a novel and was beginning to revise it. That had first priority. I had this article to do, and it was fighting the novel for first priority as the deadline approached. I had a busy schedule of teaching, traveling, and talking this spring. There was no time for poetry. But on a Saturday, when I had a clear day at home, a day when I had programmed myself to split the morning between editing the novel and drafting this essay, I spent the morning on a poem. When a poem comes, I listen. I have to remind myself that the purpose of my writing routine is to make me receptive to writing—the writing that wants to make its voice heard. That is not always the writing which is expected but I must seize the gift and toss aside the schedule.

It is my habit to begin the day grinding coffee and putting the kettle on the stove. While the pot boils I sit down and twist the dial of a pocket timer to fifteen minutes. I open a 10 by 8 inch narrow-ruled spiral notebook (National 33-008) with green eye-ease paper on my beanbag lap-desk, and uncap my pen (Esprit DLX with black ink and 0.5mm superfine point).

The tools are important. Most craftsmen are compulsive about their tools, and writers work with pen, pencil, typewriter and paper which are familiar to hand and eye. Secretly, I think most writers believe the writing is either in the page or the pen, somehow magically released by the act of writing.

---

*This essay is unedited and is reprinted here from *Composition and Teaching* (December 1980) by permission.

Time is also important. I try to start each day with a few quiet moments when I listen for writing, listen to hear the words I watch my pen put on the page. I may hear—and capture—drafts, titles, lines, leads, details, lists, ideas, memories, scenes, notes for stories, textbooks, reportage, profiles, essays, poems, plays; whatever comes to my ear is captured on the page. The quiet moments when this happens have a religious quality for me. The quiet time is made possible by habit. I do not get up eager to write. I do not get up even eager to get up. But it is my habit to turn on the timer, open the notebook, uncap the pen, and listen.

Writing usually comes—100 words, 5, 152, 18, 249. No matter. I am simply waiting, listening. If no words arrive at my ear I may think back to a moment of intense feeling—when I was eight and found Grandmother collapsed on the stairs or the moment in combat when I knew I could kill. Or I may brainstorm, catching the specific and apparently unrelated fragments—images, words, details—which pass through our minds as we meditate. I may describe the plant on the table across the room or the scene in the corridor outside the classroom yesterday, because description best ignites writing. I may also play with words. For example, in thinking about my mother's militant Christianity, I was interested when I heard two words collide: angry prayers. Those words may give off a poem, a story, an essay, or flicker out and die. It does not matter, at this time, what—if anything—is produced.

If no words come that is fine. I suppress the panic I feel at silence. There will be another day; the writing will come if I wait, and I often do have to wait minutes which seem like hours. My students tell me after they write in class that they had to wait ten minutes, fifteen minutes, half an hour before they could get going. I have timed their long periods of waiting; it seems a long time to them, but it is often only 30 seconds, 105 seconds, 90 seconds, sometimes even 120 seconds. We are educated for busyness, not educated for listening to our own minds at work. I worry more, in fact, when my words come too easily. It is important that I discipline myself to sit down and be quiet, but I am not an assembly line, I do not have to produce. The irony, of course, is that the more peaceful I am, the more quietly receptive, the less I drive myself to produce, the more productive I become.

I try to come to my 15-minute appointment with the blank page as empty of conscious intent as possible. I want no internal noise—the carping of the critic at my last piece, the echoes of past failure or past success, the sandbox bickering of campus politics, the endless listing of what isn't done and must be done—to interfere with what I may hear. External noise does not bother me and I usually write in the morning with the television news or a classical FM music program in the background, but the internal noise of my own busyness can create so much noise I cannot hear my own voice and therefore cannot write.

Of course, I do not really come emptyheaded to any morning's writing. When I am most clear of intention, my life lies raw and open to my pen. The other evening, at a poetry reading by Heather McHugh, my notebook was open, my pen uncapped. The better the poetry reading, the more likely that unexpected lines of poetry will arrive. I was ready for the line that rose from within myself: "The dead swim in the earth."

The next morning these four lines slowly arranged themselves on the page:

the father who has buried his daughter
knows the dead swim in the earth
whale shapes of memory rising
to make him stagger as he walks

I have to listen to my autobiography, no matter how painful it is. I must hear the writing which demands to speak.

Every writer—student or professional—comes to the page with a personal history as a human being and as a writer; I am well-aware of how my autobiography brought me, on that Sunday morning, to the poem which is central to this essay. I have been a writer since I published a fourth-grade newspaper by hectograph. I have wanted to be a drawer and a painter, and still do. I have long been concerned about the making of art. New poetry usually arrives in bunches, like a car full of uninvited relatives.

Three other forces had impelled me towards a poem. I had made notes on a plane flying home from Charlotte, North Carolina, playing with the idea of a book of poetry called, "An Essay on the Line," which would tell the important things about lines, dots, curves, squares, and triangles my high school geometry book left out. I had had lunch two days before with a fine artist on our faculty, John Hatch, who had talked about how a painting talks to him while he is living within the act of painting. He had given me a marvelous quotation by Cennino Cennini on how the artist discovers "things not seen, hiding themselves under the shadow of natural objects." The mail brought me word that several poems had been accepted and, like my students, I am motivated more by acceptance than rejection. So, on Sunday morning, I found my pen putting down:

AN ESSAY ON THE LINE

THE LINE
THE LINE COMES FROM WHAT THE HAND
DIDN'T KNOW IT KNEW
        LINE
THE ∧ TELLS THE HAND WHAT IT KNEW

THE LINE IS (RECOGNIZED) NAMED
IT IS A HAND
REACHING

LINES MAKE CONNECTIONS
OF THEIR OWN
IF THE HAND THAT IS DRAWING THEM
~~SEES~~
FINDS THEM

THIS LINE IS A ROCK
THAT A STONE
IS A TREE
THE LINE CRACKS THE STONE
IT

BUT THE TREE IS NOT THAT TREE
OVER THERE
THE STONE
THE ONE ONCE SEEN

IT IS THE STONE
ON THE PAGE
WITH ITS OWN HISTORY
OF FROST AND WARM
THE INSIDIOUS WATER
THE ICE
THE TREE WHICH HAS BECOME
A PART OF IT

ON THIS PAGE
IT IS NOT A STONE ←
SPLIT BY A TREE
OR A TREE SPLITTING
A STONE

IT IS A STONE TREE
A TREE STONE

MADE ONE BY THEIR
NOT SHAPED HISTORY

move earlier? THE PAGE FLUTTERS
TO THE GROUND

THIS TREE   ROCK
SPLITTING THIS ~~PAGE~~
IS TOO REAL A TREE
TO BE TRUE

THE HAND MOVES A ROCK
WHICH HAS BEEN
SPLIT BY A TREE
A ROCK OF HALVES
~~NOT KNEW~~
NO LONGER KNOWING EACH OTHER

THE HAND
TEARS UP THE PAGE

That was fifteen minutes' writing, perhaps a bit more self-conscious than normal because it was a poem about art. I was aware of how didactic the first lines were, but I suppressed the critic and did not worry at this time about how unpoetic most of the other lines were. I have to listen to the writing and nothing else. I have to try and hear the soft but true voice hidden under the loud but clumsy voice in an early draft. I have learned that writing evolving often stumbles, but what seem to be mistakes often turn out to be keys to meaning.

I was surprised and excited when one line made a rock and another line a tree. I had no idea that would happen, but when it did, I had something that was real in my mind's eye. I could study the rock and the tree to see what they meant. I felt then that the poem might grow into a piece of writing, not a statement about writing. There was no calculation which produced that rock, that tree; they weren't pre-thought. This is not automatic writing in the sense it is dictated from a spirit world, and it is not an un-intellectual act. It is both intensely intellectual and intensely emotional as language brings thought, feeling, and experience together on the page. I live in a New Hampshire landscape of rocks and trees. I experience rocks and trees, I feel rocks and trees, I think about rocks and trees. I did not, however, consciously remember that landscape, and I could not see it from the chair in which I sat. It is such surprises of sight and insight more than anything else that motivate me to write.

When I wrote, "it is a stone tree/a tree stone," I felt I was on the track of something—that I heard a true voice—but I didn't know if I had or what it was saying. There need be no conscious thought at this point in the writing process. These words are not recorded as a result of conscious decision as to their worth, there is no censor at this stage of the process, the pen writes and later the mind considers and reconsiders what the words mean.

During the process of revision the mind is more consciously engaged. We will write nothing but garbage if we do not practice critical thinking towards the end of the writing process, but it is dangerous to be too critical too early. The better educated the writer, the more important it is to suspend the critical element of that education in the early stages of the process. The crimes committed by the writer should, in the beginning, all be unpremeditated. On this early draft I was a dog cocking my ears to a strange and distant sound. Perhaps this sound could be described as a problem to be solved. But I did not rush to attack it. I kept drifting along, my ears cocked, allowing words to appear on my page, seeing the energizing relationships the arrows indicate. Then the timer pinged and I capped the pen, closed the notebook.

After breakfast I went downstairs to my desk, again expecting to work on the novel. But the poem spoke first and I had to turn to the typewriter to see how it would look on the page.

THE LINE
(for John Hatch)

the line comes from what the hand
didn't know it knew

~~the line tells the hand~~
~~what it knew~~

~~this line is a rock~~

this line becomes a rock
that line a tree that cracks the stone

but the tree is not that tree
over there
the rock
not ~~the one~~ once seen at Pemaquid

it is the rock on the page
with its own history of frost
ice water earth seed tree

this tree
splitting this granite rock
is too real a tree
to be true

the paper flutters to the ground

the hand
makes a rock split by a tree
a rock of halves
no longer remembering each other

the hand tears the paper
from the board

the line leads the hand
across the page

it is not a stone
split by a tree
or a tree splitting
stone

```
                        the line shows the hand
                        a stone tree
                        a tree stone
     not parts but whole  ◄──────────
                            ↗ face hidden from the eye
                  that ↗    is shown by the line hand
                            led by the line
```

The visual aspect of discovering writing is important but in doing the research for this article I discovered hearing was more important than seeing, at least in creating the draft which marks the dividing line between prewriting and rewriting. I had thought writing appeared on the page, surprising my eye. I intended to describe and probe that process in this article. But in using myself as my own experimental rat, I discovered I heard the writing in my head an instant before it appeared on the page. I was talking to myself when I was writing, listening to what I had to say.

As I realized the importance of this sequence of listening and then seeing, I began to understand why I usually write the first drafts of poems by hand; then, when they seem ready to be tested—to stand by themselves—I type them. It is, I suppose, the first stage in the process of detachment which must take place if a piece of writing is going to move towards its own identity.

The process seems visual, but the words are first heard in my head and the line breaks are first heard, then typed. The lines may change as I read and edit, trying to help the poem arrange itself on the page, but the final test is how the lines sound rather than how they look.

When I started this article I had a subtitle—how language leads to meaning but that doesn't seem to be the process I follow. As my colleague, Professor Thomas Carnicelli, pointed out, my process doesn't seem to be so much linguistic as imagistic, a process of seeing, then recording in language. Rebecca Rule, a writer, added that as the image is written down it is heard more clearly. In this poem I said in those first didactic lines what I intended to explore, then I heard and wrote so I could see what I had heard. As I examine what I usually do as I write, I feel there is a constant productive tension between what is seen and what is said.

Sometimes I fear my literary colleagues, whose business, after all, is critical thinking, want to know what criteria are used in accepting or rejecting a discovered thought as if the criteria were external to the piece of writing.

When writers, rather than critics, talk of their own writing to each other and to themselves, they ask what works and what doesn't work. In a real sense they ask the writing what works and listen by reading—often aloud—to the piece of writing's answer. The writer avoids external critical standards—standards which evolved from other pieces of writing in other times by other writers for other readers—and works within the piece of writing. The writer listens to the evolving drafts, "talking with the work" in John Hatch's phrase, to discover its own demands.

Some of what the writer does as he or she reads and rereads, listening to the evolving drafts (and we need careful study of just how that writers read drafts), may involve some of the following considerations:

- What information, symbolized by language, is telling us what meaning will evolve? What information clarifies or confirms that evolving meaning?

- What form, order, structure is evolving? What discipline—limits, focus—is the draft imposing on itself?

- What additional information is being attracted to the draft? What more does the writer—and eventually the reader—want to hear from the piece of writing? What questions have to be answered by the piece of writing?

- What does the voice of the draft tell the writer about the writer's point of view towards the subject?

- What is true to the draft? What is the truth—the meaning—of this draft?

It is important, however, that the writer keep such considerations lightly in mind while writing and rewriting, not to think of them too consciously or they will make so much noise the writer will not hear what the piece of writing is telling him or her to write. The writer must let the piece of writing take its own course as much as possible.

As I typed this draft, for example, I was aware I would have a problem deciding between stone and rock, and I was tempted to fiddle with it right away. But I let the draft speak and delayed the decision; I felt the poem would tell me the answer as I turned to the typewriter again.

~~The Line~~ THE ROCKTREE
(for John Hatch)

~~the line comes from what the hand~~
~~didn't know it knew~~

this line becomes a rock
that line a tree that cracks the stone

I continued to type what I heard in my head, extending the poem, but I have not reproduced it all here, for the most important changes came in the reading as I listened to the poem, pen in hand. I had typed ''rocktree'' near the end of the poem. ''Rocktree'' it was, and the title represented the fact. The exposition at the beginning became unnecessary; it could be cut away. The poem said it was strong enough to begin to speak for itself.

Towards the end of that draft I heard the poem more clearly.

the hand pulls back
from the line

not parts but whole
a nation with a common
history of winters

A ~~the~~ rocktree
hidden from the eye

Once
remains

~~it is not seen by the eye~~
~~but the hand which follows~~
~~the line~~

I saw the artist's hand pull back and that action had to be reported. The pulling back proved to be significant, for the drawing of the rocktree within the poem and the poem itself were detaching themselves from their maker. The flawed and incomplete endings were necessary. They had allowed me to hear the poem in the beginning, but now the scaffolding could begin to be removed. Elizabeth Bowen talks of ''what is left after the whittling away of alternatives.'' Listening to a draft means, in part, paying attention to what belongs, what drives it towards its own meaning.

In the next typing, the poem pulled itself together a bit more, and my ear, listening to the poem, worked out the problem of stone and rock. It was typed again—the fifth draft, and then the Cennini quotation was added in the sixth draft. There were no changes in that final typing, but I could not know that until I typed it and listened to the poem.

> . . . this is an occupation known as painting,
> which calls for imagination, and skill of hand,
> in order to discover things not seen, hiding
> themselves under the shadow of natural objects,
> and to fix them with the hand, presenting
> to plain sight what does not actually exist.
>
> Cennino Cennini c 1370

THE ROCKTREE
   (for John Hatch and Cennino Cennini)

this line becomes a rock
that line a tree that cracks the rock

but the tree is not that tree
over there
not the rock
once seen at Pemaquid

it is a rock
growing out of paper
with its own history of frost
ice water earth seed tree

still
this tree
splitting this granite ledge
is too real a tree
to be true

the paper flutters
to the ground

the hand makes another rock
split by a tree
a rock of halves
no longer remembering each other

the hand tears the paper
from the board

the hand allows the line
to lead the hand

it is not a rock cut by a tree
not a tree that can slice stone

the line shows the hand
not parts but whole
a nation with a common history
of winters

the hand pulls back
from the line

a rocktree
once hidden from the eye
remains

—Donald M. Murray

"Rocktree" tells me something I had learned as a writer but did not know until this poem told it to me: the central act of writing is listening.

The experience of the poem also reminded me that I must somehow, as a teacher, a husband, a son, a father, a friend, a colleague, a citizen, a professional, a busy-busy-busy man so proud of my busyness, find time to listen so I will hear what I have to say. If I am able to be quiet within myself, something may appear on the page which may become writing and, when that happens, my job is to listen to the evolving writing. The piece of writing will, if I listen carefully, tell me how it needs to be written. It will develop its own shape and form, its own destination, its own voice, its own meaning, and it will finally detach itself from its maker and find readers who may hear things in it I never heard.

It is important we make the student listen to each draft to hear what has to be done—and not done—next. Our normal educational pattern is to tell the students to look to textbooks or to remember lectures, although what has been said often bears no relationship to the work at hand and may, in fact, cause the student to tune out what the draft is saying and therefore ruin it. We also counsel students to pay most attention to what they learned from previous writing tasks but each piece of writing has its own history, and each new piece must be listened to as if the writer were writing for the first time.

It may be helpful, however, to articulate some of the questions which published writers no longer need to articulate while they are listening and relistening, writing and rewriting. These questions may help the student to listen to the student's own developing work. Such questions include:

- What did you hear in the draft which surprised you?
- What did you hear that was most interesting?
- What sounds best?
- What sounds so right it can be developed further?
- What is the draft telling you?
- What does the draft ask you to include in it?
- What question does that draft ask?
- What is the draft trying to say?
- What does the sound of the draft mean?
- In what direction is the order of the information in the draft taking it?
- What is the draft telling you about the subject that you didn't know before?

Too often we tell students to listen to what we have to say when students should listen to their own drafts. These questions can be asked by six-year-old beginning writers and hairy-chinned remedial writers. Neither published writers nor beginning students have much control over what a piece of writing says as it is talking its way towards meaning. Both must listen to the piece of writing to hear where it is going with the same anticipation and excitement we feel when a master storyteller spins out a tale.

In writing this, I realize that listening to a piece of writing is similar to listening to a student in conference, class and workshop. In the beginning, neither the piece of writing nor the student knows what it wants to say. If I listen well and perhaps ask a few questions of the writing I may hear what the writing says in the same way that students in the writing conference or workshop hear what they say when they are given the opportunity to speak of their writing and the process which is producing it. We teach more by listening than by lecturing, and we write better if we follow Janwillem van de Wetering's advice to "just write easily, quickly" and listen to what the writing is saying.

This process of listening is more dramatic and easily apparent in poetry than in narrative or in non-fiction, but the process seems more similar in all the forms of writing than it is different—at least the way I write.

When I draft a novel, the making of the draft goes on for months. I stop in the middle of a sentence whenever possible and try to put down three pages of draft a morning, listening to the unfolding story as I hear the words in my head describe the sequence of action and reaction. The process of hearing a novel is the same as hearing a poem.

I also go through a similar process in writing an article such as this. I may do more conscious research and structured thinking in preparation for the writing of non-fiction; I may be aware of a predetermined length or form, a specific audience, an external purpose in writing. Still, I have to listen to the writing as it evolves within those limitations—and if a strong piece of writing it may bend those limitations a bit, as it did in this case when I had enough quiet time so that when I thought I was writing a traditional educational article I found I was writing a poem and wrapping an article around it.

Teaching writing is often as unexpected. I must listen and the students must do the talking. That does not mean that I am passive, for the act of listening requires immense concentration and patient receptivity. I must create a climate in the writing conference in which students can hear what they have to say so they can learn to listen to their own writing.

Too often, when we teach writing, we give our students the misconception we plan writing, that we intend what will appear on the page. They are frustrated when they are not able to visualize before the first draft, what will appear on their page. The students think they are dumb. We must be honest and let them know how much writing is unconscious or accidental. You do not think writing; you write writing.

Of course, even as I say that, I can think of exceptions. The creative process is never too clear, thank goodness. The elements of intention and planning vary depending on our experience, our purpose, our audience, our writing tasks, but the best writing is often unintended. We usually do not know what we want to say before we say it in non-fiction as well as poetry. We should push ourselves—and our students—to write what they do not expect to say, for the excitement of writing is the surprise of hearing what you did not expect to hear.

I did not expect a rocktree. While dictating the first draft of this article I did not expect to hear my voice developing the relationship between listening to writing and listening to students. But I did hear it, and I recognized its significance. It tied together some things I have learned about writing and about teaching.

I resolve to let my students know why I find it necessary to write quietly for at least fifteen minutes early in the morning. There are 96 quarter-hours in a day, and I need to find at least one quarter-hour which I can insulate from busyness so I can listen to myself. If I do that, perhaps I will find a few other quarter hours to listen to the work as it detaches itself from me and tells me what it wishes to become. We write well, not by forcing words on the page, but by listening to those words which collect themselves into a meaning while they are recorded on the page by a good listener.

If our students are to become effective writers, then it is our job to help them find at least a few small slices of quiet time—perhaps in class—and show them how to use that time to listen not to us, but to themselves to hear the writing they did not expect to hear.

Trusting Poetry to Teach Itself: A Naturalistic Approach to Reading and Writing Poems

by Marie Wilson Nelson

In 1965 poetry walked in faded blue jeans and wore wool turtlenecks. And it refused to be ignored. Since that time I've never taught a unit in poetry. I've never *taught* poetry at all. My students hear lots of poems, though, and we read, and haggle, and respond. When I find a poem I like, I share it, no matter what we're doing at the time. And when what we're doing reminds me of a poem—my own, a student's, or an established writer's work—I bring that in and read it too. It's the only way I can teach poetry anymore, and it's something I learned from Bob Ford, back in Greenville, South Carolina, many years ago.

Bob was only about 19 at the time, a sophomore at a college in the city where I taught, but he's the only teacher of poetry I really ever had (and yes, I *was* an English major). Bob used to drop by my house evenings bringing the latest poems he'd found. He would sit on the mat-covered floor in my tiny first apartment reading newly discovered passages to my roommate and me and our friends, involving us in his pleasure at a well-phrased line, ecstatic in his approval when a passage spoke to him. The rest of us joined naturally in the talk, pointing out parts we liked or didn't, running to a college text to find a writer we were reminded of, discussing how the poets achieved their effects, and speculating about their lives. The other thing Bob did for me was share the things he wrote. He even wrote poems for me on occasion, an honor I never returned. I never shared any of my poetry with him, I don't think. I was too unsure, too new. Bob was the first poet I had known, the first person to act like a poet anyway, to share his poet self with me, the first to bring poetry to life. That's when I learned the only way for me to know poetry was to discover it for myself, and my teaching has been different ever since.

A couple of years ago my friend Sandra Worsham, short story writer (and finalist for Georgia's English Teacher of the Year Award), asked me to speak to her creative writing class. Sandra doesn't write much poetry, so she wanted a "real poet" to come talk to the group. "How I Write a Poem" was the assignment, and I stayed up late the night before, searching for the order in my knowledge of how I write.

Sandra's invitation forced me to do some things differently from the way I usually teach. My poetry teaching is spontaneous—in literature and in writing classes. I've read a lot of poems to reading classes as well, for I've found poems to be microcosms of the language occurring in less condensed prose. Poems are built from just the sorts of language effects weak readers have trouble with; and not only are most short enough to read together in class, students explore ungrudgingly imagery, word choice, inverted sentence structure, and multiple layers of meaning in the poems that they like. Equally important, they initiate the exploration themselves, in order to understand.

For my talk to Sandra's class I tried to pull together the things I do incidentally with my own classes whenever the issues arise and to make from them a coherent presentation. That experience proved valuable for me, for personally helpful insights resulted from the attempt. I now believe (and I have seen this work for other teachers as well) that a carefully introspective study of what we do when we write—whether poetry or fiction, term papers for graduate courses, or letters to our friends—is the single most reliable source of insight about how to teach writing that any teacher can seek. Research in composing can inform us of what others do when they write, and theory may enlighten us as to why; but personal knowledge of writing, when carefully examined, is always accurate. As long as we remember that differences among writers exist and don't expect all students to write exactly as we do, our knowledge is a dependable guide, for differences among writers are more superficial than profound. The similarities lie in the conditions writers need to write, in the phases their writing goes through, and in the psychological demands that writing makes on them. The differences lie more often in the rituals they use to get through the hard places, in strategies for shaping their ideas.

For two years I have been studying how writers teach writing in middle and secondary schools. I have talked to dozens of writers, interviewed 23, observed for a day or two in each of eight classrooms, and then spent a quarter (term) each observing the three writers whose teaching was most strongly shaped by experience. In these three writers' classrooms, I watched them teach, I saw their students learn, and I tried to specify precisely the relationships between the two. Personal experience with writing, I found, is a primary source of insight for teachers into what students need to write well, and the know-how that results is always dependable. During my study it became evident that the most successful teachers (and equally significant, perhaps, the ones who are most content) are those who teach writing as they practice it, not as they are ''supposed'' to teach, not as they themselves were taught, and not as preparation of their students for college or for tests. These successful ''writer-teachers'' are consistent in their approach. More important than how they teach writing, for they do teach differently, is the way they all set up the conditions necessary for beginning writers to write. They remove the stigma of the grade, find any excuse they can think of to praise students' writing, build safe writing communities where learners can take real risks, encourage and support students in their efforts, and model the role they want their students to adopt—the role of the writer.

I've learned other things, however, about *less* successful teachers who write. These ''teacher-writers'' are alike in one regard: Our talks revealed discrepancies between how they teach and how they write. All were teaching in ways their practice invalidated, some predominantly so. It is not my goal to describe in detail how the writer-teachers teach, only to emphasize one point—that relying on experience is the key to their success. Let me sketch for you, therefore, what I learned about myself as a writer while preparing for Sandra's class—not to give you more content to incorporate into your teaching but to illustrate how teachers can learn from looking closely at what they know.

What I Learned about Writing by Studying Myself

What did I learn as I pulled together what I knew about how I write? And how do I think such personal knowledge can best be taught? I'm not sure that how-to knowledge of writing *can* be directly taught, but I think awareness of more advanced writers' habits validates for beginners the experience they already have, particularly when their experience conflicts with the precepts about ''writing'' they have traditionally learned in school. Such exposure may also suggest new strategies for handling the problems students are already struggling with. I do not believe, for example, that I can show a student how to revise her poems, but I can describe the considerations I make in my own work; then she can decide for herself whether my writing improves or not.

I began by going through my notebooks, trying to reconstruct the process by which each poem had emerged. I had always thought of myself as an endless reviser, and I knew most of my poems were attempts to capture feelings, to identify where feelings came from, and to clarify their meanings for myself. I also knew my poetry usually stemmed from ambivalence or from changes in relationships. In fact, I had told my students all these things in the past. One thing I had not realized, however, was how often my impulse to write grew from reading another poem. Though I was aware that established writers often used reading to find ideas, I had not known how frequently I was using it myself. Now when I'm looking for inspiration I read poetry that affects me strongly, and I encourage my students to do the same.

"Tokyo, 1967" is a poem I particularly like because writing it synthesized forgotten feelings about my years spent in Japan. It began, however, as a disdainful reaction to one of Brautigan's *June 30th, June 30th* poems (written in Japan). "A brown cat lies/in front of a Chinese restaurant/in a very narrow lane/in Shinjuku," began Brautigan. "The window of the restaurant is/filled with plastic models/of Chinese food that looks good/enough to eat."* I decided to share my response to Brautigan with Sandra's class.

TOKYO, 1967

I remember the fat brown cat of Shinjuku
lying in the alley, Brautigan, not <u>lane</u>
where
       [damp green stones littered with bok choi]
shreads of hakusai cling
to the piss-streaked portal of the chinese bar.
We could have afforded to enter of course—
it's easy to tell by the plastic food in the case—
but we leaned against an aloof stonewall in the darkness
and skittered gravel at intruding lions.

I remember the lean brown cat of Roppongi.
We arched backwards together into the shadows
when the glittering people intruded
from the Chinese Restaurant at the end of the lane.
There are Hotel Edens and porno flicks near the station
and the Shin-Otani and the Frank Lloyd Wright on the hill
but I have discovered your hands, here in the darkness.
The chauffeur-driven limousine's eyes are still.

---

*Excerpted from the book *June 30th, June 30th* by Richard Brautigan. Copyright © 1977, 1978 by Richard Brautigan. Reprinted by permission of Delacorte Press/Seymour Lawrence.

Another thing I hadn't realized about my writing was what different amounts of work various poems require. Having earned a reputation among my friends for the amount of on-page revision I do, I was startled to discover how many of my short poems had literally floated up to me. Shortly after my talk to Sandra's class, the experience occurred again. Working late one evening, I stopped to get something to eat. As I stood by the old gas stove, lifting spinach from a bamboo vegetable steamer, the following lines overtook me, and I stopped to write them down.

> Pausing past midnight
> to steam for myself
> a rice-bowl of spinach
> dashed with my chinese sesame
> and her japanese soy,
> I wish that you were here.

Realizing from my introspective preparation that a number of poems had come to me from fleeting rather than recurrent impulses, I began training myself to identify the spontaneous feelings in which some of my poetry is found. This practice is most difficult but also most productive when the feelings occur at a normally busy hour and must vie with more persistent distractions for my attention. I remember once during dinner at a friend's a far more experienced poet than I asked for a pad of paper and a pen. Three or four times during that evening I watched the pen in the writer's hand arc almost imperceptibly back and forth above the page. It was trying to pick up a poem, like a radar sweep I thought; and each time, after a few moments, a poem appeared on the page. I am still learning to recognize potential poems when they appear, and I suggest that my students do the same.

A second type of poem I write falls near the middle of the continuum between extensive revision and effortlessness. Sometimes I sense a sudden likeness between two unlike things, and from that awareness a poem often grows. This type usually requires two or three drafts to assume its final shape, and fine tuning may continue for a month—I can never rush it. Classes generally show interest in the evolution of poems, and I've shared this next one, written shortly after my meeting with Sandra's students, several times. Asked to read some poetry and talk about how I write at the summer Governor's Honors Program for superior Georgia high school students, I read the final version while students read along. Afterwards, I traced the poem's development. It had begun with a struggle to define the limits of the metaphor forming in my mind and with some false starts in tone. After the first draft was down came a period of regression during

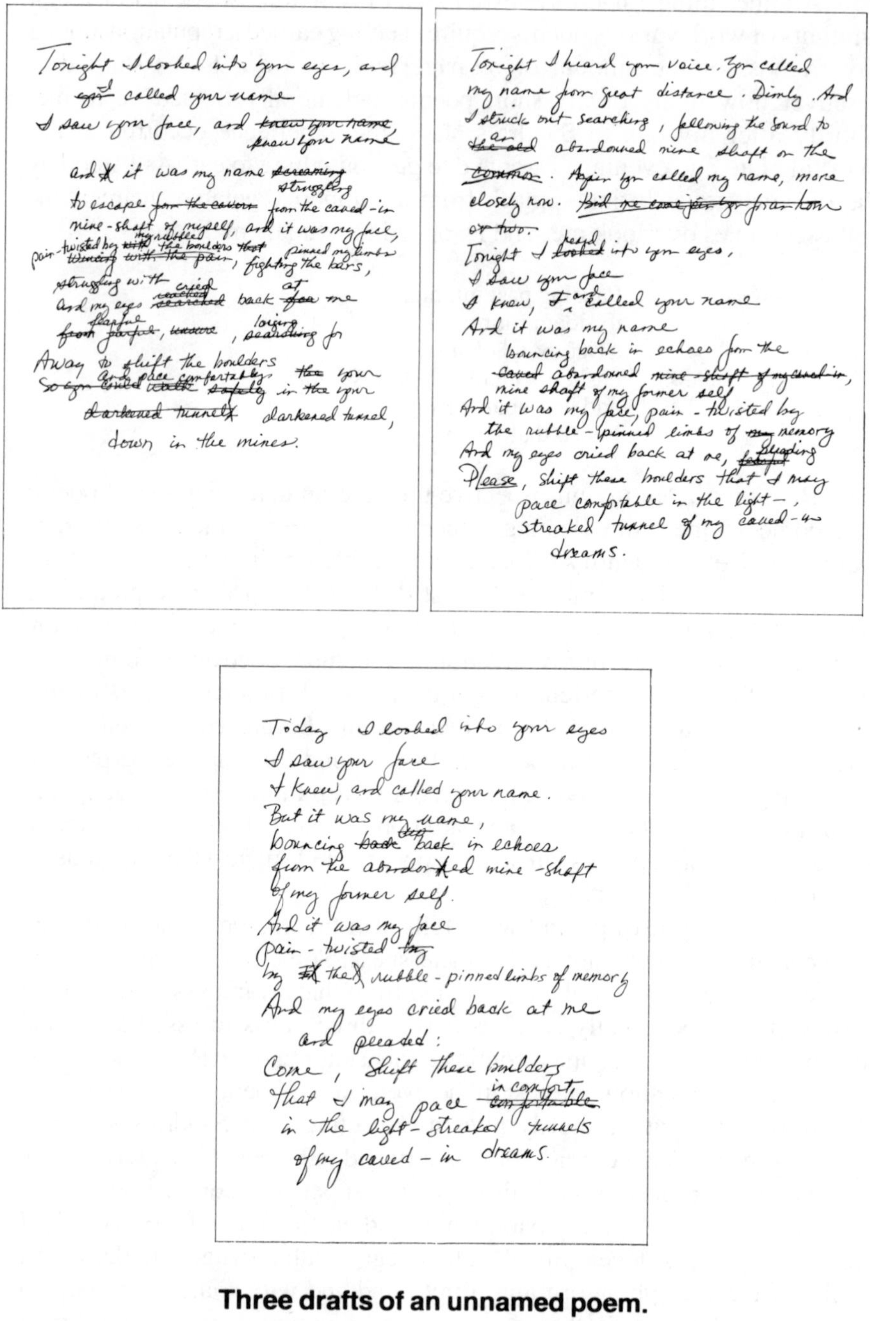

Tonight I looked into your eyes, and
~~you~~ I called your name
I saw your face, and ~~knew your name,~~
knew your name

and ~~I~~ it was my name ~~screaming~~
struggling
to escape ~~from the cavern~~ from the caved-in
mine-shaft of myself, and it was my face,
pain-twisted by ~~with~~ my rubbled ~~the boulders that~~ pinned my limbs
~~Wincing with the pain~~, fighting the bars,
~~struggling with~~
And my eyes cried ~~reached searched~~ back at ~~for~~ me
fearful ~~from fearful, unsure~~, longing ~~searching~~ for
Away to shift the boulders
~~So you could walk~~ and pace comfortably ~~safely~~ in the ~~the~~ your
~~darkened tunnels~~ darkened tunnel,
down in the mines.

Tonight I heard your voice. You called
my name from great distance. Dimly. And
I struck out searching, following the sound to
~~the old~~ an abandoned mine shaft on the
~~common~~. Again you called my name, more
closely now. ~~Bid me come join you from here~~
~~or two.~~
Tonight I ~~looked~~ peered into your eyes,
I saw your face
I knew, I and called your name
And it was my name
bouncing back in echoes from the
~~caved~~ abandoned ~~mine shaft of my caved-in~~,
mine shaft of my former self
And it was my face, pain-twisted by
the rubble-pinned limbs of ~~my~~ memory
And my eyes cried back at me, ~~fearful~~ pleading
Please, shift these boulders that I may
pace comfortable in the light-,
streaked tunnel of my caved-in
dreams.

Today I looked into your eyes
I saw your face
I knew, and called your name.
But it was my name,
bouncing ~~back~~ back in echoes
from the abandoned mine-shaft
of my former self.
And it was my face
pain-twisted ~~by~~
by the rubble-pinned limbs of memory
And my eyes cried back at me
and pleaded:
Come, Shift these boulders
That I may pace ~~comfortable~~ in comfort
in the light-streaked tunnels
of my caved-in dreams.

Three drafts of an unnamed poem.

which I kept writing determinedly though nothing I liked would come. Though all grasp of form seemed to be slipping away, I tried to keep the poem alive by repeatedly directing my attention to the feelings that had prompted it. The final stage, which students recognize easily, was the reestablishment of control in draft three.

This poem preserves for me the memory of the electric burst of empathy that flashed from me to a friend I saw struggling through a crisis much like one I had experienced before. Even though the poem is sometimes misunderstood, the fact that it serves this function for me, that the writer writes to clarify and preserve experience for herself as well as for others, is something I may never have said directly to my students, but which is evident when I share my drafts in this way. Students also see specific revisions I have made and may later consider similar strategies if they find my changes effective. Sometimes they volunteer, for example, that they would never have considered making such-and-such a change. But they recognize improvement when they hear it.

The third type of poem I will include here illustrates the revising end of the continuum. These poems go through draft after draft, sometimes resolving themselves after a week or two, sometimes requiring months. A poem about a friend's death from cancer evolved this way. In its final version it was far shorter than the earlier drafts, for I tightened and cut and condensed. Almost a year after Elaine died it began to feel like a poem. The poem "When the last door slams" represents a different kind of process. It began as a group of fragments which I sensed from the start were related, though I had to discover how. It took almost a month for me to perceive the relationships between the parts and to understand the images that would not go away. In the meantime the poem went through 18 or 19 drafts.

WHEN THE LAST DOOR SLAMS

When the last door slams behind me
on a taut week's work
and my tired sunflows like honey
on the rearview horizon
out from behind the corners of my eyes
you leap at me

dance in the quiet glint of rooftops
tin on spring grain flashing
glance off the sharp-edged hollows of my silences
but I cannot find your face.

At speed zone ahead
I downshift for the harrow

soon it's cotton dust and Sevin
as Waylon fades away.
In
        through twin channels of stereosong
you wash sudden
but I do not know your name
and there's no righthand line
on a dark Georgia road
to protect me from the glare.

What would I give to keep you near
where I might see you stumble
and what could I pay an agèd man
to tell me who you are?
Oh, I would make only new mistakes with you
none of the old ones
but who would I sell my children to?
and how betray a constant man
who knows me as I am
for one who only glimpsed the door ajar?

Helmet and goggle
the one-eyed Harley
takes me from behind
long breath slow coming
then rearing, skirts my vision's convex lens
and roars ahead.
Afar, two fan-tailed hawks
anchor competing jack-pines to the sky.
Distances hurt me softly when they fly.

    Hardly a poem I would have deliberately chosen for high school students, I impulsively stuffed my notebook under the lens of an opaque projector to illustrate my revising process. I was expecting Sandra's students to note the number of crossouts per draft and let the poem go at that. I should have known better. Unlike English teachers, students are rarely interested in revision for its own sake. They anchor every discussion of writing to content, finding no relevance in form alone. And they are right. Sandra's students wanted to read some drafts of the poem, to verify the feelings I was trying to express, to find out what hadn't been working for me and why. They wanted to know what the images meant, why I had chosen certain words. And they were fascinated to discover that I had boldly lifted the last line, which had rung in my head for months, from an otherwise forgotten poem by a friend. It was my unexpected identification with the feelings in that last lonely line that had prompted this poem in the first place.

This interest of adolescents in a content hardly "relevant" to their experience leads to a final point about teaching writing by relying on personal knowledge. Good writing is honest writing, and as such it is necessarily revealing, sometimes uncomfortably so. As a writer, though, I must not fall into the trap of disguising my true feelings, even in the classroom: it is destructive to my work. To do our best writing, whatever level of performance we are presently working at, honesty of expression is the key, and censoring what we say about our writing is to distort the writer's role. I don't mean to say it's necessary to share very personal writing with young students; I do believe once writing is shared, however, that censoring perverts the piece and that we must model that premise for learners because censoring also distorts their understanding of how the writer works.

Writing is risky business as every student knows, and sharing honest writing is riskier yet. That's why successful writer-teachers work first to create trusting communities of writers in their classrooms; it makes writing possible for their students, and it makes adopting a fellow-writer stance safe for them as well.

"But I haven't written a poem since high school," you tell me, "I'm not a poet at all. I *can't* rely on my experience as a guide." Then don't "teach" poetry writing. And don't expect every student to write poems if you don't (there's Lesson I from your own experience). It's probably better not to teach poetry directly anyway, but even though you're not a poet, you can set up classroom conditions under which poetry can thrive. Teaching poetry is nothing to be afraid of, for those of you who don't write can do much of what poet-teachers do: You can show respect for poetry and poets, bring into the classroom many friends who write, share only the poems that you love. Let the study of poetry flow naturally back and forth between reading and writing, regardless of the name of the course. Encourage students to form *on class time* a poets' group. Let them give readings of their work. Have *students* talk to your classes about "How I Write a Poem." If you model the kind of writing that you do, whatever that may be, and ensure your student poets' prestige, you won't need to feel bad about your failure to teach poetry. Poetry will teach itself.

Only a Well-Digger's Teacher

by Philip Billings

Richard Hugo had a long, excellent article in *American Poetry Review* two years ago on the subject of how to teach poetry-writing.[1] I remember three things from it: one, make them use lead pencils so that they are not in the slightest way encouraged to think of their early-draft words as permanent; two, tell them they had better have some favorite words and use them a lot, unless they are amazingly talented; and, three, coax them to have "the courage of their obsessions." I don't like it when poets can't talk about poetry without every minute quoting some other poet talking about poetry, so I promise not to do it again. But I did want to get that third idea said and credited exactly right because that is the log on the fire I want to poke at here. I want to say what I think Hugo means by "obsessions" and by "courage" and why, in poetry, the one demands the other, and why this is so important for beginning poets and their teachers to realize.

We obviously have different levels of obsession. I am obsessed with truth, with death, and with women. Less generally I am obsessed with the way truth can be so deep and beautiful as to be of no more practical use than a flower, with the deaths of children, and with stubborn, tough old ladies. Specifically, I am obsessed with the (partly imagined) sight of my grandmother lying very much like a baby in a hospital bed made very much like a crib by its safety bars along the sides, pounding her bony fist against one of those bars all night, my father sitting next to her unable to do or say anything about his love that would aid her in her fight against—or was it for—death. I am obsessed with myself, my aging, my hairline. I am obsessed with soft things beneath rough surfaces, with the very real, delicate joys of two-a-day fall football practices, with the sweet smell and cool feel of the grass during 8:00 a.m. push-ups.

It is the third, most exact sort of obsession, I think, that Hugo is talking about. It must be. I didn't feel especially courageous, didn't feel I was risking much of anything, when I told you those first two kinds. It would take courage for most people to say they were *not* obsessed with or at least seriously interested in such "topics." But that third kind: Weren't there things in it that you might find unseemly? Excesses of morbidity, nostalgia, vanity? A person's most particular obsessions, those precise gestures of mind and body he can't help but repeat, give him away in a flash. Even to himself. He hopes no one is watching; he half-wishes he himself weren't. Especially in this age that has so thoroughly refined and propagated for commercial purposes the idea of mass sameness or, if you will, of mass, "normal" obsessions (as with personal hygiene), to admit to idiosyncratic obsessions of almost any sort takes guts. You've singled yourself out. You are eccentric, unhealthy, noncommercial, which is nearly the same as unpatriotic.

To come at the subject another way, I think Richard Hugo advises poets to have the courage of their most particular forms of obsession because my favorite poems, including some of his own, are full of them. They are what people literally read first and remember longest. Ironically, it can often be the best literature students who most consistently forget this. We teachers make them. The good student turns to Keats' "To Autumn," sails through line after line of precise images of the man's obsessions— heavily ripe fruits and vegetables, drowsy afternoon boys, buzzing gnats— then writes in the margin "attempts to accept death." That's probably the nice safe *idea* the teacher will ask for on the next test. Or, if the teacher turns out odd enough to actually ask about images, the good student learns to talk about them as if they were totally conscious devices to convey theme. Keats needed something, again, to symbolize "Beauty: the narcotic power of"; so he went again to his dictionary of literary motifs and found "the fume of poppies." The man who made so sane (and old) a poem couldn't have been *really* hung-up on gorgeous narcotics, could he?

My answer, and I believe Hugo's, is a resounding yes. He not only could but also *should* have been. Writing out of real, personal obsession of some kind, that is. Almost any kind would have served, so long as it was honest. Why? Because that's the major way to write sentences that don't sound quite like anyone else's. It is the source of the intensity that makes images, metaphors, ironies, rhythms, repetitions, and all other verbal tricks spring to genuine life and then stay under control. It is the only material you've got to clothe and thereby make visible those oh-so-popular but elusive "feelings" that everyone knows you go to poetry for. While the proper, disciplined pupil of your eye is focusing on just what its supposed to in the night sky, the thematically significant constellations, the rowdy, careless peripheral vision catches the biggest, deepest, most mysterious and (thus) interesting stars of all. It does more than catch them, actually; it helps to *make* them.

I can imagine three objections to this obsession-oriented poetic think-ing, especially as it might be applied to teaching adolescents. First, there is something else besides specific, obsessive imagery in great poetry, namely, wisdom. General, universal truth asserted in the most appropriate form, whether it be plain or baroque, ingenuous or ironic or whatever—this, too, is something that makes sentences eminently worth reading. It wasn't just Pope or Frost who thought so, either; Mark Strand is always saying wise things like:

> His pursuit was a form of evasion:
> the more he tried to uncover
> the more there was to conceal
> the less he understood.
> If he kept it up,
> he would lose everything.*

This is no place to get into the old battles between Romantic and Classic, Imagist and Meditator. I'm not only willing to grant the place of overt wisdom in poetry; in fact, I love and would defend to my figurative death that place. But not in teaching adolescent poets. Wisdom and its concomitant ability to freshen and control abstract truths is something those kids just don't have. When they try for it, what you get is the stuff of warmed-up athletic banquet speeches and disinterred American Legion essay contests. They say what they think you want them to in ways as stuffy and stern and self-righteous as they think your old-fashioned life is. Do I have to give examples? Young people's bodies are wiser than their minds. I can hardly think of any of the overtly wise poetry I love that was written by people under 35.

But, someone might counter, isn't the "courage of your obsessions," the strength and willingness to damn conformity, equally beyond the adolescent grasp? Who more than the teenager literally buys all those commercials, clings more desperately to the crowd's hem, feels more acutely the screws put to him by peers? Kids who sign up to write poetry have already gone out on a limb, because everyone "knows" what poets are like; now you want them to saw it off with real self-revelation in the things they actually write?

I admit the case is a bad one. Something like the old question of whether it's easier to make a handsome boy smart or a smart boy handsome. But (not knowing which of those alternatives it more closely corresponds

---

*Reprinted by permission of Mark Strand from "The Untelling," in *The Story of Our Lives* by Mark Strand (New York: Atheneum, 1971, pp. 42–43).

to) I choose the truth of obsessions in their most particular form over wisdom in its most general. For one thing, there might be a better chance than you think that the very courage that made the kid sign up for or, if it wasn't optional, even pay attention in your poetry-writing class gives evidence of the capability for even more courage when inspired by a good subject or teacher. For another thing, the risk once taken might lead to self-revelation of a positive nature; peer groups often try, after all, to enforce inferior, stupid, or insensitive self-concepts. The exhilaration of finding them wrong can become a life-long habit.

Furthermore, promising young poets often resist genuine involvement in the discipline of writing seriously exactly *because* they have been told that THE POET first and foremost shows forth WISDOM—the very thing their innate honesty and common sense tell them they are fresh out of. If they are hard-boiled enough to suspect that adults come up short in this area, too, then THE POET described only in relation to WISDOM is an even bigger fake than their principal. Faking it in class may be fun for awhile, may even be mandatory, but it finally isn't as good as the real thing you get at the auto-repair shop, ball game, or senior class play. One more consideration. Once teenagers get in tight enough with a crowd, they can get remarkably reckless, loose, crazy. Besides being the most conformity-minded among us, they may also be the most self-conscious; and, when that quality gets turned inside-out in the peer-group's safe confines, they can wear their obsessions like five coats of Clearasil. Maybe the poetry class can eventually turn into a group like that.

The final complaint I can imagine against teaching poetry-writing in this obsession-oriented way is that what you will get is trivial or neurotic or quirky stuff best left to the therapist or the peeping Tom. Who cares, finally, about aberrations? Schools are meant to civilize kids, teach them how best to fit into the common, productive scheme of things, how most thoroughly to blend in with ''society.'' My response to this belief is pretty simple: anyone who believes it whole-heartedly should not teach poetry-writing to anyone. I understand the assumption behind all art to be, simply, that it is not ''civilized'' (in the sense just described anyway); it is chronically child-like. The single case is always more important than the group norm. The aberration art publicizes proves some other, more important rule. The truth it cherishes is always a little quirky.

But not, finally, limited or trivial, not *merely* personal. That star that the corner of the eye sees better than the pupil does belongs to the whole universe which includes each of us; and each of us helps to make that star. Without us it is dead. Or to choose a more utilitarian metaphor: poetry is water that the whole community needs in order to fully live, and the best way to get at it is just to drill straight down from where you are standing. It takes a good deal of faith, especially at first, but it works every time. If your efforts have brought up nothing but trivial, sick, or incomprehensive sludge so far, it's a simple (though exhausting) matter of trying harder, drilling deeper. If you hit solid rock, you were unlucky this time. Move over a little and try again. The water table is down there somewhere, for sure. Have courage.

First of all, then, teach beginning poets to "have the courage of their obsessions." That's what I'd advise. They will want to write about their convictions, instead. They'll want to say Uncle Ray was sweet; don't let them; get them to tell you about the pungent odor from some kind of plant that always makes them remember Uncle Ray's back yard. They'll want to write about the importance of victory; make them describe instead the sight of the pitch that almost took their head off last summer and that they still have dreams about. Or make them describe the act of having thrown it. They'll insist on saying they're in glorious love or nobody understands them or life is what you make it; ask them what they practice in front of the full-length bedroom mirror, the one on the back of the locked door, every night. If the answer would be *only* embarrassing—don't worry, they would never tell you in 1,000 years. They will want to use rhymes; let them if it doesn't interfere with the truth. (It probably will.)

The biggest draw-back to this "obsessive" method may relate more to the teacher than to the young student. Since kids learn best by example, the teacher him- or herself cannot finally avoid showing the same kind of courage she or he is demanding. I have been playing teacher of this method here and have, therefore, used myself by way of illustration near the beginning to an extent that would otherwise be inappropriate. Let me end out on the same limb by citing one of my poems.

THAT LOG

Ringed full of a sleep
no rounder or longer than the others'
but at least twice as heavy,
that log
was the last one hauled in.
It never got really caught up
in the pale yellow-blue exhibition
that crackled briefly beneath it.
For hours afterwards it shrank and grew
black-gray-white by itself.

Now, just before we click off,
follow as usual the last light up,

then smooth and tuck ourselves finally out,
that log
cracks itself open to the heart
and blooms its own flame.
And that flame
quivers once, then stands:
deep gold-purple, tight with attention,
ready for the long night.

I don't claim a lot for this poem. I wrote it when I was even more of a beginner than I am now. I think now I can do better. But I am not ashamed of it either, and I can't imagine ever being ashamed, because I feel something true to my best self and to something more in it. You may check the poem against the personal obsessions mentioned earlier in order to get a psychologist's eye-view of some of the roots that lead up to this sturdy feeling. That analytical view was not at all mine, however, when I wrote the poem. All I could see was that log. I watched it for hours one night, first out of the corner of my eye, then directly, when I "should" have been doing something else, I forget what. Then I couldn't stop watching it with my mind for days afterwards. Finally I saw a scary white sheet of paper that I could make safe with words that fit that log as well as I could make them fit. When I have shown the poem to writing classes, none seems to have found it trivial or embarrassing. Most seem, miraculously to me still, to have recognized either from experience or from intuition what the poem is about. At the same time, miraculously again, they seem to have learned something new from it. And not primarily about me at all. About real logs. And "real life." A few even thought they learned something about writing poetry.

Reference

1. Richard Hugo. *American Poetry Review* 8 (2) (March/April, 1979): 21.

APPLICATIONS

Introduction

Hearing what poets have to say about their craft and about their feelings for poetry is useful, but there remains the basic problem that all instructors face when they enter a classroom: *I* have an appreciation and an understanding of poetry, but how do *I* communicate these to young people who, more often than not, resist any thought that poetry might be important to them? Is it important, after all, that nonreaders and writers who so frequently populate our classrooms even know that poetry exists and that it may speak to many of their concerns and wishes? The answer is obviously yes, and the suggestions of how to make this connection appear in this section.

A common thread runs through the discussions of applications which appear in this section: namely, that one of the first things that has to be done in the classroom to help students become interested in poetry is to make it accessible to them. One way of accomplishing this is to help students understand the importance of words. For many students, as Tom Liner points out in his anecdotal account of working with low-level students, being able to use words to communicate feelings and ideas is a totally new experience; once the contact with words begins, however, an entire new world begins to appear and students tend to embrace it eagerly. Jim Heynen, Ron McFarland, and Ingrid Wendt share their experiences as poets in the schools, explaining the different techniques they use to introduce language play as the first step toward understanding poetry. Coming to grips with the possibilities of words, of their combinations, and of their meanings can lead gradually to more extended use of language and a greater understanding of the power of language to communicate. Raymond J. Rodrigues, Charles R. Duke, Helen J. Throckmorton, and Denny T. Wolfe, Jr. provide practical applications for systematically building upon language play to make poetry more accessible.

Introducing poetry to students should be done in gradual stages, beginning with language play and then moving on to the intellectual exploration of meaning in poems. James S. Mullican outlines an approach for involving students in unlocking the meaning of a poem. Suggesting that many poems remain a kind of riddle until the clues are put together, Mullican shows how this "riddle approach" can be applied easily to the classroom study of poetry. However, sometimes it is necessary to go beyond the poem itself to obtain an understanding of the culture in which a poem originated. Jeffrey F. Huntsman suggests the importance of this approach in his exploration of the basic principles to be found in Native American poetry.

In addition to understanding the role of language and meaning in poetry, students eventually will need to develop an understanding of form. David Sudol describes a classroom approach for making form accessible to students. His description of a collaborative writing of a ballad suggests how students may begin to bridge the gap between reading and writing poetry while also coming to an appreciation for form. Suzanne J. Doyle provides an outline of how a complete poetry course might be developed, focusing on the lyric poem as its principal form.

With form comes a need for understanding meter, rhythm, tone, and voice. Joseph E. Price suggests ways to introduce the concepts of meter and rhythm to students, while R. L. Barth provides an explanation of the more technical aspects that students will need to comprehend as they become more sophisticated in their reading and writing of poetry. Rose M. Feinberg outlines an approach which, by combining drama and poetry, provides ways for students to explore the importance of tone, mood, voice, and rhythm in poetry. David C. Schiller outlines a testing method for evaluating students' understanding of how poets' styles and perspectives may vary.

Finally, Thomas G. Devine offers a summary of the roles poetry may play in the classroom and suggests some fundamental principles for teachers to keep in mind as they develop their own applications for teaching poetry to young people.

The Outlaws . . . and Jonathan, Smiling

by Tom Liner

Fourth Period. Half of Gainesville High School was at lunch, and it sounded like most of them were in the hall outside my room at the end of third wing. My class was coming into the room. Like Jackson Browne singing from the tape player in the corner, I felt like I was "running on empty"—already tired at mid-day, frustrated, worried about this bunch of seniors in a class called Practical Writing. They, and I, knew that meant it was a basic level class for seniors who had trouble with English, especially with writing. All but one of them (who was misscheduled and couldn't get out somehow) had to pass this one to graduate. Most of them had been in trouble with other teachers and the principal, some with the law. They were mostly male, mostly tough and street-wise, mostly negative about school, about themselves, about writing. I had known them only a week, and I was having serious doubts about the structure of the class—an open writing workshop with daily free writing in a journal, sharing my reading aloud, and editing for in-class publishing. I often used the workshop-developmental model with gifted students and average students in elective creative writing classes, but I didn't know if I could make it work for these hard-core "basic" kids.

Yet, they came in smiling. I think they liked being there. I had no way of anticipating it at the time, but my Outlaws, as I called them and still think of them, were to be the most rewarding class I've ever taught. From that bright Friday in January until June, I saw them grow as writers. More importantly, I saw them grow *together*, writing and sharing their writing and themselves in an atmosphere of mutual support and openness. I'm not sure where the magic came from but part of it came from Jonathan, the Outlaws' poet.

He came in late, as usual. He was a tall, handsome Black kid, and he always dressed "sharp." He was as street-wise and street-tough as any kid

I've known. But beneath that brittle outside was something genuine and vulnerable. Maybe I already sensed it, I don't know. I liked him.

"Jonathan, my man, where've you been?"

His teeth flashed, the loose-jointed walk kept its slow pace to his desk. "Be cool, Brother Liner, the little girls needed some attention."

Instead of getting mad, I laughed. We laughed together and began the bond of trust and acceptance and affection that would reach to the whole class. The ritual greeting at the first of each period was established. I always called Jonathan "my man," he always responded with "Brother Liner." It was never a problem.

I started the class, as I always did, with a 10 to 15 minute free writing. We wrote together before I checked the roll, made assignments, or performed other clerical duties. And I did not allow anything to interrupt the free writing. We were 10 minutes late for one fire drill. Astonished teachers, students with messages, even the assistant principal were told to "come back in 10 minutes, we're writing now."

After the first few days, I'd say, "Give me 10 minutes, gentlemen— and ladies," turn on the music, and sit and write with them as they fell to work. They were some of the most pleasant times I've spent in the classroom. A noisy student in the room was usually silenced by neighbors before I could call him/her down.

I wrote my first poetry with them in class that Friday. Actually, I started a poem I never finished. Neither form nor subject was prescribed in the free writings. And most of the writing I did and the students did during the semester was prose. Yet, all but one of them, including Allen, who was blind, wrote poetry at one time or another. Only two of these kids had ever written poetry of any kind before, and that was in grammar school. The forms of their writings literally grew out of the flow and substance of the developing writings themselves—with a lot of encouragement and sometimes with a lot of work.

After free writing with them each day, I read aloud what I had just written to them. Good or bad, confused or coherent, I read it straight off the page and talked about where the writing came from, what I thought about it, what I would like to do with it next. Especially I talked about the problems of a writer faced with the blank page and the tentative, difficult, searching, but joyous work of writing. And today I read a rambling free writing that finally turned my eyes to the bright January sky out the windows.

> "People need some reason to believe"
> —a hard day to get it going, so it goes—in this
> writing business, trying to catch a hook and start
> something—O, well, there are those days.

if I were to pick an object that represented *me*
right now, what would it be? How about that coffee cup—
a thing of little value, wearing my "sign" I guess.
I've grown from peace signs to rainbows. Maybe that's
growing?
What do you want to be when you grow up, Tom?
I don't know yet. I just like to play.

jet stream cumulus, fingers of the sky

a nice line, I guess—now what?
and the cold opened its hand to touch me

Winter song

the wind rattles in the broom sedge
jet stream cumulus hold the sun
        in an open hand
the sky's touch is cold
wind from the west

                ?

I told them I wasn't happy with the writing and probably wouldn't finish the poem. Jonathan was smiling. Then I asked, "OK, anybody have anything you want to read?" The invitation was usually met with silence, but today Hub, a White kid who sat by the windows and wrote turned toward them looking out, read in a halting and almost shy voice a description of the hill, the gym, and parking lot behind the school. I remember one phrase about "the light glare on a hundred windshields hurts," and I remember how quiet the group got when he started reading. When Hub stopped (his piece was very short) I started to praise him, but Jonathan beat me to it. "Man, that was *something*! You sure can *write*!" Hub grinned and looked at me for affirmation. All I did was nod and say, "Listen to the man."

Jonathan didn't read that Friday, but I felt the class come together because of his listening ear, his generous spirit, and his smile. Hub turned into a fine descriptive and narrative writer by the end of the year, his voice growing stronger in his writing each week. I discovered Jonathan's writing voice when I read his journal over the weekend.

The sky is grateful . . . Daydreaming All day,
Daydreaming All night Wake Up in 4th period,
ready to write . . . You feel crazy & you feel
great, Just let your pen move and not Hesitate.

> Right On! Right On! Right On! . . . The Halls
> are Ambitious! . . . A Voice here, A Voice there.
> Why can't it consume quietness . . . The Act of
> Togetherness was really there . . . Will the
> World stand still? . . . Thinking. That's what
> I'm doing, Thinking . . . OOH, What a Crazyful
> World. On your toes, on your feet! You've got a
> special duty to meet. That's the law around here,
> You have to wear your sunglasses and you have to
> be on your toes. Why did I put toes first and
> sunglasses last?*

I could "hear" him places, and his phrasing struck me. At the end of his journal for that first week I wrote, "I think you're going to be a *natural* poet!"

For the next few weeks, I pushed the Outlaws to read aloud in class because of the positive feeling in that room when they shared their writings. Once a week, I pulled them into a circle for a "quick round," calling on each of them in turn. They could pass or read. I encouraged. Gradually they began to read. Often I heard Jonathan's "Hey, Man, read the thing" in those sessions.

They were invited to read after each free writing, but no one was called on. When someone did volunteer, that was the best reading we did together. At the end of the second week, Jonathan volunteered his first poem to the class.

> Daydream, Daydream, Daydream
> lady, lady, lady, Wondering, Wondering
> Wondering, will you be there real soon

As he did with me when I read poetry, I asked him to read it the second time. It didn't get any better with the second reading, but it was a start. And his journal that week was open and honest, reaching to an audience that he was suddenly aware of and had many things to talk to about. I wrote in his journal that week, "The man can *write*!"

I don't know who the "lady" was in the first poem, but he was in love and had lost her. A few days after he read in class, I was thinking about his daydream, and I sketched out a rough daydream sequence of my own about lost love. When I read the first version to the class, I told Jonathan, "I'm working on your daydream idea, my man. You've got me hooked." I spent a couple of days writing with them, putting this poem together.

---

*Excerpts from the journal and other writings of Jonathan Butts, Gainesville, GA, are published with his permission.

WAKING DREAMS: A SEQUENCE

I paint these pictures on the walls of my mind
and the colors tremble when I touch them

your memory is like singing at the edge of night
in your hands are two perfect white stars

I follow your footsteps in the sand like sunset
but the tide is sleeping where they end

this fire dances yellow in the wind
sparks tangle in the trees like midnight

I keep losing your face in the dark
when your voice goes out like a candle

clouds are walking down the sky
and sleep is easier than dreams

the wind touches the window wanting in
I smile and tell it lonely secrets

my life is an empty room in a deserted house
dust and shadows wait behind the door

children write on the empty walls
I hear them laughing in the mote-still light

I close my hands without touching you
the fire is dying sparks fly up like wings

the clouds are passing I can see the stars

We talked through the drafts together. Jonathan took an overseer's pride in the process. It was his idea, after all. And he wasn't shy about his criticism of the final product. "Man, I don't know about that poem. It just don't get itself together." Then he smiled. "You got better stuff than that, Brother Liner."

He was right. I never published it. But we did talk a lot about writing poetry and the *process* of writing that week.

Meanwhile, he was writing longer poems in his journal and reading them proudly to the class. Most were about girls, but there was also this sensitive exploration of a 19-year-old's feelings about his relationship with his father.

FATHER

Though capable,
but never,
releasing the tensions
brought about between us,
Or shall I say
Though wanting,
but hesitant to—
To square me away,
To Live,
To forget my past,
To accept me,
     Once Again,
For you have
all of the World's
greatest reasons

It's Love
It really is
Though we hardly confront it,
but often thinking,
Our love
only grows stronger

To say, I love you,
is a phrase
waiting to be heard,
but Afraid to be
     given,

What shall be,
     Will be,
Through thick,
Through thin,
I am his Son,
a Son indeed,

Waiting for my father,
Who is waiting for me.

     Daddy.

I especially like the ending of this poem— "I am his Son,/a Son indeed,/ Waiting for my father,/Who is waiting for me./Daddy."—and what it says about the assumption of manhood and the subtle, often painful, love of sons and fathers.

The class was moving, writing and talking about writing together, and taking a great pride in being writers. During the fourth week, I decided it was time to publish in the class. All of the free writings and other writings had been done in single drafts in their journals. By now, many of them were being read to the group and talked about, and I responded to them in writing each weekend. But we had done no editing.

We managed to publish only twice in Fourth Period, all the dittoed writings eventually going into a small book for each student. Some pieces were written, some printed, and some "two-finger" typed with the indulgence of a friendly typing teacher down on first wing. Spelling and language usage in the journals were exactly what you'd expect in a basic level class of former "nonwriters." Editing was slow and frustrating, for them and for me. I remember one short piece by Chris, a lumbering White kid who liked to fight and whose handwriting was the worst scrawl in class, that went through at least five drafts and five conferences with me before it was finished. I insisted that the published pieces be as good, and as correct, as we could make them. It was the hardest work we did, and probably the most important. Their words in print made them, officially, *writers*.

With the daily free writing continuing and other activities going on, it took us three weeks to publish the first time. Sometime in early March, I wrote this poem in response to something Jonathan had said about the class in his journal.

4TH PERIOD

Mid-day passes quickly
in sunlight
Spring rises this morning
and waits for your
smiles

"Man, that's *us*!" he said Monday when he read it, and he insisted I publish it with the class.

But he refused to show me the piece he was preparing for publication. "Now, Jonathan, my man, it better be good. And no mistakes. This is important," I told him when I called him over for an editing conference. "Be cool, Brother Liner, this poem is *bad* [i.e., very good]. It's a *surprise*. Darryl'll help." Some of the others in the class looked up and grinned knowingly. I knew Darryl, the lanky basketball·player, spelled almost as badly as Jonathan did. But I left them alone. I had insisted on proofing final "copy" on the dittoes and running them off myself before the pages were punched to include in their books. Somehow, Jonathan and Darryl got to an unguarded duplicating machine. They proudly marched into class a few days later bearing the finished copies.

"This goes in the *front*," Jonathan smiled and handed me the stack of copies. I was surprised all right.

MR. LINER

From one great poet
to another
From one self-contained youngman
to his brother.

Our lives are alike
in such a way
That we live beside each other
Day by day
The way we live,
The way we laugh,
The way we cry,
Our tears are together
in that single drop
for to let us know
Our brotherhood will not stop

For the Day will come
when we will depart
but until that day
We are heart in heart

Be Cool, Brother Liner

When I read his journal that weekend, I found three carefully worked over drafts of the poem on three successive days. I know he spent hours writing and editing the poem. For many reasons, it makes me feel good when I open a small yellow binder on my desk and see his poem first.

The Outlaws grew together into the spring and lived up to their nickname. Chris got into another fight in the hall. Tony, the long haired rock musician who had been married since he was 14, changed jobs and was having trouble getting to school on time. Alex showed up one day barefooted because the dog had chewed up his shoes. Martie dropped out of school suddenly. I was never told why. Hub was in trouble with the principal again. I think everyone in the room was in danger of not graduating at one time or another. Jonathan seemed to fall in and out of love on a weekly basis, and he spun out poems about all of them.

In early May we were editing and getting ready to publish again. I still reserved time for free writing to start each class. We enjoyed it, for one thing, and they were volunteering to read aloud more all the time. I began writing sketches of each person in the class. I don't know what started it, but my writings were quickly done during the free writing and took the form of impressionistic prose-poems. I tried to write one a day, and I read it to the class and to the student, looking right at him/her as I read. The result was electric! Soon everybody was writing about everybody else in the room, and voluntarily *reading them aloud*. I felt the class hold its collective breath each time one was read. They were all positive, very personal statements, and many were gentle and moving. They asked me to publish my sketches in the last publication. By unspoken agreement, none of theirs was published. They were too personal, and shared best read aloud by the writer to his subject.

Jonathan's smile was never brighter than when I read this one to him.

> JONATHAN is my darker brother—"Jonathan, my man,
> how are you?"—poets talking living smiling the
> day into tomorrow. I will envy you the journey.
> You are honest. I write and teach, only two things.
> Movement and *yes*-saying, singing is smiling,
> running to catch the sun rising.
>
> Jonathan, my man, thanks for the teaching.

A few days later he read a very nice, personal piece to me. But, he said, "I done yours before. It's in the *book*." The finest moment for me in that class came unexpectedly on another sunny Friday, this time in late spring, when Jonathan read his poem to Chris. Their friendship had grown over the semester. Chris was big, boisterous, and White. Jonathan was street-wise and cool, sharp and tough, and Black. And never more beautiful than when he read in a clear, cadenced, and completely sincere voice:

> CHRIS
>
> To be a friend of yours
> is to be a friend of many.
> The security you give,
> the friendliness you share,
> the smile you win,
> For to be Chris,
> shall I say,
> is to be champion in many ways.
> For the things you do,
> you will never know,
> For the thing you share

is to accept us all.
I do not face you
as a different race.

Instead I face you wrapped within
closed tight the texture
of my own receiving face

Chris, through the tough
time and times we've both seen

Through the extent we've made
our Mothers be a Mother,
Shall I not be halted to say

I simply love you as
my Brother, Brother.

"Jonathan, my man," I said when I could trust my voice, "you make me proud."

They all made me proud. Except for Martie, all the Outlaws graduated. And scattered. Most are working, or I hope they are. A few are in college and probably having a hard time of it. Maybe their pride and new confidence will keep them going. I haven't heard from Jonathan. He was thinking about college, but he knew it would be very difficult, both academically and financially. I hope he's still falling in love and still writing poetry.

I was going to include a series of *do's* and *don'ts* about teaching poetry to "basic" kids, but that doesn't feel right now. I hope the "rules" of sharing the experience of writing, accepting the young struggling writer, growing together in a caring and safe community of writers, and reaching up for something we didn't think we could do but are proud we did—I hope these *basic* rules of writing and teaching writing are expressed in my relationship with and my love for the Fourth Period Outlaws and Jonathan, my *Man*.

Shimmering Chartreuse

by Jim Heynen

Let us be realistic about teaching poetry to young people. Part of teaching for most of you is survival—financial and personal. When the black dog of poverty is not at your heels, you are facing a classroom of potentially diffusive energy that threatens bedlam at any moment. You think of ways to stay ahead of your students, to anticipate their disruptive and sometimes cynical moves. Still, for many of you, teaching poetry is a way of trying to salvage lives and minds and potential talents, of somehow finding a path toward beauty through all of the brambles. A few of you may be in a precious setting with well-disciplined, dedicated, and gifted students. Your task is not easy either, since you have to guard against complacency, against the easy divisions of life and art, against a kind of honor student decadence. But most of you are in some way on the defensive. Because you are nevertheless still possessed with love and dedication, you read essays like this one and believe you can effect change, that both you and your students can grow through the dynamics of the classroom. Thank God for you. I hope in some way I can help you.

For several years I have directed a poetry workshop program for gifted students. After a few years of the program, I realized that the best young poets were consistently coming in clusters from certain teachers. I began to wonder if, instead of providing workshops for gifted students, we were simply confirming the results of gifted teachers.

One obvious conclusion was that the writing of good poetry can be taught. However, I began to wonder how we might recognize potential in students who do not participate in such programs. I sent out a questionnaire to scores of American poets asking them to characterize the young poet whom they thought would be potentially good. I assumed that many of the poets would recall their own childhood obsessions, and I am sure many of them did. The sampling was quite representative, including Pulitzer Prize and National Book Award winners, as well as young poets just starting to publish nationally.

What characterizes the potentially gifted poet? By far the most fre-quent response had to do with "delight with the language." Answers took the form of such phrases as "likes to play with words," and "is interested in words for their own sake." Other answers which tallied high were (a) broad reading interests and habits and (b) a general curiosity about the world. Interestingly, hardly any of the poets surveyed said anything about feelings or sensitivity. This survey confirmed some of my hunches and made me feel more comfortable about my own inclinations. I like to have fun in the classroom, and the survey seemed to suggest that my predilection for using language games just might be all right.

I remember well a one-week visiting poetry engagement I had in a Washington suburban school where this predilection worked to my ad-vantage, as well as to that of the students. I am not sure how typical the high school classes were that I visited, but there seemed to be an extraordinarily high level of frivolous obsessions over hair and clothing styles, over cars, over "in" parties, over recreational drugs, and over social cliques. So much snobbery and so little reason for it, I thought. My label as "poet" was one strike against me, since, among other things, it obviously meant that I did not make much money and that I probably did not have very much power in the world. I read them some poems by teenagers. I wrote poems on the blackboard, impromptu, on any topic they wanted. They were clearly impressed, the way they might be by someone who did card tricks, but they were not turned on to poetry. Noticing that the classroom was filled with cliques, many of them mildly hostile toward each other, I told them to rearrange themselves in the room so that they would be with their best friends and to form into groups I called committees. The teacher cringed seeing the likes getting together into conglomerates of like energy. I then told them that each of the committees was assigned the task of providing a list of new color names for next year's line of lipsticks to come out from some prestigious cosmetics company.

The assignment was no more—or less—than a competitive word game, and one which accepted all the baser social and snobbish qualities of the group. Of course there were the "dead-frog greens" from the smiling-tough males and the "pleasant peaches" from the 1950s-nice females. But then there was the "shimmering chartreuse" group, a basically ambivalent and sassy committee of young women who, I guessed, had tried every teen-age fad by the time they were 15 and had come out the other side bored. This assignment was clearly for them and they came out, by my pronouncement, the glittering and excited winners.

Sizing up the group, I made my committee word assignments which would at some point give every group a chance to shine. Advertising slogans for motorcycles. Bumper stickers on a wide range of topics. Ironic (real or imagined) road signs. The delight in language was fantastic.

At some point, the "playing with words" guideline will fall short, but if you are in a classroom setting where attitudes toward writing and poetry are still major obstacles, you will feel more comfortable with the seemingly trivial word games which may come to mind or which you may find in any number of writing handbooks.

The following days in that suburban school, I had no trouble building on the good spirit created by the competitive word games. One day we wrote country-western songs. Most of them parodies, of course. Round-robin. I supplied first lines ("Checkerboard square on the table—your move"; "I'm a little dog caught in the kennel of your heart"; "Your coat hanger left a twang in the closet when you left me"; etc.) and would help bring a song back on track—or off track—if it seemed to be getting lost. Five songs were circulating simultaneously around the room, and I had one going on the blackboard that students could work on when the circulating songs were not in front of them. Whoever came up with the next line for the song on the board simply ran to the front and wrote it down. There would actually be a scramble of people rushing to put the next line on the board. We wrote rock lyrics the day after that. The students were indeed turned on, and the assignments produced some big class hits.

The transition from word play had begun. Already I could see hints of the new and more mature form emerging: personal touches in the song, real feelings and experiences crouching within the cliched images from contemporary rock songs. For some, of course, the transition from the rather frivolous activities will never progress into serious attempts at their own poetry. For others, the word games are simply a delightful aside to what is already a commitment to using language toward more personally meaningful and even ambitious ends. But the shimmering chartreuses! And their counterparts, male and female! These are the ones who challenge the teacher in me and who make my idealistic vapors rise! And I suppose these students are "most students."

This may sound outrageous, but if you can help that mass of students see the relationship between words and power, you may be opening the doors to more personal and committed writing. Much of the success of the word games is owing to the students' sense of having a creative power and control with words. Competitive word games—especially ones hinting at a commercial market—emphasize even more the possible relationship between words and power in society. And I do not think I am being carelessly out-of-touch with youth when I nearly equate *money* and *power*. Bending a rather base motive just a little, you can assign poems in which students have the power to effect change. For example, any variety of poems which call for transformations or directives: How to . . . or Instructions for. . . . This chain of subtle shifts and variations can go on *ad infinitum*. It can lead to rewriting fairy tales in verse as several contemporary poets have done; it can lead to poems about the love affair that might have turned out differently; it can lead to rewriting parents into people the students wish they had been. Most primitive cultures knew that the word, that poetry, is power. Once we return to that realization, we also realize just how "heavy" word games can be, for by acquainting and delighting students with the weaponry of words we are equipping them with the kind of power that none of us will ultimately be able to do without.

Following is a How to . . . poem which I wrote and which I have often used with students as a transition from the word games to a more personal poetry. It has in it the kind of word play they may have come to enjoy, and yet it also has a kind of menacing power: the reader can feel at some point that he or she is the tourist controlled by the world created by the poem. (One of the many good responses to this poem was one entitled "Student Guide: How You Can Tell For Sure When A Teacher Is In A Bad Mood").

TOURIST GUIDE: HOW YOU CAN TELL FOR SURE
YOU'RE IN SOUTH DAKOTA*

You drive down Main Street
of the first town you come to.

There's a traffic light.
Always. Prestige.

When it sees you coming,
it turns red.

You stop and you're exposed,
and you know it.

A thin cowboy's rabid dog
eyes you from the pool hall.

Then a thick old man
thumps down from the curb.

He's in front of your car
when the light turns green.

*"Tour guide: How You Can Tell for Sure When You're in South Dakota" appeared originally in *South Dakota Review*. Reprinted by permission of the author and *South Dakota Review*.

Something slow meets your eye.
An eye meets your eye.

You smile.
It doesn't.

You start to drive away.
The whole world stalls.

Glancing over what I have presented thus far, I see that I have espoused an approach to teaching poetry from the outside in. Starting with words and forms and working toward the students' felt experience. Very well. But I can imagine someone achieving similar ends with a totally reverse approach! Indeed, I can recall an argument among teachers of poetry which broke down into two camps: those who would start by encouraging self-expression and those who were more inclined toward emphasizing ways of writing, or technique. I was acquainted with the results of some of the teaching from both camps and knew that some teachers had students who wrote beautiful poetry from a premise which was pretty close to *just write what you feel!* These teachers made extensive use of journal writing, automatic writing, meditation, dream recording, and other methods of probing the inner self. The technique camp were more intrigued by my approach. [Though I use all the other methods too when I have time (shh).] Alas, the two camps do in some way represent that old distinction between the poet as maker and the poet as seer, as craftsman or visionary. But I do not believe that distinction has ever been very useful for the making of poems or even for the instruction and inspiration of young poets. Truth is, many poems of vision or substantial ideas have been written by poets concentrating on form, and many formally interesting and exquisite creations have accompanied the poet's concentration on subject. One may hold one concern more consciously in focus in one poem or another, but the other side will be there, even if at a subconscious level. And who would dare to say whether it is the conscious or subconscious energy that provides the greater contribution to the process of creating a poem?

What I am saying, really, is that the debate is a silly one. When it comes to successful teaching of poetry to young people, the only intelligent and, probably, workable decision is to go with one's own passions and what one perceives to be the passions of the students. That is, finally, what I do when I go to the classroom and it is, finally, what I would encourage others to do. A personal, passionate involvement with poetry, whether the teacher writes poetry or not, is perhaps the most essential prerequisite to successful teaching of it. Rather than using someone else's gimmicks and formulas out of a fear of one's own inexperience or whatever, the act of teaching poetry writing or reading should be very much like the act of writing a poem: a steady alertness and allegiance to the moment and to one's inner vibrancy. And whatever ideals give rise to that vibrancy are ones that you will have to trust. At some point that trust may be as basic as accepting who you are. I accept my ideals and passions, even if I do have to make fun of them to keep from being consumed by them. My hot air. But it keeps me aloft. If my approach seems wrong for you, I hope you trust your own passions—and fly with them.

A Word to the Wise

by Ron McFarland

When I begin poetry workshops, or any course in poetry writing, my greatest problem is overcoming my desire to communicate everything at once. If I could pull it off, I would prefer, godlike, to do it all in an instant: fresh language, vivid imagery, well-attuned ear, keen sense of rhythm and line, dramatic presence. Then I could spend my time picking at things, building nuances, pruning impertinences in my students' writing. I would urge greater and deeper insights, visions, ineffabilities. That, however, is fantasy.

I suppose that a successful writing session is the result of a compromise between what the students expect and what the teacher expects (both of the students and of himself or herself). In trying to find what student expectations are (in order to see how much compromising I'll need to request to them), I usually discover that what they want is a sympathetic ear. They want a reader, not just their mother or their friends, who will tell them that they're good. Somewhere, too, someone has told them that poetry is (a) emotional and (b) therapeutic; in effect, that poetry can be a sort of emotional purge. I would like to blame Sir Philip Sidney, of look-into-thy-heart-and-write fame, but the source is both more ancient and nearer to hand, and, besides, Sidney's poems are hardly the sort of emotional gush to which I am referring. "Write about something or someone you know really well and feel very strongly about." That's about how it goes. Writing of this sort bares one's feelings and that, presumably, makes one feel better. It's sort of like kicking a locker. It's great, if you're not a locker or a janitor. Along with the premise that writing is therapeutic comes the corollary, discreetly unspoken, that whatever is uttered or jotted is "okay," maybe even "good," and quite possibly "publishable."

Right away, therefore, I try, as nicely as possible, to get my students to put their poetic pasts behind them. The older they are, of course, the more difficult the task, but I do not want to read a poem about how sad a student was that rainy day when Rick broke up with her. In fact, I want to convince my students not to get involved in writing "about" something. The worst poems most of us will ever write are those "about" love or death or mom or spring. I don't want my students to go wandering in search of a "proper" poetic subject. That they can do later, when they write their epics, if they must. A poem can be about anything, and in some ways, especially at first, the more trivial, the less momentous, the less emotionally stirring, the better.

That appears to be step number one, to get my victims to relinquish their commitment to subject matter—pet ideas, hobby horses, great themes of Western or Eastern culture, feelings, impulses from vernal woods, and all. Next, I try to get them to compromise their need to sound "poetical." Everyone has some notion of what a poem sounds like, or looks like, so this is an even more difficult compromise to come by than the first. Some students will pretend to yield, but in their hearts will always want to say, "Behold yon cotton-candy clouds!" A majority of the class, however, given some bullying and browbeating, will surrender. If there are sessions later on, I will have exercises on accentual-syllabic rhythm and use of rhyme, but for my first meetings (since I am compromising, after all, my own desire to accomplish everything at once), I beg them not to show off. This is also my opportunity to caution my students against archaisms, including outdated contractions ('gainst) and inversions in phrasing. By now they are wondering what's left for them. The answer is "too much." The more beginning writers divide themselves among image concoctions, rhyming, metrics, and message, the more their bad habits will crop up. I want to head off these preestablished habits at the pass. To do this, I simplify. Poetry is terribly complex, much more complex than most young writers suspect, and I do not want my students mired in its complexity.

Now I get to my own expectations. Knowing that I cannot possibly accomplish what I set out in the first paragraph of this essay, I ask what is most important for the students (whether they know it or not) and what I would most like them, eventually, to get out of me. The answer: For each of them to find his or her own voice, to find a way of written expression that is (sounds, feels) uniquely like himself or herself. Ideally, the poet finds what fits and wears it and urges others to try it on. The delight of being a poet is that (almost miraculously) the garment nearly fits many, various people, and the frustration is that the garment fits no one exactly, except for the poet him or herself.

To extend this metaphor just one step further, to the point of my compromise, the fabric for this garment is language. "Poetry," writes Wallace Stevens in one of the several definitions scattered in *The Necessary Angel*, is "a revelation in words by means of the words."[1] I want my students to *deal* with language. I want them to do that first of all and above all else. I want them to do that before they worry about theme or imagery or sound. I would have them say it before they think of what they're saying. They should not worry about meaning, for meaning attaches naturally to language, it is unavoidable; and so far as sound is concerned, let them hear William Stafford in *Writing the Australian Crawl:* "all words rhyme, sort of; that is, all sounded words are more like each other than any word is like silence."[2] And if it's imagery they want, consciously legislated imagery, let them write "blue" for now and get fancy later.

When students say they don't know what to say (or write), they may actually think they mean that they have nothing to say about this or that subject. Composition teachers sometimes think that a good essay, or class discussion, or both will give their students "something to say." The truth, however, as it invariably surfaces when those students try to write poems, is that they don't have the language. Or, as some poets have argued, they're afraid of what they do have. Someone might laugh at them. While they might eventually share Stafford's "intense distrust of language"[3] it is important that beginning writers participate in its pleasures. Teachers of both poetry writing and composition, therefore, might do well to offer some fabric instead of merely patterns and embroidery needles.

Fortunately, there are many ways of alerting students to the felicities and pitfalls, and even pratfalls, of words. When it comes down to the first serious session of poetry writing, a few words for the wise. I may use a favorite poem from John Donne or Wallace Stevens or Theodore Roethke simply to say, "Look . . . see . . . ah, now, *there's a word*!" Another popular device is to present the class with a poem from which the most effective words have been removed or altered for the worse:

> Yes: but the color of the heavy *trees*
> Came *walking*.
> And I remembered the cry of the *birds*.

The underscored words in this passage from Stevens's "Domination of Black" replace "hemlocks," "striding," and "peacocks," respectively.

Sometimes I like to try a poem or two of my own to illustrate the importance of grappling with language, since I can usually recall the torturous match and can recall my reasons for having tried this or that hold. I don't bring much of my own work into class, primarily because I think such a practice may throttle some student writers while others may resent their teacher showing off, using them as a compulsory audience. The following poem, however, has proven useful for this sort of session. "Asotin Girl Still Lost" concerns a teenaged girl who was reported missing after the county fair a couple of years ago in Asotin, Washington.[4] She has not been heard of since.

> When the Ferris wheel pins itself to the moon
> a twelve-year-old girl might pass
> for a woman.
>   Pedaling her bike along
> Snake River, Christine might see the moon
> trickling downstream, feel
>   that sudden response
> to the moon
> and rear up high on the pedals and sing
> rare tunes like a Danish merry-go-round.
>
> Then she would peel herself away from
> farmboys' animals lowing at the moon
> in their ribbon-blue
> simplicity, as if a lucky cast of glossy eyes
> or human-sounding notes
>   might save their throats.
> Christine, you rode The Hammer
>   throwing your glad
> screams into a night of men and moons.
> You were young and old at once.
>
> What happened later, when the gears of The Whip
> stiffened?
>   I think, Christine, you heard the moon
> ring out eternity,
> and your bicycle sliced its choppy trail,
>   its river-silky light,
>   its doubtful path,
> like a hand over a mouth.

In commenting on this poem, I begin with a couple of obvious points, for example, my repetition of the word "moon," which (I hope) haunts the poem in a way. When I wrote the poem, I was also thinking of the connection between the moon and the menstrual cycle, and so of Christine's coming of age, but whether I go that far with my observations depends on the class. I also talk about my use of carnival rides, and how the poem moves from the standard pleasure rides like the Ferris wheel and the merry-go-round to the more "thrilling" (but also menacing, in this poem at least) Hammer and Whip. Why "Danish"? First, because Denmark associates well with frivolity (Tivoli Gardens), pastry, pleasant or peaceful notions in general, and I want to start the reader (disarming him or her) on that level, singing and so on. Second, Christine is of Scandinavian extraction, though I doubt that that can be seen in the poem.

Next, I examine words and phrases that appear, to me at least, to be especially powerful, to have an extra weight of connotation, or to be of interest because they are used in an unusual way. These include "pins" (1.1), "trickling" (1.6), "peel herself" (1.11), "ribbon-blue/simplicity" (11. 13-14), "stiffened" (1.22), "ring" (1.24), "sliced" (1.25). I won't go into what I say about each word or phrase here, but what I try to do, I suppose, is justify my choices. I want the students to see, for example, not only how "sliced" works with "choppy" to introduce the notion of cutting, perhaps the unstated possibility of Christine's throat being slit, but also how it "resonates" (as Stafford might say) with "bicycle." Usually, I make some observations on line when I talk about this poem, especially on my conviction as to the importance of maintaining some sense of surprise or excitement at the ends and beginnings of lines, e.g., "moon/trickling" (11.5-6), "ribbon-blue/simplicity" (11. 13-14), "glad/screams" (11. 18-19), "The Whip/stiffened" (11.21-22).

What I hope to achieve from this sort of study is to aim the students in the direction of powerful (connotative, evocative) diction. I usually expose them to some of Ezra Pound's advice (the 'Don'ts") on Imagism, especially where he cautions against the proliferation of function words. I want my students to be aware of heaping up mounds of function words (articles, prepositions, auxiliary verbs, verbs of being in general, expletives like "there is"), abstractions, and throw-away words like "things." This is a good time, too, to warn against clichéd, trite, euphemistic, and vague diction.

For the most part, however, I want my students to see what can be done with words, and I want the lesson to be positive (what they *can* do) rather than negative (what they should not do). For an initial assignment, therefore, I sometimes resort to a trick which I suppose a number of poets and teachers have used successfully. I will compile a list of a dozen or so words selected, perhaps, from a poem by Wallace Stevens or maybe from thin air. I usually list the words by part of speech, but I let the students change parts of speech (also tense or number) by altering word endings, and I allow some flexibility with the list, requiring that they use 10 out of 12 words to compose their poems, or just "as many as they can," depending on the class and the time available. For example:

NOUNS	ADJECTIVES	VERBS
harvest	invisible	slice
stomach	muscular	sharpen
hawk	pungent	expect
edge	cold	confuse

The list above is essentially composed at random. I try to spread a few monosyllables around, and I avoid abstractions (generally) and erudite or esoteric words. This sort of exercise is useful not only to alert the student to interesting language (one might, for example, use the opportunity to slip in one's "favorite" words, though I have not done so in the example above), but also to dissolve that "writer's block," which seizes so many of us at one time or another, especially in "must write" situations. Going back to the list, it is important that the student not feel overly restricted, but also that he or she not feel too much at liberty. A student may use "harvest" as a verb, for example, or she or he may change "muscular" to "muscle." One may always be more liberal than I am inclined to be, perhaps asking that the student use only six out of the twelve listed words. The poems that result from such exercises are rarely fine works of art. They usually run from 10 to 20 lines, however, and they provide a reasonably sound starting place.

Now I do not intend to illustrate "what can be done," what sure-fire, publishable-in-*The New Yorker* poems may emerge from the list. If the lesson is any good, if it "works" in any significant way, you will find out once you try it. I do not really suppose that the old proverb, "A word to the wise is sufficient," holds up as one of life's great verities, though of course I would like to think so. It is probably not even true that the wise use of words, Coleridge's "best words in their best order," is sufficient to the end of writing good poems. That is, I recognize that there must be something beyond lexical skill or luck, that along with those biscuits Sandburg spoke of there must be hyacinths. The teacher of poetry writing, however, cannot go much beyond the nurturing of craft, and there, it seems to me, the initial focus should be on words.

References

1. Wallace Stevens, *The Necessary Angel* (New York: Random House, 1965), p. 33.

2. William Stafford, *Writing the Australian Crawl* (Ann Arbor, MI: University of Michigan Press, 1978), p. 26.

3. Stafford, p. 58.

4. Ron McFarland, "Asotin Girl Still Lost," *Confrontation* 22 (Summer 1981): 93.

First Attempts: Free Association into Free Verse

by Ingrid Wendt

clock

The word stands alone, its letters large and confident, near the top of the chalkboard with plenty of space all around. You, the teacher, have just put it there, and your class of fourth- or ninth- or twelfth-grade students (or even adults) has paper and pencils ready, desks cleared of everything else. They're expecting to write a poem, but a poem different, you've promised, from anything they've ever written before—a kind of experiment in thinking as poets often think—in letting ideas flow unhindered; in writing quickly without a thought (at the moment) to punctuation, spelling, neat penmanship, making sense; without any of the self-censoring mental devices that keep us from writing as fast as we can or from trusting our own spontaneity. Today you've told your students to forget, for a while, all other poems they've ever read or tried to write. Today they'll be writing "chain poems."

"Clock," you say and point to the board, chalk in hand, having volunteered to write an example. "What does the word 'clock' remind you of? What one single word comes into your mind? The first one."

"Time," someone says, and someone else, "tick tock." Slowly at first, answers start to leap out: "grandfather," "mouse," "alarm," "minutes." There's no right answer, you encourage, and no wrong one (unless it belongs to someone else).

clock
time

You write another word under the first: "time" in this case, instead of other answers, because it was the first word volunteered, not because it's the best. There is no best. No worst. Word choice doesn't even have to make sense. (But you could also have used the last word offered, or the second, or third; as a teacher you know how a little classroom structure goes a long way.)

What's next? (You've guessed it.) "What does 'time' bring to mind?"

"Lunch." "Late." "Machine." "Magazine." And so on, until everyone knows what's expected, what to do—until everyone has gotten involved and there's a list on the board something like this:

> clock
> time
> lunch
> awful
> monster
> movies
> popcorn

But it could have looked like this:

clock	or this:	clock
tick tock		grandfather
cake walk		old
carnival		shoe
Ferris wheel		hole
umbrella		well
rain		deep

You try a few more lists on the board, for illustration. Not poems yet, you admit, but chains of words, each word like a link connected to words just below and above.

Notice (you point out) how the topics keep changing: how the first word doesn't really relate to words farther on down the line. It's almost like dreaming. (Who dreams, you ask. At night? In the day?) You start out with one idea or one picture in your mind; before you know it, you're off the subject. One thought leads into another, one picture changes to something else. Who knows what will happen?

And isn't that part of the fun—of dreaming, of thinking, of seeing a movie or reading a story—where the unexpected is bound to occur? Variety, anticipation, surprise all hold our attention. The same thing can happen, in a different way, in poems, which makes them a pleasure to read and (believe it or not) sometimes even to write.

Moving now toward individual work, each student gets ready to write his or her own list, just like the ones on the board, this time using a different first word—most likely a noun, and a noun that is "open" enough to avoid predictable, dead-ended responses. Everyone, furthermore, starts with the same word, making it not only fair but allowing you to point out that everyone *is* unique: Everyone will almost certainly end up with a word different from everyone else. (Maybe our minds are like filing cabinets, storing similar images, memories, words and ideas, but organized each in a personal way.)

Getting ready to copy the word you put on the board, younger students might first draw a short black line near the top of the page, as close to center as possible. This is where the first word will go, and the rest of the list—underneath—as many as six or eight or ten words. More than that, for older students. But not many more. You'll want to set limits.

And while they are writing, you're busy, too. You're writing as fast as you can on the chalkboard, filling in spaces around the original "chain," so when students look up at the end of their lists, they'll see something like this:

> When my grandfather clock ate
> the time and I missed
> my lunch, I
> felt as awful as
> a monster
> at the movies when no one
> will share popcorn with him.

It looks like a poem. It sounds like a poem. No one would call it great, but that isn't the point. The point is that again, as in making the chain, you've shown how it's possible to write something off the top of your head—something you hadn't planned to say. There's lots of stuff in your head, you tell your students. Some of it's bound to be good, and surprises are interesting. How will you know what might happen unless you try?

In fact, this same chain could have produced an entirely different poem. For illustration, you might erase everything you've written except for the original chain, and ask students to help fill in the blanks this time with their own words—maybe one sentence per line, instead of one long sentence. Possibilities can go on as long as attention spans, until each student has turned back to his or her own paper, filling in around the chains, producing what looks, sounds, and feels like a poem. Here's one example of what happened with the word "fence" in a fifth-grade class at Dunn School in Eugene, Oregon:

> The fence sits
> by a stick, guarding
> the garden of
> blue grapes changing
> to wine over
> chilled ice.
> Peaches burn to
> a city of raspberries.

> Don't fence me in,
> for the gate is locked, and there
> is no other door.
> Not even a window to look through.
> Let me see. Help me recover
> from blindness. I have
> no imagination.

> The fence
> trapped someone.
> Don't be afraid, even
> though you're care-
> less like a monkey
> swinging on a swing
> in the park
> on the playground.

Compounding such variety by 20 or more "chain poems" from the same class, each starting with the word "fence," the point has been made by the students themselves: they *can* write something that resembles a poem; they *can each* be original, mainly by being themselves. Engaged right from the first in a nonthreatening, noncompetitive, indeed a playful writing exercise, everyone "wins." With exceptions too few to mention, everyone who is able to write, at whatever level of proficiency, is able to do this assignment (which is one of the reasons that in my role as visiting poet I make this the first assignment each time I meet several dozen new classes each year). Likewise, I believe that every teacher—at whatever grade level, with whatever background he or she has or hasn't had in poetry—can have fun with it in the classroom (another reason for the editorial "you" of the preceding pages). You can do it and introduce poetry in a way that's both instructive and entertaining.

Fun is one of two main objectives here: fun for both teacher and student, writing the poems and reading (or hearing them read) aloud, noting the many directions thoughts can go, even when they've started all in the same place. *Later* you and the students can recognize room for improvement. *Later* they will care enough, it is hoped, about their work to want to learn to revise, to learn technique, to correct their spelling, to make a "neat sheet" out of their "sloppy copy." In fact, within a very few classroom meetings I approach other things: musical language, rhythms, patterns of repetition, metaphor, and other formal techniques. But first, students have had a chance to discover some of the reasons for learning these things; they've discovered that they have something to write about, even when they think they haven't.

And perhaps this discovery, made early enough, or strongly enough, will help prevent some of the agonies, some of the stumbles we as teachers no doubt have experienced in our own writing careers: the uncertainties and self-doubts about the merits of our ideas; the feeling that we can't begin to write until we know exactly what we're going to say; and what we think of to say has already been said before. (Sound familiar?)

Frustrated once myself (and not just for the first time), I found myself one day with unexpected free time, private space, a restless urge to write a poem, any poem—and with nothing to write about. Nothing came to mind. At least nothing I thought was any good—until finally, out of desperation and a need to do something, I started to follow the advice I'd been giving my class (of college students, at that time), and I wrote down the objects of my attention: the things that were keeping me from writing, the things immediately around me that were so ingrained in my total feelings of the moment I couldn't ignore them. I fully expected to throw away what I wrote, thinking I was just using my words as catharsis, and that the "real" poem would come after I'd cleared my head. It came. But not in the way I expected, for not only did the list of frustrations show some unity, some cohesion in imagery, but it led into the theme of the "real" poem itself.

FEELING DRY

To want to write, but to lack words.
More accurately, to lack some
thing to feel.

This unpainted
desk, cars outside
proving themselves on the hill,
smoke from burning fields
slipping unnoticed under the sun
until someone drowns
in his own breath.

To listen for some wind.

To feel responsibile for listening
and to be unmoved, an air sock
limp as an unfilled dunce's cap
waiting some change in the weather,
something full as the river
you fished last weekend
without luck

and then swimming saw
the whitefish
grazing on stones

the flickering trout steady
as mobiles suspended
on more levels
than you thought water
could contain.

What I hadn't expected when I began to write was that I'd remember the river experience—a very real, very beautiful time which I'd wanted to write about when I was living it but hadn't the words right then, or the approach, and so had let it go by. In fact, I didn't think of writing about it again until I'd written the phrase "something full as . . . ," which itself came directly from the image of the "unfilled dunce's cap." I wanted an image that would be the opposite of empty; I needed an example from my immediate experience. It was natural to remember the river.

But again, what wasn't planned (indeed I wasn't conscious of it until teaching the poem, some months later) was that the image of the river, with the accompanying images of fishing, swimming, and seeing the fish (something that really happened), would turn out to be so appropriately symbolic of the creative act itself. Trying so hard to get a fish, to catch one with my "blind" line, and failing to get one, I'd concluded there weren't any there. But having donned face mask and snorkel, and letting myself drift with the current down the Middle Fork of the Willamette River, I was both surprised and chagrined: How could I have been so wrong? (How could I also have thought, writing, I had nothing "to feel"?)

Learning to write quickly, to take notes as fast as I think, to give whatever pops into my mind a chance to enlighten the rest (by comparison or juxtaposition), has been perhaps the single most difficult thing for me to learn about writing. Every time I write I still have to remind myself it's all right to proceed even when I sometimes don't know what I'm saying, to use the margins, to scribble if necessary, to trust stray thoughts, even if off the subject, because (who knows?) they might just be valuable. And in this I suspect I'm not alone. Judging from conversations with friends and statements made by other writers, I've discovered that many things can get in the way of the creative process. Until one is free to drift with the current, to see the many levels "water can contain," it's unlikely we'll see any fish.

Perhaps even more important than fun, then, is this second objective in writing "chain poems": to learn that writing can be truly an "act of discovery"; and that if we can just relax enough to let ourselves *be* ourselves—to trust our sometimes wildly erratic impulses, getting off the subject and following tangents when necessary—we'll usually find something to say. That something might be funny, or serious, or sad; ordinary or sparkling. But it probably wouldn't be found by adhering to an outline or knowing in advance what the poem was going to be about or "to mean."

Different from what most of us have been taught to teach, writing poems depends somewhat on forgetting the rules, on not struggling to do it the "right" way, to say the "right" things. Not that technique isn't important, nor that form and function don't often go together; often I find that technique leads me into using certain words, which in turn prompt new ideas, and so on, happily! But I would prefer to let technique act in the service of words, rather than let it control them. To let students discover that by finding their own things to say, they might someday find ways to say them better: to learn, first, to trust themselves—which, I discover, having written all this so far, I find is what I'm really writing about.

Teaching Poetic Appreciation Is Like. . .

by Raymond J. Rodrigues

The key to teaching students some appreciation for the poet's craft had been sitting in front of me for several years, and while I recognized the undeniable phenomenon, I must have some mental block in taking so long to overtly adapt it to my teaching. The key lay in this simple fact: Those students who seemed to appreciate poetry more than any others were those who had taken my creative writing in poetry class the year before. They were the ones who knew what it meant to seek the exact word, the best simile, the metaphor with the greatest impact, the image that could best evoke the "aha!" response. It wasn't that they were brighter than the other students in the literature classes or harder working or necessarily more creative. It was just that they had traveled the same road, had journeyed to the same place that published poets had been, and they knew what it meant to create the poetry of those anthologized poets.

Perhaps the difference between those students and the ones who had never tried to write poetry is the same distinction that separates two football fans, one who has at sometime played football, even if the greatest accomplishment was only suiting up and sitting on the bench throughout the season, and one who has merely watched football on TV. Or perhaps the respect the weekend jogger has for the marathon runner. Or the awe we feel for the musician who has mastered several instruments while we have to admit failure in learning to play the recorder. Regardless of how thoroughly we explicated poetry in my classes, few students could discuss poetry as well as those who had been writing poetry. So when I finally made that connection in my teaching, I sought exercises that would simulate the creative writing process, exercises that would not emphasize the artificiality of poetry, but exercises that would generate the types of language that typify the language of poets.

I began with what I believed to be the simplest poetic device—the simile. A simile is just a comparison using the word *like* or *as*. Item X is *like* item Y. Students can memorize the definition of a simile easily enough. Given a list of similes and nonsimiles, they can pick out all the similes. But in back of their minds—and often at the front of their mouths—is that perpetual question, "So what?" And it is not an unreasonable question. If we cannot help students understand *at a gut level* what the point of all this is—the similes, metaphors, images, synecdoches, and all the rest, then having them memorize definitions only serves to raise scores on tests; it does not develop a poetic sense.

A simile is also an analogy. Analogies help us stretch our brain muscles a bit more. They give us insights we might never have had. They force us to view things from a different perspective. One simple exercise that develops the analogizing process is the following: With the class, pick a topic or thing that you all would like to perceive more clearly, for example, the problem of energy supply and demand or the school football team. Then find an object in the room that you all could compare to that topic or thing, for example, the door or the blackboard. Now ask the question, "How is the energy supply and demand problem *like* the door?" Accept any answers that the students give, no matter how fantastic. One student might say, "When you open the door, you let in light, but it takes energy just to open it." Another, "Until you open it, you don't know what's on the other side." Or "It's like 'The Lady, or the Tiger.' " Trying to test the analogy, a student might say, "They both have rusty hinges." Don't let the far-fetched throw the class. Pursue the analogy. Reach for the insights. "How is the energy supply and demand problem like a rusty hinge?" "You have to use a little oil to get it to work." "What is the oil in the energy supply and demand area?" "Money . . . AWACS planes . . . defense treaties. . . ." Pushed a bit and allowed to speculate freely, students come up with many fine ideas.

Take one object and list on the blackboard, without judgment at first, as many comparisons as possible, again using objects in the room. "Our football team is *like*. . . ." "books . . . this class . . . a lightbulb . . . chalk dust . . . the window. . . ." Then question the similes. "What do you mean by this comparison?" "How is the football team like the pencil sharpener?" Often insights come when least expected. "Well, if you let your pencil get too sharp, it breaks off . . . the point, I mean. I mean, it's like our football team . . . they practice and practice and practice, and come the game, they just fall apart. . . ."

Make assignments that require similes. "Generate a list of similes comparing yourself to as many objects as possible. Be prepared to defend each of those similes in class tomorrow." "Choose something to use in as many similes as possible. As you go home tonight, keep picking out objects around you and comparing them to the thing you have chosen. X is like . . . a sidewalk . . . like a tree . . . like a cloud . . . like, like, like. . . . Tomorrow we'll talk about and write about your similes.''

Now, are these exercises going to generate poetry? Not necessarily, but perhaps. More importantly, they will generate words that are poetic, and we are striving toward that poetic sensibility. When students ask me to define poetry, I say I can't, but I can define poetic devices, and perhaps, then, a circuitous definition of poetry is that it is language that employs poetic devices. Someone is bound to say that some prose piece we just read in class used poetic devices, so, by my definition, some prose is poetry. Right.

On to metaphor. All metaphors are basically similes without the *like* or *as*. The difference is one of strength and impact. Consider with the class two lists, one of metaphors and one of similes, both based upon the same comparisons or analogies:

> Happiness is like a warm puppy—Happiness is a warm puppy
> Writing is like an octopus—Writing is an octopus
> This class is like a garbage pail—This class is a garbage pail

And so on. . . . Then, after trying to understand any that might be a bit obscure, consider which is stronger, the simile or the metaphor. Consider whether there might be times when a writer would rather use the weaker. ''Why does Wordsworth write that Milton's 'soul was like a star' instead of ' . . . was a star'?'' This type of discussion begins to relate the technique to both audience and purpose, in short, the context in which a poet employs a given technique.

Assignments to develop the students' sense of metaphor can be similar to those growing out of the simile discussions. Have students not only generate their own metaphors, but also look for metaphors around them. Perhaps looking for brand names might be the easiest way to begin. Or names of rock groups. Pull out the sports section of the newspaper. How much of the football is poetic? Wing-T's. Weakside linebackers. Strong safeties. The blitz. Screen pass. The shotgun. The Flea flicker. Even the stock market is poetic with its bulls and bears. Students will discover poetry all around them.

Imagery is language that conjures up mental images. Have students take ordinary words and seek variations. How many of these alternative words provide us with images, pictures that help us see things more accurately? Take some simple words and, with the class, generate alternatives. ''He *walked* into the class.'' How many other ways can we say *walked*? Slinked, slithered, strutted, ambled, marched. . . . Instead of using the abstract pronoun, attach a person's name to the statement, a student in the class, a character from their reading, or a famous personality. How would we best describe this person's *walk*? Why is that such a good image?

Have the students look for additional sources of imagery in the world around them—advertisements, morning bulletins, political comments, newspaper cartoons. Compare political cartoons. How do cartoonists portray leading political figures, depending upon the point they want to make, the image they want to convey? Lead the students to notice how language is manipulated through imagery to produce the results desired. What, for example, is the difference between an "enhanced radiation device" and a "neutron bomb"?

Reserve a spot on the blackboard or bulletin board for an "Image of the Week" or a "Metaphor of the Day" or a "Simile of the Season." Appoint student committees to seek those out, collect them, and judge them. Publish them in the school newspaper or announce them over the public address system. Encourage some students to draw the visual images they get from verbal imagery. Post these in prominent places and talk about them with the class.

If you can cause your students to be more aware of imagery, metaphor, and simile, you will have taken a great step toward accomplishing that other goal of literature teachers: appreciation of the poet's craft. But what about all the other poetic devices that we have to teach: synecdoche, metonymy, onomatopoeia, rhythm, rhyme, rhyme scheme, metric pattern, and the rest? First, aside from certain departmental or school district curriculum guides, there is no law that states that we have to teach these terms. Requiring that they be taught is more of a tradition than an inherent need. Second, if they must be taught, they should be taught within the context of poetic use. Like grammar, terms taught out of context are dead weight. All of the terms can come alive if we devise ways for students to use the techniques they stand for creatively and meaningfully.

The key elements of modern poetry are imagery, metaphor, and simile. If we can lead students to use and appreciate those, we will have accomplished the essential. Then we can move on to the other devices. Sound devices alone do not make poetry, nor do all the witty words imaginable. The poet's vision of the world as revealed through language choices grabs our attention, illuminates life a bit more, and makes us appreciate our world through a greater insight. If our students cannot begin to see with the poet's eyes, then no amount of memorization will help them appreciate poetry more.

Maybe, then, when they run across some poet working words in a unique way, they will not respond with a shallow, "Why doesn't she just say what she means?" but with something like, "Yeah, yeah, I see. Hey, that's not bad!"

Teaching poetic appreciation is like: replacing a light bulb, hanging a door, executing a successful pass pattern, learning to drive a car, baking bread, building a house, fly fishing. . . . Your assignment is to fill in the details.

Language Play and the Teaching of Poetry*

by Charles R. Duke

English teachers have probably read more poetry than most other people and yet continue to find it one of the most difficult forms of literature to present to students. Student attitudes have much to do with this difficulty. Almost inevitably when a teacher announces that a class will be reading poetry, universal groans and grimaces occur all over the room.

We may be able to trace this attitude to previous experiences with a widely used approach called "what does it all mean?" The assumption upon which this approach is based is that students are automatically interested in poetry sufficiently to want to "dig" into poems to criticize and analyze line by line what they find. But putting analysis before appreciation and response with students usually invites a negative attitude. Common sense tells us that not all automobile drivers need to become mechanics before they learn to drive; why, then, should we insist that all students become poetry analysts before they have an opportunity to enjoy poetry?

What has been forgotten in trying to interest students in poetry is their need to discover that the poet at heart is a profound player with language. Most students never have the opportunity to see that even the most cerebral or lyrical of poetry has its playful elements and deliberate contrivance to make us wonder at its form. We have neglected to introduce students to this world of word play and make them fully aware that because it aims at language creativity, word play encompasses the highest skills of poetry, exploiting the full resources of the language—sense, musicality, structure, movement—to spark the mind and the spirit.

The rich language background which most children bring to school often disappears once children have been exposed to "school ways" with language. The spontaneous conversation of the young is marked by poetic

---

*This essay is unedited and is reprinted here from *Indiana English* (November 1979) by permission.

images, magical colors and unique word usage; but somehow, by the time students reach the middle grades, their poetic "insides" have been tampered with, often to the point of producing dull, rhythmic conformity. Because words have sounds, shapes, rhythms, and ambiguous meanings, they can be juxtaposed in ways that not only tease thought but also create something which can be looked at, toyed with, and responded to on its own terms. Word play is meant to be fun, but it is also a significant part of any language arts curriculum because at its best, word play is also a creative response to experience; when words are the play things, language power cannot help but increase.

Teachers who subscribe to such a view of language should take the time to build a climate in which language play is natural activity. Time spent in creating such a climate reaps benefits later on when students begin to make connections between their own word play and that engaged in by poets. The following activities should be useful in establishing such a climate and connection. What emerges from some of these activities will not necessarily be poetry; instead, what we look for in these activities is the freedom to experiment, to see words as building blocks, and to stretch students' imaginative uses of language. Once these things have been accomplished, we can expect to make the poetry connection with far less difficulty and much more positive reactions.

The Image

One of the primary building blocks of poetry and prose is the image. So often we ask students to be more specific in their writing, to let us see what is happening. The concrete image, however, often proves elusive. To help students with their production of images, we can begin with a simple concrete noun and verb—ie., "The girl runs." Then, with students, begin asking questions and seeking answers, all with the intent of expanding the basic image. As the figure begins to emerge as a character, create a context for the character and a problem that must be solved. The familiar Who, What, When, Where, Why, and How will serve well in this exercise. Consider the following sequence:

> The girl runs.
> (what girl? Who?)
>
> The wan-cheeked, slender girl runs.
> (where does she run?)

> toward home
> (how does she run?)
>
> She staggers and limps
> (Why does she stagger and limp?)
>
> She's crying, gasping for breath,
> and she has only one shoe

Here we can stop and put together what we have developed so far:

> The wan-cheeked, slender girl,
> gasping for breath, her eyes
> glistening with tears,
> staggers and limps home,
> her small bare feet cut and bleeding.
>
> (where has she been?)
> school
>
> (does she have books with her?)
> Yes
>
> (Why is she all alone?)

She cannot speak clearly and other children at school ganged up on her and made fun of her. Frightened, she ran away from the school yard, losing her shoes as she crossed a stream.

Finally, we might have the following:

> The wan-cheeked, slender girl,
> her eyes glistening with tears,
> staggers and limps toward home.
> She walks painfully now because her
> bare feet are cut and bleeding.
> Her two thin arms hug her school books
> against her heaving chest; sobbing
> and gasping for breath, she does not
> see the figure on the other side of
> the fence; the sound of a dog barking
> causes her to lift her head; seeing
> the frisky dog prancing next to the
> familiar figure of her mother, the
> girl breaks into a tear-stained smile
> and begins to run toward the out-
> stretched arms of her mother

Such expansion of images can be done as group activities or by individual students; placing the results on the blackboard or on transparencies which can be projected for the entire class will help to demonstrate that a basic image can be expanded in many different ways. Students, if they wish, may look at several of the expanded images and then compile one major image by extracting details they like from other versions; the more combining, comparing, and building which go on, the more likely students are to get the feel for working with language to expand meaning.

Still another possibility for dealing with concrete words and images is to have students produce catalog lists. These lists may focus on objects, people, or events which students strongly dislike or like. Students can look at excerpts from Rupert Brooke's "The Great Lover"[1] or John Peale Bishop's "The Great Hater"[2] as possible models. Emphasis should fall first on building the list as specifically as possible; once the list is completed, students can return to work with what they consider the most effective arrangement and order. Here is one girl's catalog about things she loves:

> . . . Things that I love:
> The rustle of taffeta,
> Tchaikovsky's Concerto in E flat number one;
> Deep snow brightening in the sun;
> A foal gently lipping new spring grass;
> A fellow who'll take me to Sunday mass;
> Football games in November air;
> The touch of a certain hand on my hair;
> A "Lexington, Kentucky" postmark; New
>   Year's Eve romancing;
> A cadet's icy buttons against bare shoulders
>   while we're dancing;
> Men six feet and over; big dogs; chocolate
>   cake;
> Swimming without a bathing suit in a hidden,
>   sky-blue lake;
> The smell of a freshly lit pipe; rain splashing
>   in my face;
> Stuffed dogs tied wth satin bows; Christmas
>   and Christ;
> Beauty and grace.
> And of all the things that I most love,
> To top all those I've named above
> I should have put . . . John.

A variation on the catalog poem is to rhyme the items such as in the following:

I like T.V. . . .
A.M. or P.M. I'll turn on the set
For Barbara Walters or Carol Burnett
Abernethy, Brinkley or Walter Cronkite,
Push the button and make the screen bright
With Mod Squad's capers or Archie's quotes,
Weather predictions or precinct votes,
Rams and Lakers and New York Knicks
Hammy wrestlers for extra kicks,
Happy commercials in fast or slow motion,
Making a pitch for beer or lotion,
Daytime or nighttime, so much to see;
That's why I simply adore T.V.

A natural part of any image building, especially in poetry, is the use of figurative language. No attempt is made in the previous exercises to introduce the idea of metaphor or simile although either may appear on its own. Instead, students may explore the possibilities for metaphorical expression in the following activity.

Have students form groups of four. Each group will receive a natural object. They are to examine the object carefully, tapping it, scraping it, holding it—all the avenues of sight, sound and touch should be explored. Group members should share their observations with each other—what does the object smell like, look like, feel like, sound like. Encourage comparisons. Then each group member is to write two sentences about the object; place the following form on the blackboard for the groups to use:

The _____ is (a, an, the)_____/ _____. Students are to place the name of the object in the first blank and then their vision or insight in the second. They are to show that the object is equivalent to something else that is basically different; then in the third blank, they are to show how that "something else" is basically similar to the first object.

"The *egg* is a *white stone/worn smooth by water.*"

When members of the group have each completed two sentences, they share the sentences within their groups and then decide upon the best order to place the sentences, one sentence to a line. No lines may be dropped (there will be eight) but first words of a line may be dropped or changed to make the finished product read more smoothly. After groups have finished their poems, share them with the class. Placing the finished poems on transparencies will facilitate this process.

Encouraging students to look at words in new ways and explore methods for using words in unusual combinations is vital to increasing student sensitivity to the poetic possibilities of language. One exercise which encourages this view calls for inventing new word combinations. Students receive a list of words, usually short ones with very few abstractions; students are asked to take as many of the words as they can from the list, getting at least one from each column and then scrambling them in order to produce images; they are encouraged to put words together in a way that no other human being ever has. Nouns can be changed into verbs, endings can be added and prepositions and articles may be used. Such a list might look like the following.[3]

red	snarl	wind
quick	coo	swan
still	sing	velvet
broken	weep	pickle
bright	tease	puppy
silent	race	lion
blue	smile	dishes
gold	stink	giraffe
clean	lie	wart
rotten	fly	leaf
high	sail	ring
green	bump	rubber
sticky	surprise	ocean
delicate	lick	ribbon
icy	chuck	steel
sleek	shoot	birth
silver	pound	hippopotamus
purple	dream	bullet
white	shout	peanut butter
brittle	sparkle	ghost
wee	chime	monkey
loony	chase	blood
rusty	scratch	wheel
cross	crackle	angel
humongous	mutter	junk
jagged	dance	wizard
cool	flapdoodle	clown
flaming	open	moose
stringy	grow	petunia
juicy	waddle	cake
deep	mooch	prissy

This exercise is particularly valuable for students who suspect they have no imagination. Variations on the game also can be used: word-poker, where a word is printed on each card of a deck and then each person receives a hand; from the words dealt, the individual makes as many different images as possible. Examples from any of these approaches might include "a pound of purple petunias," "the silver pickle spills its juicy ocean," and "delicately chiming earth."

Still further development of vocabulary can be stimulated by the use of rhyming synonyms and antonyms. Students build two lines of words; the first line consists of a series of synonyms or antonyms for the title word; the second line offers a personal comment on their use or meaning.

FAT

Fleshy, thick, obese, or plump;
In any case, the frump's a lump.

DULL

Shiny, incisive, keen, acute:
The cutting word can execute.

Arrangement

Once students have been introduced to the idea of language play, it will be difficult to stop them from asking for more. One way to begin to channel this motivation toward more formal poetry concerns is to begin to explore the possibilities of word arrangement. John Ciardi once claimed that "white space" helped to make a poem. Certainly many poets have followed this principle, some of them with startling interpretations of the relationship between words and arrangements on paper. An exercise which provides an excellent bridge between word invention games and the considerations of how words might appear to a reader to produce certain visual effects can be accomplished through an activity suggested by Dorothy Hennings.[4] The exercise begins with brain-storming. Students respond to uncompleted statements by recording several random impressions for each statement. For example, one statement might be "To me loneliness means _____"; then students are asked to use only one word to complete the sentence "Loneliness is _____."

Next, students react to "When I'm lonely, I'm _____." A student is then selected to collect half the class's responses while another student collects the other half. Additional concepts like love, blue, peace are then provided and the same format followed; each time two different students collect the answers; eventually eight students will have a number of answers from the class. At this point, discussion can occur about possible arrangements for words on a page; sometimes it is helpful to diagram a few of the possibilities on the blackboard:

From this point, students move into groups, with each student who collected answers serving as chairman of a group; all the responses are read aloud in the groups and each group is asked to select the three to six impressions that seem to fit together best because of the sounds of the words or because of some apparent relationship; words can be added, deleted or re-arranged; then an order for the impressions must be decided upon and the impressions arranged into some appropriate block design. Upon completion of the task, a member from each group can place his or her group's "impression blocks" on the blackboard for reaction from the whole class. Students are usually surprised at the effects they have been able to create.

After such an exercise, the teacher might want to talk about other forms of poetry such as concretism. In concrete poetry, the concentration is on letters, or a word or words by which a visual impression becomes as important as meaning. Concrete poems produce an object to be perceived rather than just words; hence, the term ''picture poem'' is sometimes used to describe the result such as in the following:[5]

THE CITY QUESTION

<pre>
                    Wino?
        sidewalk.   Junkie?
            on   Hurt?
          face   Sick?
          on   Knife
        Man   in
                              pocket?
                          Danger?
                          Medicine
                          in
                          pocket?
                        May
                      die
                    without
                  it?
                  Forget
                  him?
                  Leave
                  him
                  to
                  the
                  cops?
              Or try to help?
</pre>

Found poetry is closely related to concrete poetry; the found poet takes words, phrases, and sentences that are discovered in public communications, such as advertisements, menus, signs, and reports, and arranges them into lines and stanzas that form fresh commentaries on or insights into life. The following example is taken from a restaurant menu:

TAHITIAN FLING

A zesty taste treat
that wafts you to Paradise
Fresh strawberry ice cream
and lime sherbet surfing
on half a pineapple
with white caps of whipped cream
and orange crunch.
Good enough to make
the natives restless.

Even traffic signs may form the basis for an effective commentary in a found poem.[6]

> Yield
> No parking
> Unlawful to pass
> Wait for green light
> Yield
> Stop
> Narrow bridge
> Merging traffic ahead
> Yield
> Yield
> Yield

Providing students with magazines, various food containers or labels, newspapers and other public material will spark a number of interesting and often provocative found poems; in fact, once started creating found poems, students may never look at words in quite the same way.

While students are engaged in the exploration of word arrangements through concrete and found poetry, the teacher may also find it useful to introduce them to some poets whose works rely heavily on typographical arrangement. Probably the most accessible examples of the style are by e.e. cummings; a poem such as the following will provide a good starting point for discussion of such style and how it may or may not contribute to meaning.

> un
>   der fog
>   's
>   touch
> slo
>   ings
>   fin
>   gering
>   s
> wli
>   whichs
>   turn
>   in
>   to whos
> est
>   people
>   be
>   come
>   un

Students trying to read the poem* aloud will encounter difficulties initially; once the two sections of the poem are identified (the "slowliest" and the rest of the words), students will begin to see that cummings has actually engaged them in the very process the poem describes.

Along with their positions on the page, poems, like prose passages, have aspects of internal consistency, coherence and order. Once students realize that poets tend to use language in ways that we may not commonly expect, they are ready to begin studying the structure of a poem. Scrambled poems are helpful in demonstrating the importance of structure. For example, ask students to take the following words and turn them into a poem, (the capitalization is as in the original):

a	face	river
Asked	for	the
calm	kiss	The
Cool	me	of

The actual poem by Langston Hughes called "Suicide's Note" looks like this:

> The calm,
> Cool face of the river
> Asked me for a kiss.

Still another poem "puzzle" is the following one which also forces students to engage in some sentence combining activity:[7]

1. The moon is a basketball.
2. The basketball is dribbled.

3. The dribbling is too much.
4. The basketball is worn.
5. The basketball is waxy.
6. The basketball is smooth.

7. The wearing is from floor boards.
8. The wearing is from sweaty palms.

9. The moon hangs.
10. The hanging is in the air.

---

11. The hanging is a hook shot.
12. The hook shot is slow.

13. The hook shot is speedless.
14. The hook shot is breathless.

a soft shadow arching across

the sky

of aching

anticipation . . .

Students more familiar with poetic structure can move on to more complicated exercises. One which works well is to simply take an unrhymed poem, label each line of the poem with a random number; then cut up the poem line by line; place the strips in an envelope; several different poems can be handled this way by groups and then the versions can be compared with the originals; the purpose is not necessarily to come up with the original order of the lines but to force students to examine lines carefully to detect possible relationships and movement; students engaging in this exercise will do a great deal of talking about poetry and structure before they finish the activity.

At this point, the teacher may well want to stop and take stock of what students have learned. To determine this the teacher may present the following for reaction by students.

> O poet
> Blush like a rotten skin;
> Brighten like a dusty tower;
> Wail like a happy earthworm;
> Dream like an enormous flood;
> Tremble like a red locomotive;
> Flop like a damp gate! . . .
> The beaches are praying.
> Listen! How they stifle their enormous
>   lips! . . .
> The river
> Winks
> And I am ravished.

After students have had an opportunity to examine the poem, ask for their reaction: What pictures or images do they like or dislike, why? What feeling do they receive from the piece. The purpose here is to get students to articulate some of the feelings about order of words, about arrangement of words, and ultimately, about what they suspect ought to go into a poem and how it should work. The words they are examining were arranged by a computer—"The Meditation of IBM 70 94-7040 DSC—which had been programmed with simple grammar, assorted stanzaic patterns and a vocabulary of 950 words drawn from a random section in classical and avant-garde poetry.[8] Whether electronic circuitry is better than the human brain is immaterial at this point as long as the creation sparks student discussion—and it will.

If all seems to be going well, students can move on to some of the easier poetic formats such as cinquains, haiku, tanka and then to ballads, other formal verse patterns and free verse. Occasional reminders and even returns to some of the exercises mentioned early should be made to help students remember the importance of language play in poetry and keep alive an interest in how each poet they encounter is a language player and creator.

References

1. *The Collected Poems of Rupert Brooke*. New York: Dodd, Mead, and Company, Inc., 1917.

2. *The Collected Poems of John Peale Bishop*. New York: Charles Scribner's Sons.

3. From David Anderson. *My Sister Looks Like a Pear*. New York: Hart Publishing Company, Inc., 1974, pp. 122–123.

4. "Pre-Poetry Play: Building Impression Blocks," *Elementary English*, (December 1972), pp. 1149–151.

5. Robert Froman. *Street Poems,* New York: McCall.

6. Ronald Gross. *Pop Poems*. New York: Simon and Schuster.

7. James Hobbs from Barnett, Hobbs, Parker, and Johnson. *Sentence Combining*. Colorado Writing Power Company, 1978.

8. *Time*, (February 1971), p. 77.

Language Can Do What We Want It to Do*

by Helen J. Throckmorton

In my experience, students most enjoy learning, and learn best, when they feel they are discovering something for themselves. Whatever its limitations, such learning is at least authentic. This is especially true when students study what for them are unpopular or difficult subjects or concepts. Poetry is one of these.

The exercises which follow were originally designed for students in a freshman English composition course, most of whom frankly admitted that they seldom understood and therefore almost never read, let alone enjoyed, poetry. Moreover, they did not see any particular reason why any writer would choose to write poetry instead of prose to say what he wished to say, or why any reader would choose to read poetry instead of prose when to them poetry seems more to obscure than to clarify communication.

Yet one major purpose of the course was to examine ways that language works, and to examine ways that language works in poems was an integral part of that purpose. As I saw it, my task was to help students (1) realize that the language of poetry differs from the language of prose in kind, of course, but also in degree; (2) develop confidence through competence in reading and talking about poems; and (3) learn to recognize and to do some of the things that "good" writers do, to achieve writing that works.

It was not intended that we study "elements" of poetry. However, we found it convenient to use some terms commonly associated with concepts of poetry. Students remembered some terms they thought they had forgotten, others they thought they had never learned, and used them with increasing facility to describe qualities in words and sentences that accounted for what was happening, what was working.

---

*This essay is unedited and is reprinted here from *Exercise Exchange* (Fall 1980) by permission. Copyright © 1980 by *Exercise Exchange*.

Nor was it intended that we study "definitions" of poetry, although more than one classroom comment began, "This is poetry, because . . . " or "This is not poetry, because . . . ," an acknowledgement that poetry is characterized, or perceived to be characterized, by certain definable attributes. Certainly it was altogether unexpected when one student proposed an operational definition that no one challenged: "Poetry is what poetry does."

At most, these exercises may have led to "an heightened prizing." At the very least, they led to greater awareness that those "imaginary gardens with real toads in them"[1] that Marianne Moore describes may be worth inspection, after all.

Exercise 1

1. Using the overhead projector, I presented the following assignment:

> Imagine that you are traveling swiftly from east to west, across
> Kansas, as a passenger in a bus, a car or train. As you travel, you
> are looking at Kansas—and thinking about the mountains that lie
> ahead.

In one sentence describe Kansas as you see it.

2. When students finished writing, I asked them to read their sentences, then select what they considered to be key words and phrases. These I listed on the chalkboard in the order given. With all students responding, and few duplications, a list emerged:

flatland	flat barrenness	monotonous
dry land	sun-dazed farmers	vast prairieland
rolling flat plains	unmerciful sun	grassland
hot	tawny yellow desert	many wide open spaces
dusty	treeless	golden wheat
unpicturesque	hot	grassland
buffalo	windy	wheatfields
sod	quiet	old tattered patchwork quilt
rolling plains	barnyard	sun beating down
level	flat	lonely
miserable	warm-dry	rough patches
hot-dry	endless blank plains	no end, no purpose
dust	no contrast	drab
sand	no color	scattered trees

3. In an effort to open, but not direct, discussion, I asked: "What do these words and phrases reveal?"

Comment

Students expressed surprise at the length of the list and at the variety and diversity of words and phrases. They went on to observe that most were uncomplimentary, a few relatively neutral, and relatively few positive. Not all agreed about which was which, though. Is the phrase "many wide open spaces" neutral? Positive? Is the phrase "old tattered patchwork quilt" neutral? Positive? Or even uncomplimentary, pejorative? What did the writer intend? How did the reader or listener perceive? Are intentions and responses congruent? In what ways do the writer's experiences or perceptions affect his choice of words? In what ways do the listener's or reader's experiences or perceptions affect his response?

In considering these and related questions, students applied, and frequently stopped to clarify their understanding of, the following terms: *denotation* and *connotation*, *concrete* and *abstract*, *literal* and *figurative*, *nouns* and *verbs* and *adjectives*. Students especially liked the phrases that "suggest more than they say" and that "help us see." *State, suggest, infer,* and *imply* were recurring terms.

Exercise 2

1. Again using the overhead projector, I presented the next assignment:

> In your imagination you conjured up a fairly graphic picture of Kansas. The sentence you wrote conveyed that picture. As you were looking at Kansas, you were asked to think about the mountains that lie ahead.
>
> In a second sentence, describe the mountains either as you "see" or "perceive" them.

2. Again, students read their sentences, then selected key words and phrases. Again, all students responded, with few duplications, and we had this list:

coolness	high green blue timberline	snow in August
running streams	tower endlessly	haze of purple

ground squirrels	adventures	terrifying mountains
rugged	cool large	trees
steep slopes	rocks	snow
deep valleys	nature's heaven	shade
blue peaks	stately majestic	pine
crystal blue sky	adventure	picturesque
cool respite	cooler	exhilarating
	fear	

3. Again I asked the question, "What do these words and phrases reveal?"

Comment

As before, students remarked on the effect of certain words and phrases, noting the predominance of expressions evoking positive, pleasant, even euphoric responses. Someone questioned the kind of experiences underlying the choice of "fear" and "terrifying mountains." Another observed the use of abstractions: "nature's heaven" and "cool respite." Some of the terms used earlier were used again, most notably *concrete* and *suggest*. So, for the first time, were the terms *image* and *metaphor*.

Exercise 3

1. I distributed the following take-home assignment:

Here are three sentences written by someone who is as familiar with western Kansas, and the mountains that lie beyond, as you are. In the first sentence, the writer gives us his perception of western Kansas. In the third sentence, he gives us his perception of the mountains beyond. Compare your first sentence with this writer's first sentence, and your second sentence with his third.

The telephone poles have been holding their arms out a long time now to birds that will not settle there but pass with strange cawings westward to where dark trees gather about a waterhole. This is Kansas. The mountains start here just behind the closed eyes of a farmer's sons asleep in their work clothes.

2. All students completed the assignment, and I duplicated and distributed excerpts from their papers, with this request:

As we read each one of these aloud, let's see if we can discover precisely what it is that the writer is trying to tell us about the way that the language of the sentences being compared seems to work and with what effect.

These are some of the excerpts we examined:

> The feeling of 'farminess' and of 'wide-open-spaces' comes across in both passages, but both passages leave unanswered the question of whether or not the people really like Kansas.

> Two main differences show the basic weakness of my sentences. First, the paragraph brings Kansas to life by conveying the idea that people really live in the state. My sentence mentions scenery alone. Second, my terms are ones that everyone generally uses when speaking of Kansas and mountains, but the paragraph uses unconventional terms to convey similar ideas. For example, the telephone poles standing with arms outstretched suggested to me the picture of a flat, seemingly endless highway lined by telephone poles, and this, in turn, suggested great expanse.

> Obviously it is the wording that makes one better than the other for words are all we have and if one is better than the other it must be because the words are more informative or more conveying of a feeling. The most significant difference that I can see is that I just describe an area but in that writer's sentence the words make lifelike objects alive and real. An example is 'the telephone poles have been holding their arms out.' This suggests a very real feeling that the poles are alive. Also, 'dark trees gather about a waterhole' suggests live animals which are capable of moving around.

> I was thinking of Kansas as a whole without the details that make that whole. Mine was a statement that could be said of any time and place. The other writer implies the monotony of watching a countryside by how that person has picked a detail that doesn't change each quickly passing mile. He has stared at those telephone poles for so long that he knows the birds that light there, stay for just a moment and then gather at some other place.

> With mountains behind the closed eyes, that writer can make them anything he wants. The sentences in this passage set the imagination flying.

> The writer's sentences are more open to investigation and interpretation than my sentences, which are definitely very clearcut.

> The similarities between the students' and that writer's sentences seem great to me. The essential part is in being able to interpret his sentences to understand the inner meaning.

> I tried to explain how Kansas and the mountains actually looked to me. The unknown author, however, gives a skeletal framework which forces the reader to fall back on his experiences and take these experiences to the skeleton to form the flesh. My sentences are purely descriptive. One reads my sentences and that is it. They stand still. The unknown author's sentences, though, move and work.

I, through a rather unskillful manipulation of thoughts, managed to scratch out nearly fifty words which communciate nothing other than exactly what the words say.

It is interesting to me that such a short passage as the one presented can say so much for being so short. It gives just as much detail as mine did in about a fifth as much time.

Comment

Discussion revealed students' belief that language used to suggest, connote, compare, or personify worked with particular effectiveness. They were unusually attentive to, and admiring of, those uses of language that either stimulated, allowed, or required "interpretation" and "imaginative play" (or as one wryly put it, "imaginative *work*"). A number felt that they themselves had achieved these effects with some degree of success; even they, however, found more differences than similarities between their sentences and "the writer's" sentences. Finally, they demanded to know "the writer" and the source of those sentences before taking one more step or taking on one more "assignment." Nothing for it, then, but to present the original text.

CROSSING KANSAS BY TRAIN [2]

The telephone poles
have been holding their
arms out
a long time now
to birds
that will not
settle there
but pass with
strange cawings
westward to
where dark trees
gather about
a waterhole. This
is Kansas. The
mountains start here
just behind
the closed eyes
of a farmer's
sons asleep
in their work clothes.
　　　　　　—Donald Justice

Reactions to the poem were immediate, intense, and diverse, reflecting outright glee, discovery, satisfaction—or dismay.

"Aha! I knew it was a poem!"

"Well. So that is a poem. But it made good prose, too. Only, well subtle. And the way the poem looks might make it more difficult to read but doesn't necessarily have to, if we pay attention to the fact that the lines are parts of sentences."

"That wasn't too hard to understand. But why didn't Mr. Justice just write it the way you did? I can read sentences!"

"You expected us to compete with a true poet? Not fair!"

We considered the effect of the arrangement of words on the page, not just the words in relation to one another but, as one student succinctly put it, "in relation to the reader." Then I presented my "arrangement" of two students' sentences paired in sequence.

1

The flatlands

of Kansas

with its dry lands

one can see for miles

2

I sure do wish we'd

hurryandgetoutof Kan-

sas!

Click! Typography—space, shape, and distribution—not only works for poets but can be *made* to work for us. Further, in these arrangements one student heard rhythm, another rhyme. "They were there all the time, but I missed them before!"

It was time to go fishing. Behind the eyes of those farmer's sons, of course.

References

1. Marianne Moore, "Poetry," in *A Little Treasury of Modern Poetry*, ed. Oscar Williams (New York: Charles Scribner's Sons, 1946), p. 311.

2. "Crossing Kansas by Train" by Donald Justice from *Selected Poems*. Copyright © 1961, 1962, 1963, 1964, 1965, 1967 by Donald Justice. Used by permission of Atheneum Publishers. [Editors' Note: New permission, as follows, was secured for this volume:] Copyright © 1963 by Donald Justice. Reprinted from *Night Light* by permission of Wesleyan University Press. This poem first appeared in *The New Yorker*.

Poetry and the Composing Process: An Instructional Approach

by Denny T. Wolfe, Jr.

According to legend, Robert Frost once sat in the back of a one-room schoolhouse in New England, listening to a teacher "teach" his "Stopping by Woods on a Snowy Evening." By "teach," I mean dissect and particularize the poem's elements. At the end of the lesson, the teacher—breathless, smug, and content—said to the poet, "Now, Mr. Frost, tell us what you really meant by that last stanza." Frost reportedly rose from his seat, stretched, hesitated dramatically, and declared, "What I *really* meant was that it was time for my little horse and me to get the hell out of there." At least Frost was invited to respond. That's much better treatment than most students probably received in that classroom. Yet instruction in poetry must be response-centered if teachers are ever to penetrate the prejudices which students hold toward the genre.

Further, students must be led to see how and why some people actually spend agonizing hours writing poetry, as well as how and why some people actually spend equally agonizing hours reading what poets write. And they must be led to see that the reward for the agony is delight, ultimate and serene. Obviously, in the beginning, instruction should emphasize the delight and minimize the agony. But honesty must prevail, and if the teaching approach goes right, students will move on their own, at their own individual paces and levels of readiness, from delight to agony and—we must hope—back again to delight. The best chance we have to help students end with delight is to establish a process for teaching that reflects the way real poets construct poems and the way real readers read them.

On the following page is a pattern, followed by discussion, which illustrates such a process.

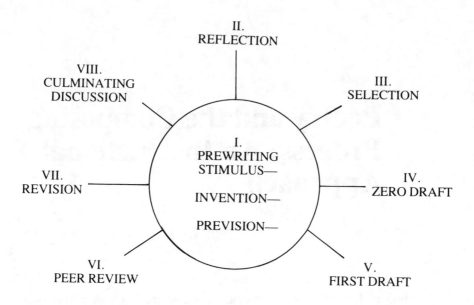

I doubt seriously that Wordsworth bounded out of bed one morning in the English Lake Country, ran downstairs and announced to his sister Dorothy that his "heart leaps up" each time he "beholds a rainbow in the sky." And, even if it did happen that way, I'll wager that Wordsworth didn't say such a thing without ever having seen a rainbow. It is significant to recall how he defined poetry in the Preface to *Lyrical Ballads:* ". . . the spontaneous overflow of powerful feelings; it takes its origin from emotion *recollected in tranquility*" (italics mine). The writing of a poem begins, then, with an *experience*—an event, an encounter, an engagement, a connection, a discovery, a dilemma. In short, the writing of a poem begins with a *stimulus*. The stimulus is at the core of the way the composing goes and the way instruction should go. It is the first phase in moving students toward composing poems, as well as toward reading them.

A clear charge to teachers, therefore, is to create an experience which can stimulate the student's thought, feeling, and imagination. As an example, a teacher might ask students to rise from their seats, stand in a comfortable posture, close their eyes, and relax. They must think of nothing—perhaps a blank movie screen will do. The teacher suggests that they concentrate on relaxing their toes, ankles, calves, thighs, upper torsos, necks, and shoulders (much tension gets stored there), their fingers, forearms, biceps. They must begin to feel numb, floating free. "Now," they are told, "concentrate all your psychic energy into your *left* thumb. . . . You *are* your thumb. The rest of you is gone. All that is left is your thumb, and that's you. Now, open your eyes and pair off with a partner." At this point the teacher suggests several encounters: "Meet the other person as a friend." (Some students will forget they are their thumbs, so they must be reminded.) "Meet the other person as a boxer, a wrestler, a slithering snake, a blind person, a flesh-eating plant, a robot, a fish, an invisible person, a lover." At this point the students may sit down. The stimulus has been provided.

In the second phase, students are asked to *reflect* on the experience— to *recollect in tranquility*. They must recall the encounters and think of what they did and felt. They must remember which encounter they felt most strongly about, or which one perhaps triggered a thought or memory worth pursuing further.

The students are almost ready for the next phase in the process. So far, two crucial steps have been taken: (1) the teacher has provided the *stimulus,* and (2) the students have begun to respond to it and to *reflect* on how it made them feel. Before students move to the third phase in the process, however, the teacher provides a bit of "direct" instruction about haiku poetry, pointing to its structural requirements of three verses with a 5-7-5 syllable count in the sequence of lines, for a total of 17 syllables in the poem. The teacher should also mention certain characteristics of the content in haiku, i.e., what the haiku poet is attempting to achieve. There are almost invariably two or more images which somehow merge to create a sense of universal harmony and unity as an overall effect of the poem. Perhaps the most famous haiku poem in Japan, which Japanese people know as well as Americans know nursery rhymes, goes this way in translation (the English does not contain the 5-7-5 syllable count):

> Old pond
> Frog leaps in
> Splashing water

Amy Lowell's "Staying in My Room" is an example of American haiku, which does conform to the 5-7-5 syllable count, and there are many others for students to see. Several excellent sources include: R. H. Blyth (ed.), *A History of Haiku* (Tokyo: The Hokuseido Press, 1963); Harold G. Henderson (ed.), *An Introduction to Haiku* (Garden City, NY: Doubleday, 1958); *Issa, The Year of My Life,* trans. by Hobuyuki Yuasa (Los Angeles: University of California Press, 1972); and Kenneth Yasuda, *The Japanese Haiku* (Bloomington, IN: Indiana University Press, 1975).

The third phase of the process has to do with *selection*. The teacher has assigned the form. Each student will write a haiku (obviously, other forms could be used: cinquain, concrete poetry, "guided" poetry, based on phrases to complete or short questions to answer—many options exist; I am using haiku as an example to define the process approach). The students must select an image from the several encounters with their thumbs: friend, boxer, wrestler, snake, blind person, flesh-eating plant, robot, invisible person, lover. Who knows where the images will lead? The actual poems which students write may contain no direct references at all to the specific stimulus. The stimulus may serve strictly as a mnemonic device, triggering a memory of another experience, real or imagined.

Phase four is a *zero draft*, a jotting down of possible images, phrases, comparisons, descriptive words—in short, a "bank" to draw on for the first draft. The zero draft may be a series of questions, a sketch, or an outline. It may be a word association game that the student plays with himself or herself—perhaps written as a "cluster" with a "core" word or words (images, really) placed in the center of a blank page and associative words encircling it. (My diagram of the process I am describing might be viewed as an exercise in "clustering.") Then the associative words may lead to still more associations, until the student discovers some direction for the next phase.

In the fifth phase, students write their *first drafts,* attending to both the structural and content requirements of the haiku form. Line by line, students will be making diction choices which may be changed as they go to conform to syllable counts and to achieve the harmony of images which the haiku demands. Revision often occurs during the drafting process itself—it is not always a separate and distinct phase.

The sixth phase calls for a *peer review*. Students exchange poems with their partners in the "thumbs exercise." As they read each other's drafts, they are to make at least one complimentary comment and at least one suggestion for possible strengthening of the drafts. The quality and amount of feedback one gets largely depend upon questions the writer asks of the peer reviewer. The teacher should ask students to consider diction choices particularly, noting Coleridge's famous distinction between prose and poetry: *prose,* words in their best order; *poetry*, the best words in their best order.

The seventh phase is for *revision*. Students get their poems back and consider the feedback they have received. The feedback comes both from peer reviewers and from the writer's own continual reflection. The writer will reconsider the stimulus, the tentative selection of images he or she has made, and the "bank" created by the zero draft. The writer always functions as executive decision maker; that is, only the writer can decide which feedback to use and how to use it in making revisions.

As a *culminating activity,* in the eighth phase, the teacher asks for several volunteers to write their haiku poems on the chalkboard. An added ''wrinkle,'' though, is that the volunteers are instructed to leave out every third word, drawing lines to equal length in the spaces left by the omitted words. Once the poems appear on the board, the class attempts to supply the missing words in oral discussions of the poems. This activity enables students to ''publish'' their work, enlarge their vocabularies, further recognize the importance of revision, further engage in critical and creative thinking, and—certainly not least—begin to appreciate the craft of making poems. After a discussion of each poem, the writer reveals his or her own answers to the missing words. The writer is the lone ''authority'' as to the ''truth'' of the missing words.

Haiku poems that secondary students have written when I have conducted this activity include the following samples:

> My self met her self,
> Wrestled playfully awhile,
> Suddenly to love.
> > (ninth grader)

> Photosynthesis
> Spectrum of light invading,
> Making the world green.
> > (tenth grader)

> Serpents entangled,
> Slithering for advantage,
> Conquering their fears.
> > (eleventh grader)

> Venus sits waiting;
> A lightning bug approaches—
> The strongest survives.
> > (twelfth grader)

> Man making robots
> To do his labor for him—
> Just one soul to share.
> > (twelfth grader)

Engaging students in the practice of making poems as a prerequisite to reading them can combat the difficulties I cited at the beginning. Students who write poems can learn to relate to poets, thereby breaking down prejudicial stereotypes which have made poets seem dilettantish and unfathomable. And teachers, discovering that their students can and will actually write poems, may not be so inclined to begin instruction reductively. Finally, poems which students write do not seem to abhor instruction. Like Frost in the New England classroom, the poet is present to express his or her own ''truths'' and to untangle confused intentions. From a writing approach to the teaching of poems, teachers can lead students toward higher levels of meaning-making with poetry in the classroom.

Solving the Poetry Riddle

by James S. Mullican

Too many young people profess to hate poetry. As children they loved nursery rhymes and stories in rhythmic, rhyming verse, and as adolescents and young adults they retain their affection for verse in popular songs. Yet in the English classroom they profess to hate poetry. For these young people, poetry consists largely of "deep meanings" understood only by teachers. Many of these young people don't like what one of my students called the "shredding of poetry" for the purpose of sifting out that last bit of meaning in a poem. I'm sure that this student and many others like her would agree with Wordsworth that too often we "murder to dissect."

We can, I am sure, lure some of our students into a renewed liking for poetry by returning, with appropriate adaptations, to their childhood loves. We can read to them narrative poems and light verse. We probably should do more of this kind of exercise, since a good story, rollicking rhythm and rhyme, and humor are attractive qualities in many poems, and students should be made aware of these qualities. Not all poems are "deep."

Yet too much lightness can be a cop-out. Experienced teachers know that much of the best poetry is complex, subtle, and difficult and that some of the pleasure of reading poetry resides in wrenching meaning from complex, dense, and puzzling poetry. We teachers would like to share our enjoyment of excellent poetry with our students, and we would like to assist our students in gaining the skills necessary to read such poetry. Our problem is to find ways of presenting such poetry in a pleasing, non-threatening manner. One solution that I have discovered is to present poems explicitly as riddles. I begin by reading aloud some of the riddle poems in May Swenson's *Poems To Solve* (New York: Charles Scribner's Sons, 1966). After reading each poem aloud, I ask students to suggest answers to the riddle and "prove" their solutions by citing specific words in the poem. Sometimes I stop after a few lines and ask if anyone can solve the riddle before hearing the entire poem. I find that after a little practice both high school and college students become quite adept at solving these poetry riddles.

My next step is to present several other poems that are not explicit riddles but that have puzzling aspects that need to be solved. For example, I ask who are the narrators in Wolcott Gibb's "Declaration of Independence," in John Crowe Ransom's "Blue Girls," and in Theodore Roethke's "My Papa's Waltz." Sometimes solving the riddle consists of supplying titles to poems whose titles I have omitted: Plath's "Mushrooms," Yeats's "Father and Child," Tennyson's "The Eagle," and Langston Hughes's "Mother to Son" have proved excellent for this exercise. I cite these examples because they are rather well-known, but I find some of my best poetry riddles in current magazines. Somehow poems seem more real and relevant to students when they are located in current magazines. For several years, for example, I used Richard Peck's "Nancy" (*Saturday Review* [June 21, 1969]: 6) as a riddle or puzzle; students tried to discover who Nancy was (an alienated high-school or college student), who the narrator was (a teacher), and what dramatic action was implied in the poem (a confrontation based on "relevance" and "the generation gap"). Students in the early 70s found much to empathize with in the antiestablishment protagonist portrayed in the poem. By the mid-70s, however, I found students required "historical" background to understand the poem, and its day in my classroom was done. An advantage of using magazines is that they permit us to exploit the interests of the day; unfortunately, the occasional nature of many of these poems condemns even the best of them to obsolescence.

After the foregoing exercises, students are ready to become involved in locating riddle poems. I ask students, in groups of three, to search out poems, not usually taught in school, which they find puzzling in some way. Sufficient copies are to be brought to class so that everyone can have a copy. I've found that having three students lead the discussion diffuses responsibility among the students and relieves the pressure on them. The selectors are at least potentially more expert concerning their poem than anyone else in the classroom, including the teacher, since only the selectors have had certain access to the poem before class.

Once three high-school students in our honors seminar brought Sylvia Plath's poem, "Metaphors," from *Crossing the Water: Transitional Poems*, (New York: Harper & Row, 1971) to class. This poem proved perfect for my purposes, since it explicitly proclaims itself a riddle. The class struggled through the poem, admiring the imagery but not solving the riddle, until someone suggested tentatively: "Could the narrator of the poem be pregnant?" Once the question was asked, the answer was obvious, and many students joined in to show how each detail fit in with the suggested solution. Someone pointed out that even the nine syllables in

"I'm a riddle in nine syllables" were not arbitrary, since they corresponded with the nine months of human gestation. Then someone discovered that there are nine lines in the poem and nine syllables in each line.

In setting up the ground rules for solving poetry riddles, I have found Laurence Perrine's "The Nature of Proof in the Interpretation of Poetry" (*English Jounal*, 51 [September 1962]: 393–98) most helpful. Perrine contends that we should consider all the details in a poem as data in demonstrating proof for any interpretation. Any solution to a poetic riddle must account for all the details in a poem; the interpretation that accounts for all the details in the simplest way is the best. Class discussion thus has a rational basis and a norm for testing the validity of answers.

After the experience of working with poetic riddles in the classroom, I discovered an article that offers some reasons why this approach can be successful: S.I. Sackett's "Poetry and Folklore: Some Points of Affinity" (*Journal of American Folklore*, 77 [April/June 1964]: 142–53). In this article, Sackett contends that the appeal of metaphor stems from its nature as a riddle, something that all cultures find attractive. We enjoy solving riddles because "It is only human for us to feel pleased with ourselves for having solved a problem." Approaching the poem as riddle, according to Sackett, can also induce the reader to cooperate in the enactment of a poem: "Through the use of metaphor, the poet brings the reader into the poetic process as a participant, and the reader must guess the metaphor before he can read the poem with any degree of comprehension." By regarding some poems—or parts of poems—as riddles, Sackett has located at least one source of the enjoyment of complex poetry: reading such poetry is "a natural human activity deriving from natural human impulses and appealing to natural human instincts." If Sackett is correct—and I think that he is—treating some poems as riddles is not merely using sugar to make the medicine go down. Decoding the metaphor—or solving the riddle—is the essence of reading and enjoying some poetry.

My proposals for teaching poetry riddles are modest: (1) use the more familiar and more attractive term: a riddle is less intimidating than a deep meaning; (2) begin with riddles that students can solve and work gradually toward more difficult poetry; and (3) involve students in locating and solving poetic riddles, giving them the opportunity to become the experts.

As teachers and students work toward meaning through questioning, probing, offering tentative solutions, making errors and correcting them, they solve more than the riddle before them. They come to understand something of the reading process and the ways in which we arrive at meaning, using the poem, as I.A. Richards suggested, as "a machine to think with." In the process, we can all rediscover another pleasure of childhood, solving riddles.

Teaching Native American Poetry*

by Jeffrey F. Huntsman

The rich and enduring literary art of Native America is, unfortunately, seldom encountered in American schools. Although there are several differences between the literatures of Indian peoples and the more familiar ones of Europe and America—differences that must be understood before the fullness of Indian verbal art may be appreciated—such literature can be both accessible and moving when presented effectively. Like that of most other small traditional cultures around the world, Native American literature was, and is today, fundamentally oral in composition, presentation, and preservation. Even those Native Americans who now compose in English typically create for the ear and not the eye, and the literature of past generations was wholly oral in its original context.

Most of us forget that all literature was primarily oral until just a few generations ago. What makes literature literature is not its mode of preservation as writing but its status as the enduring art in words valued by a people. Even in the English-speaking world, which has for centuries enjoyed a higher degree of literacy than most cultures, much literature was intended to be read aloud, although it may have been printed for easy and broad distribution. But the literature of cultures that have done without writing systems are totally presented through the oral-aural channel. Thus we might best begin to think about Native American literature with a consideration of aspects of oral presentation.

Oral performance is distinct from other kinds of language use. Ordinary speaking is an act which our hearers evaluate chiefly in terms of its effectiveness in transmitting information. But oral performance is both an *act* of speaking and an *event* of speaking. Performances are evaluated both for their information and for their conformity with cultural expectations about honesty, social appropriateness, effectiveness, and beauty.

Because of our own overriding experiences with literature in its printed form, we have come to think, like Platonists, that the "real" work is the ideal abstract text which exists somewhere "outside" its various kinds of manifestations in print or performance.

For Native Americans, however, performance is itself the "real" event, and as such must be given thoughtfully and respectfully. Understanding this, I believe, is one of the critical keys to teaching Native American literature so that the results are both effective aesthetic experiences for non-Indians and translations that are as faithful as possible to the forms and values of the original works. Until recently, it has been difficult to appreciate the full dimensions of traditional Native American literary performances because they were available only in bald renderings from anthropologists' field notes. In the past few years, however, research on performance conducted by scholars in disciplines such as sociology, anthropology, linguistics, and folklore has resulted in new approaches that have direct import for teachers.

Performance for Native Americans involves more than the simple repetition of a text. Even the simplest-appearing story is embedded in a cultural framework that allows the teller to make only the scantest reference to details that all in the community understand. Most tellings take place at special times and in special places. People of the Southwest, for example, do not tell stories about the kachina spirit-beings except in the dark of the year, when the kachinas have withdrawn to their winter village, for to speak the names of the kachinas is to summon them to the speaker's presence. The inflections of the songs that frequently are part of the performance, the subtle physical and vocal gestures of the teller, even the smells of cooking food and burning piñon, sage, or sweetgrass are all vital parts of each recitation that cannot easily be replicated. Perhaps only a few of these dimensions may be shown to our students, but we enhance our chances of successful teaching by including as many as we can. Naturally, slides of areas students may not know will help—the vibrantly colored deserts and mountains of the Southwest and the seagirt cedar forests of the Northwest Coast—but the key is to be found in the literature itself.

It is possible to approach the *feeling* of a traditional performance in the classroom by attempting to read the literature in a way that presents some of the major aspects of a performed work. One fine example is Dennis Tedlock's translations of eight tellings in *Finding the Center: Narrative Poetry of the Zuni Indians* (Lincoln, NE: University of Nebraska Press, 1978). Tedlock's edition uses a variety of different typefaces, words compressed or elongated, and lines printed above or below the normal line to indicate something of the variations in the teller's voice. A feeling of being part of a performance may be achieved by having the class read such texts aloud.

So far I have not used the term *poetry* that is in the title of this article. This avoidance has been deliberate, for, in one sense, "poetry" is foreign to all traditional Native American cultures. Poetry in our Western sense does not exist formally; there is simply no body of uniformly metrical literature in any Indian culture that is distinct from prose in the ways our poetry is. But there is another, functional way of defining poetry that does find counterparts in traditional Indian literatures, and those counterparts are songs and ritualized prose recitations.

Songs for Native Americans do exhibit the formal properties of Western poetry, and song for all Native American cultures is of paramount importance. Indians composed songs for all purposes—the celebration of the rising sun each day, of the birth of new people, of success in hunt and battle, of the living presence of beings of spiritual power and significance. Such songs are so central to Indian ways of life that one old Navajo expressed his abject poverty by saying that he did not own a single song. But Native American music is different from ours, and it is difficult for students on the first few hearings to appreciate its complex rhythms and phrasings because they are so alien to their own experiences. Playing recordings of Indian songs is one way of introducing students to those things that are central to Indian literary expression. After only a short while the effects of drums, rattles, flutes, and voices (even in foreign languages) begin to be felt.

The closest western counterparts to Native American ritualized prose recitations may be found in prayers and sometimes sermons (especially those in the Black tradition). Prose in our tradition is typically much like conversation—casual, unpatterned, and too easily forgotten. Few of us can remember the precise wording of even very familiar prose pieces, such as "fairy" stories. Instead, we remember the gist of the story and reinvent the diction anew with each repetition. Native American prose narratives, on the other hand, are typically remembered and repeated with little variation and thus have the effect of "narrative poetry," although in print they correspond more closely with prose.

Furthermore, some narratives, especially sacred ones, often are changed in a rhythmical way that is not quite song but is very distinct from normal conversation or even formal speech. An early scholar of Indian rituals, Frederic Webb Hodge, described the differences in the *Handbook of the American Indians North of Mexico,* (Bureau of American Ethnology Bulletin no. 30, Washington, DC: Government Printing Office, 1907).

> Prose rituals are always intoned, and the delivery brings out the rhythmic character of the composition. Rituals that are sung differ from those that are intoned in that the words, in order to conform to the music, are drawn out by vowel prolongations . . . In many [secular] songs the words are few, but they have been carefully chosen with reverence to their capability of conveying the thought of the composer in a manner that, to the native's mind, will be poetic, not prosaic.

Naturally, no single technique will guarantee our students a native appreciation of these works, but rhythmical recitation of some prose-poems may provide a comparable experience.

Thankfully, living traditions do not die easily, for culture is characteristically a set of deeply engrained habits of thought and action, not a set of artifacts or historical experiences. Today, there are many gifted Indian poets composing in both their ancestral languages and in the common European languages now spoken in America—English, French, and Spanish.

One such poet is Simon Ortiz, an Ácoma Pueblo from New Mexico. A bilingual, Ortiz composes poems in both English and in Keres, his ancestral language, and during his reading he may begin to chant or even to sing his poems in either language. Ortiz's poetry, like that of other major living Indian poets, is immediately understandable to most students because he writes of things common to contemporary America, even if they are things colored by his unique bicultural heritage. Several anthologies, containing the works of such modern Indian writers as James Welsh, Leslie Silko, N. Scott Momaday, Duane Niatum, Ray Young Bear, and Wendy Rose, are easily available. They are powerful voices for all Americans, and their poetic creations, like those of their ancestors, are splendid examples of high oral art.

In sum, Native American poetry is especially accessible because it was meant, from its inception, to be shared. Native American verbal art is very much a part of the communities from which it developed; the common experiences of both poet and audience, their mutual concerns, and their congruent aesthetic expectations give such poetry a cohesion that poetry from the more disparate majority cultures of contemporary America often does not have. It is intended to be heard, not read, and therefore lends itself to classroom presentation. The easy availability of musical and visual aids, which present accurate and appealing insights into Indian life, also facilitates an understanding of poetry in a holistic way. Rich and vibrant, Native American poetry provides an unusual perspective on an undoubtedly American but too often unknown way of life and art that most students find inherently interesting, stimulating, and rewarding.

On Teaching Narrative Poetry: My Collective Ballad Bard*

by David Sudol

Teaching poetry to my tenth grade English classes used to be like force-feeding reluctant geese. The honks of complaint were deafening, and all I gained for my effort was frustration. This past semester, however, I hit on an idea that has transformed the teaching of at least narrative poetry into a pleasure instead of a chore. What I did, simply, was to teach my tenth graders to write collective narrative poems—classroom ballads.

First, I introduce narrative poetry, dividing it into two general categories—epic and ballad—and explain each. Second, I state that, since it is impractical to read an entire epic in class, we'll concentrate on ballads. This statement yields a sigh of relief, as any lightening of the burden of poetry is welcomed. Next, I pass out copies of Alfred Noyes' "The Highwayman," and we read and discuss it in class, emphasizing such elements as the story line, the sad or tragic subject matter, the stanza form, the rhyme scheme, and the refrain.

After the discussion I return to my epic ploy and state that, since it is equally impractical to write an epic in class, we will instead write a ballad. This yields mixed reviews, as my students realize that the lightened load of poetry is a load nonetheless.

At this point I begin by asking what is the essential element of a ballad—indeed, of all narrative poetry; to which someone invariably replies, "the story." From there I proceed to solicit the rudiments of a story line. Collectively we decide on characters, setting, and plot. I have found that choosing a student from class—willing or otherwise—as the main character piques student interest. Likewise, the setting should be local,

---

*This essay is unedited and is reprinted here from *English Journal* (October 1980) by permission. Copyright © 1980 by the National Council of Teachers of English.

perhaps the school or home town. Concerning the sad and/or tragic plot, I have no trouble getting kids to produce weird, strange, macabre, slightly obscene scenarios. In fact they seem to revel in the bizarre (I suppose everyone is a black humorist or a sadist at heart); and to my way of thinking, the more outrageous the story, the better.

Examples of two of the story lines my classes produced are the following:

1. John Boy Mortonio arrives at his second hour English class one morning and becomes immediately enamored of his attractive young substitute teacher. His heart, burning with desire, aches to tell her of his love. He spills his guts to her; at first she plays him like a fish. Then, no longer able to control her mirth, she laughs in his face. John, wounded and angry, punches her out, stomps out of the school, and sets it on fire. Realizing the error of his ways, he rushes into the inferno to save his true love but dies in the flames, alone.

2. Crazy Mary, the shapeliest sophomore around, is the object of Ken and Scott's undivided affection. Unable to choose between the two suitors, she presents them with a proposal: let them fight over her, and let the winner take all. Ken and Scott go at it until they notice two fine-looking young ladies passing by. They immediately call a truce and leave with the girls for the night, leaving Crazy Mary shocked and alone.

Once the story line is firmly established and is sketched out step-by-step on the board, we move on to the refrain. Although the students know that the refrain is optional in any ballad, I insist that we do one, and so it goes. As a rule we try to come up with a refrain that somehow summarizes the essence of the story—its moral or theme. I find it easier, and usually more fun for the kids, to write the refrain as a couplet. Examples for the above story lines are:

1. John Boy wanted her flaming love/Now he's roasting up above,

and

2. Crazy Mary made them wait/ Now for Mary it's too late

After the refrain is polished, we must decide on a stanza form. Again I find it easier and more entertaining to write in couplets, and for the sake of simplicity we stick to a six-line stanza, including the refrain.

Finally, after all that legwork, we start the actual ballad writing. From experience I've found several ways to approach it. With especially bright and eager kids (those who by this time are really "into" the assignment), I let each student write a line or a couplet, and we simply move around the room until everyone has had a chance and/or the poem is completed. This approach, however, is admittedly idealistic and not very practical. Another way to handle the writing is for me to suggest the end rhymes for each couplet or stanza and then let the kids fill in the rest of the lines. Or I may write the first line of the couplet and then let a student finish it with his/her own rhyme or one I have suggested. These latter approaches put me in a position of control, which may be unfair to the kids, but they allow me to offer some direction; to keep the ballad on target, not allowing it to take off on a tangent; and to set up lines in such a way as to let the students write vivid images with metaphors and similes.

Of course, and unfortunately, not all of the students participate in the actual writing of the poetry—not everyone is poetic. However, I have found a way of preventing two or three kids from stealing the show. At every stage in the composition—after every couplet, every stanza—I ask the one student who has volunteered as secretary to read back to the class what we have written so far. Then I ask as many students as possible for their opinions on the rhyme, the rhythm, the phrasing, the syntax, the story, and so on. In brief, every student, whether he/she is actually writing rhyme or not, is editing and criticizing—and *everyone* likes to criticize. Thus, without fail, by the end of the ballad nearly all have had their say, and, without doubt, all feel as though they own part of the authorship.

And, speaking of the finished product. What are the rewards of this corporate poetic effort? The ballads themselves, of course. Here are two of my favorites.

THE BALLAD OF JOHN BOY MORTONIO
by English 10, period #2

John Boy fell in love with the sub,
Even though she was shaped like a tub.
When he saw her flaming red lips,
He felt his heart do an inside flip.
John Boy wanted her flaming love;
Now he's roasting up above.

John Boy walked up to her and said,
"Marry me, baby, or I'll drop dead."
The teacher looked at John and smiled
And said, "We'd better wait awhile."
John Boy wanted her flaming love;
Now he's roasting up above.

John said, "Baby, I just can't wait.
Can we please go on a date?"

Then the sub laughed in his face,
Making John feel so disgraced.
John Boy wanted her flaming love;
Now he's roasting up above.

John blew a fuse and knocked her out,
Punched her squarely in the mouth,
Went outside and lit a match,
Burned the school like it was trash.
John Boy wanted her flaming love;
Now he's roasting up above.

John Boy knew he'd made a mistake;
His teacher was broiling like a steak.
And so he ran into the fire
To rescue his true love's desire.
John Boy wanted her flaming love;
Now he's roasting up above.

John was captured by the flames;
He could not rescue that dazzling dame.
So he sighed a dying lisp,
And then he burned up to a crisp.
John Boy wanted her flaming love;
Now he's roasting up above.

THE BALLAD OF CRAZY MARY
by English 10, period #6

Crazy Mary had a real fine body,
Shaped like an hourglass, not a bit shoddy.
Ken and Scott were hot for Mary;
Things were looking hairy and scary.
Crazy Mary made them wait;
Now for Mary it's too late.

Ken said, "Mary, go out with me.
I'm better looking as you can see."
Scott said, "Mary, forget that scum.
He's nothing but a filthy bum."
Crazy Mary made them wait;
Now for Mary it's too late.

Crazy Mary couldn't decide,
So she let the question ride.
Then she said, "You guys brawl,
And let the winner take it all!"
Crazy Mary made them wait;
Now for Mary it's too late.

Ken punched Scotty in the nose.
Scott exchanged some powerful blows.
Then something happened to catch their eye—
Two shapely blondes went strolling by.
Crazy Mary made them wait;
Now for Mary it's too late.

Ken and Scott forgot their fight
And left with the girls for the night.
Crazy Mary stood there in shock;
Her mouth hung open, she couldn't talk.
Crazy Mary made them wait;
Now for Mary it's too late.

Obviously, these ballads are not great poetry—if they were King George's men, the Highwayman would still be riding on his ribbon of moonlight. Nevertheless, I think they are good examples of what tenth graders can do with a little direction. And for me they are even more—they are proof that tenth graders can master the concepts of narrative poetry and that they, and I, can have some fun in the process.

After finishing this exercise in collective ballad writing, I'm tired: oral composition and spontaneous poetic direction are energy-sapping activities. More than tired, though, I'm satisfied. I don't feel the frustration that comes from spending hours cramming poetry down a student's throat. I feel rather as though I've just finished a wonderful holiday meal—the main course, a fat roasted goose.

Teaching the Lyric to Grades Nine through Twelve or Why I Left the Classroom

by Suzanne J. Doyle

I know few good poets who have any business in the classroom. Which is not to say that I think poets should not work, nor that I think poets should claim as their chief occupation the writing of verse; that way madness lies, not to mention lousy verse. It is to say that I think good teaching, as good poetry, is born of concentrated, single-minded devotion of the spirit to improving one's craft and anyone exposed to the reality of either vocation knows the near impossibility of doing both well. Yet the classroom offers the poet a respectable professional guise and a salary, which poetry itself never will provide, and the poet of a scholarly bent often chooses the classroom with the naive expectation that daily exposure to literature will somehow be more conducive to sustaining the muse than waiting on tables or editing technical copy. My own experience, when the classroom in question was one in a secondary school in the private educational sector, has proven otherwise. Such schools demand an inordinate number of hours of classroom and paper work, extracurricular activities, and administrative responsibilities of their junior faculty members, offering an embarrassment of a salary as recompense. If you are a poet, you assume such a position at the peril of your art. I say, "Go to night school and learn word processing."

If as a poet you are already caught in such a compromising position, or if your vocation is teacher rather than poet, what follows may prove useful to you as an outline of a simple, effective structure I used for four years to teach the history and composition of the lyric poem to grades nine through twelve.

The rare, untutored genius might (although I've never seen it done), write a good poem without being aware of the tradition that precedes him or her. Even so she or he runs the risk of being brought up short by the discovery upon reaching, say, the poetic equivalent of the South Pole, that a foreign flag was long ago firmly sunk into the polar cap; someone did it before and did it better. As a matter of pride, if nothing else, any explorer or poet who claimed the title would be shamed by the experience. And if the odds are slight that one might write a good poem without having studied what has been done before with the form or the subject, preferably both, then the chances that an uneducated reader will deeply appreciate a good poem without instruction in the history of the form and ideas are even more slight. As a teacher in writing classes, therefore, I always assumed that the educating being done was of readers of poetry, not writers, not poets, for even if any of those graceless, sprawling adolescent minds were of a poetic inclination, it seems wisest not to encourage them between the ages of 14 and 18 to embrace the identity of poet, chiefly because of the sentimentally self-destructive romantic attitude toward the occupation still pervasive today.

If the teaching of verse writing is to serve as the means of creating educated readers of poetry, as with any other art, learning appreciation of the skill involved most quickly means trying one's hand at the discipline through imitation. How deceptively simple it seems it will be to imitate W.C. Williams' "Poem," for example. Although the consequent appreciation such an exercise achieves does not breed affinity or reverse aesthetic tastes, it is, as all education is, the groundwork for respectful judgment of another's endeavor to shape the truth, without which teleology the efforts of teachers and poets alike are pointless.

My own syllabus grew out of a course called "The Lyric," which was taught by the poet and scholar Helen Pinkerton at Stanford University. It is organized generically, i.e., "The Nature Poem," "The Letter Poem," "The Love Poem," and "The Rejection of Love Poem." Within each topical division, the poems are presented in chronological order, and an attempt is made to illustrate the evolving history of the idea of what a "nature poem" or a "letter poem" should consist. I include here only a partial listing of the best of the poems I taught under a few of the categories, for the hot pursuit and felicitous discovery of poems that suit the categories, or demand creation of new ones, are the greatest part of the fun in preparing this course. All desultory reading of poetry is legitimized, especially slumming for outstandingly poor examples of each genre. I have, sad to say, often taught more from a particularly abysmal example than from a dozen outstanding representatives.

Writing assignments in my classes were weekly and submitted to well-mannered class scrutiny; that is, unless a student could make a suggestion as to how the poem could specifically be improved, she or he was not granted the privilege of criticism. Students were required to submit a minimum of two poems per week, at least one in imitation of a specific poem written in traditional form. The second poem could also be written in traditional rhyme and meter or it could be written in free verse, but it was still required to be an attempt to imitate a particular stylistic aspect of the model poem. This exercise in specific imitation of rhetorical devices or meter or, more elusively, tone forced a careful stylistic analysis of the poem on the part of students and required them to learn the tools of the trade quickly. Before students could even begin to fulfill the assignment by writing their own poems, they had to understand the rhetorical structures supporting the model, which brings me to the much disputed subject of meter.

Robert Frost thought that trying to write verse without meter was like trying to play tennis without a net. If so, trying to teach poetry without first having taught meter is like taking the whole class out onto the court at once without not only the net but rackets and balls as well. Everyone mills around confusedly wondering what they're doing in the middle of all of those purposefully drawn white lines. Poetry is language in lines, and as lines, probably originally musical measures, they have been for centuries (in English at least since Chaucer) metrically defined. A poetry course at the secondary level that does not include rigorous instruction in meter and scansion can do no more than prepare a generation of readers of greeting card verse.

Before I assigned any work, I gave a crash course in meter and scansion with illustrations of iambic lines from monometer to hexameter, trochaic trimeter to pentameter, and whatever I had most recently discovered best illustrating the unusual anapestic and dactylic measures. The iambic lines, most simple and natural, are the most important to teach, of course, and the majority of time was spent discussing them in connection with the metrical substitutions with which we found them so gracefully or glaringly embroidered. For reference on meter and invaluable examples to teach from I recommend James McAuley's *Versification: A Short Introduction* (East Lansing, MI: Michigan State University Press, 1966); James McMichael's *The Style of the Short Poem* (Belmont, CA: Wadsworth Publishing Company, 1967); and with brief, but accurate definitions alone, the entry on "Meter" in M.H. Abrams' *A Glossary of Literary Terms* (New York: Holt, Rinehart, and Winston, 1971). The first two are fine sources for explanation of how meter alone does not mean but becomes an expressive tool in the hands of the skilled poet. I saved discussion of purely accentual or syllabic forms until well into the course, unless some apt student discovered them earlier during examination of one of the more experimental or modern poems assigned. When discussing the poems in class, I began with the simple and objective question of how to define the form of the poem most precisely. For the first few weeks this consumed time while students furiously marked and counted meter, diagramed rhyme scheme, but soon enough this became second nature, and a more sophisticated discussion of form and content became readily available to us than would have been possible without firm grounding in the formal rules of the game. My former teacher, the poet Edgar Bowers, once said that poetry was, like chess, one of the most complex arts because the rules were so few and so simple. And it is my experience that there must be rules so that there is then a tension of some sort created, for the only state of being which is devoid of tension is death itself or a snoring reader.

What follows is an abbreviated and briefly annotated excerpt of the reading list to accompany the poetry course I have been discussing. These poems were taught to grades nine through twelve and, although many were finally beyond the complete grasp of even the most able and mature students, as well as myself, I thought it wiser to overextend us than to risk complacency. In their inimitable adolescent absolutism, they are always too certain, along with Keats, that what they already know is all they ever need to know and I thought it most healthy to admit my limitations to them honestly so that they would not need to waste their time trying to stump me with merely academic questions. Sometimes it worked.

The Letter Poem
(This category proved to inspire the best poems.)

Horace, Usually the epistle on *The Art of Poetry* by way of the briefer I. 19, "To Maecenas"
George Gascoigne, "Woodmanship"
Ben Jonson, "Inviting a Friend to Supper"
Emily Dickinson, "This Is My Letter to the World"
Ezra Pound, "The River-Merchant's Wife: A Letter"
Janet Lewis, "Lines With a Gift of Herbs"
J.V. Cunningham, "To What Strangers What Welcome, #4"
Mary Baron, "Letters for the New England Dead"
Robert Hass, "Letter" and "Not Going to New York: A Letter"
Robert Lowell, "After the Surprising Conversions"

The Love Poem
(This category usually produces the worst poems when written to or about people, some interesting poems when written about vegetables or fruits.)

Sappho, "An Equal to the Gods He Seems to Me"
Ovid, From the "Amores," I.iv, "Your husband? Going to the same dinner?" and others in that vein
Anonymous, "Alison"
Anonymous, "Westron Winde"
Petrarch, The most elaborately figured sonnet you can find
Philip Sidney, "With How Sad Steps Wan Moon"
Thomas Wyatt, "They Flee from Me"
John Donne, "The Flea"
Matthew Arnold, "Dover Beach"
Ernest Dowson, "Non Sum Qualis Eram Bonae Sub Regno Cynarae"
W.H. Auden, "Lullaby"
W.C. Williams, "Love Song"
J.V. Cunningham, "To My Wife"
E.A. Robinson, "Eros Turranos"

The Rejection of Love Poem
(A category they rarely can yet appreciate, taught for my sanity's sake after "The Love Poem.")

Thomas Wyatt, "Whoso List to Hunt"
Philip Sidney, "Thou Blind Man's Mark"
Ben Jonson, "My Picture Left in Scotland"
William Shakespeare, "The Expense of Spirit in a Waste of Shame"
W.B. Yeats, "Sailing to Byzantium"
Robert Bridges, 'Eros"
Edgar Bowers, "Amor Vincit Omnia"
J.V. Cunningham, "Epigram #75"

The Persona Poem
(I encouraged them to choose legendary or mythological characters.)

Tennyson, "Ulysses" and "Tithonus"
Robert Browning, "My Last Duchess"
Thomas Hardy, 'The Haunter"

E. A. Robinson, ''Luke Havergal'' and ''Rembrandt to Rembrandt''
Yvor Winters, ''Sir Gawain and the Green Knight''
T.S. Eliot, ''Gerontion'' and ''The Love Song of J. Alfred Prufrock''

Other topics that interested me were The Retirement Poem, The Epicurean Poem (not restricted to the gastronomic but dominated by it), The Short Satire and Epigram, The Brief Narrative (chiefly ballads), Poems on Death, Poems on Nature (which, if you exclude most of the Romantics, can actually be a manageable category), and Poems on Works of Art (including the inevitable ''Ode on a Grecian Urn'' and the challenge of ''Lapis Lazuli''). This list is by no means meant to be exhaustive. Each year I added and deleted from it extensively, always trying to include as much contemporary work as I could with any conscience. To do so required no small effort in endlessly scanning intelligently edited literary periodicals with an eye to finding the most current and suitable examples, as well as keeping abreast of the publication of volumes of verse by minor but educated new poetic voices. The latter is considerably the easier of the two activities but both constitute one of the anomalous occasions upon which the duties and desires of both teacher and poet successfully merge.

Ninety-nine Bottles of Beer on the Wall or How to Count the Feet

by Joseph E. Price

One of the recurring experiences of teachers is dealing with students who simply do not like poetry. The hostility toward poetry may vary in its intensity, but it is present in almost every literature class. Part, if not all, of such feelings stems from students' frustration at not being able to understand the enthusiastic endorsements for poetry that many teachers offer, particularly when those endorsements are followed by seemingly unintelligible discussions of prosody. As literature teachers, we may be guilty at times of not anticipating how prosody, especially, can heighten students' frustration with poetry. In fact, we may compound the difficulty by leading students to believe that understanding prosody is, after all, the most important aspect of understanding poetry. As a matter of fact, however, prosody should be introduced only after other elements such as syntax, metaphor, sound, and performance have been considered and students seem to feel reasonably comfortable with them.

When the time comes for students to become familiar with rhythm and meter, there is no need to launch into a complicated, technical discourse on the subject when more immediate and familiar methods may work far better. To begin with, let us consider some of the basic concepts that students need to know about rhythm and meter.

For practical purposes, let us operate with the assumption that the feet of a poem are isochronous; that is, the stresses occur in a musically regular tempo, similar to the regularity of the beats of a metronome. Now, when we analyze rhythm and meter, we are analyzing the repetitions of something in the language. In English, and in other Germanic languages, words have stress; that is, they have an increase in the length, preciseness, and pitch of the pronunciation of a syllable in a word or of a word in its clause or phrase. In traditional poetry at least, the syllables arrange themselves in patterns of stresses alternating with one or two lesser-stressed syllables. This accounts for the actual workings of feet, commonly called iambic, trochaic, dactylic, and anapestic. If we determine the strong stresses, we usually discover that the lesser-stressed syllables fall into a regular pattern as well.

It is necessary, of course, to proceed slowly with students when making the distinction between rhythm and meter. Meter, actually, is an abstraction and is related to rhythm in much the same way that an ideal blood pressure and the actual reading of a sphygmomanometer are related. Meter (and an ideal blood pressure reading) exist only momentarily in the world of observation and, for the most part, as a mental concept or idea. Rhythm, on the other hand, is what is there all the time, like the fluctuations of actual blood pressure.

For students, this relationship is not always easy to see. One very practical demonstration of this relationship, however, can be achieved by having students count aloud from 21 to 30. From 21 to 29, the metrical unit will be *x x /*; that is, two lesser-stressed syllables between, or followed by, the primary stresses. But when the counting reaches "thirty," the established rhythm forces what can be called "compensatory lengthening," and the words "twenty-nine" are stretched out to fill the missing space between the stresses which, now, have no unstressed syllables to meet the requirements of the established pattern. And the word "thirty" is often pronounced as if it were one syllable, stressed to be sure, with the next word, "thirty-one," conforming, once again, to the pattern.

Another practical application may be useful in helping students grasp the distinctions between meter and rhythm. Almost everyone has, at some time or other, heard a version of the old song "Ninety-nine Bottles of Beer on the Wall" (origin unknown). However, in this case, the words to the song are replaced with the letters of the complete alphabet, which fit exactly into the pattern (or meter) of the song. With a bit of practice, and no concern for polished peformance, both teachers and students can bring it off nicely. After the tune has been sung with the letters of the alphabet a sufficient number of times, so students are comfortable with it, variations can be introduced. For example, one group can sing the letters while other groups sing nursery rhymes to the same tune. Most nursery rhymes fit nicely into the pattern of the song. Of course, in those cases where the nursery rhymes do not fit, discussions can be held on what prevents the words from fitting. In the case of "Jack and Jill," for instance, the second and fourth lines of the song are a bit short for the nursery rhyme, and the tendency is to fill the gap by lengthening "water" and "after." The adjustments students must make in lines of the nursery rhymes illustrate "rhythm," while the counterpoint singing of the alphabet "keeps" the meter. In some instances, though, such as with "Hickory Dickory Dock," students will discover that the lines are so much shorter that the performance will fail. The basic problem is that the regularity of the lesser-stressed syllables between the strong stresses is broken, for it is somehow difficult to hold the syllables of "dock" and "clock" to fill the silent spaces.

By using such basic devices instead of heavily technical explanations, teachers will discover quicky that the introduction of meter and rhythm will be received more readily and will lead to much more student interest and involvement. Employing such an approach, one can establish that there is a dominant meter to a poem or to any group of words with similar stress patterns. Students can determine this metrical pattern by simply pronouncing the words according to normal speech practices and then marking the stresses. Then the exact pattern can be identified. Next, students can perform the poem—read it aloud—and note where the actual rhythm of the syllables differs from the meter. With a bit of encouragement and practice, students will discover for themselves that the differences between rhythm and meter, between what is expected and what actually occurs, is part of the charm and delight of poetry.

Teaching Meter to the Reader

by R. L. Barth

Pray thee, take care, that tak'st my booke in hand,
To read it well: that is, to understand.
Ben Jonson

It has been my experience that very few teachers—on whatever educational level—teach poetry, or are capable of teaching poetry, as if it were poetry. This is no idle paradox: to such teachers, the poem is an organized group of words essentially indistinguishable from prose. They "discuss" the intellectual content of the poem, its symbols, metaphors, similes, images, and so on, with a kind of bucolic innocence, assuming they have done justice to the poem and the poet. In fact, they have not "discussed" the poem at all. While it is perhaps an obvious fact, I might nevertheless remind the reader that, however useful, metaphors, symbols, and other forms of figurative language are not essential to the poem. Indeed, some of the most moving poems in the English language—and I am thinking of various poems written in the plain style—largely dispense with them. A poem is a poem, and not prose, precisely because of its more tightly organized and controlled language, that is, its rhythm. In the case of formalist poetry, which is my concern here, that initially means meter. The poem is a species of metrical composition. Furthermore, rhythm carries much of the emotion of any given poem. If one has not attended to that rhythm, then, one can hardly say with truth that the poem has been either "discussed" or understood.

Before proceeding with my own methods of teaching meter, I wish to make clear that meter and rhythm are not synonymous terms, though they are occasionally used as such for convenience. Meter is the ideal of the line; rhythm is its actuality, the way in which the line is heard. Take the following hypothetical line:

Ĭ aím, Ĭ aím, Ĭ aím, Ĭ aím, Ĭ aím.

The meter is obviously iambic pentameter, and the line is as ideal as anyone could wish. Here, there is little, if any, divergence between meter and rhythm. Even supposing it were possible to duplicate this line a number of times and create a poem, the result would be stiff and, even, boring. Such an instrument could not provide an economic or subtle medium for thought. Of course, such an ideal poem could not really be composed (though perhaps any number of versifiers have come uncomfortably close). Rather, one must account for rhythm, which may be achieved in either or both of two main ways: *variation* and *substitution*. When accounting for rhythm, the most obvious fact is that in a line of, say, iambic pentameter, neither all of the accented nor unaccented syllables will be exact equivalents. Furthermore, since one *measures* syllables only in relation to other syllables within the foot, there will be times when the unaccented syllable of one foot might well receive a heavier degree of stress than the preceding accented syllable. Let me quote Catherine Davis's "Insight 2: To the Spirit of Baudelaire."*

> *Wind of the wing of madness!* What is this?
> O you that shuddered then, what mantic bird?
> What travesty, dark spirit, of the Word?
> What last cold exhalation of your bliss?
> What passage to what end? Speechless abyss.

In line four, the accented syllable of the fourth foot ("of") receives less stress than the unaccented syllable of the fifth foot ("your"). One has the effect of four degrees of stress gradually rising to a culmination in "bliss." This aspect of rhythm is achieved through *substitution*. To take the final line from the same poem: "What passage to what end? Speechless abyss." The fourth foot ("Speechless") is a trochee used in place of the expected iamb. (It is worth noting in passing that a substitution in the fourth position is rather rare. Here, it is adequately prepared for by the strong caesura immediately preceding. Finally, one should note that caesural placement and varied line endings also contribute to rhythm.)

These opening comments are meant only to provide the merest sketch of the prosodic workings of a poem. Much more could—and perhaps should—be said, but space limitations militate against it. For I must come to my subject: How shall meter be taught? One thing should now be obvious: Meter must *be* taught. It is basic to an understanding and perception of rhythm (in the traditional, formal poem, at least, though it should be noted that good free verse poems, of which there are not as many as a

---

*Reprinted from "Insights," in *Second Beginnings* (Alexandria, VA: King's Quair Press, 1962). Every effort has been made to contact Catherine Davis for permission to quote from her poem "Insights."

reading of contemporary journals and anthologies might suggest, also have clearly perceptible rhythms).

My own teaching of meter—hence, rhythm—centers on three distinct though necessarily interrelated tools: Most important is audible reading, then terminology, and finally, examples. First, students must hear poems read aloud, frequently; and they must be encouraged to read poems aloud themselves. Only later will they be able to hear poems properly in their minds. If this approach sounds relatively easy, there are real problems associated with it. Teachers must train themselves to read poems aloud and correctly in the first place. Generally speaking, I confront three types of audible reading in the early stages of a poetry class: reading poetry as if it were prose, not attending to the rhythm at all; sing-songing (often taught by Miss Jones somewhere along the educational lines as a stirring exercise in Longfellow); and reading dramatically (that is, oral interpretation as an exercise in acting). All are incorrect; the third method is the most danger-ous, for it carries the sanction of "feeling" and highly wrought emotion—in other words, it is "poetic." In fact, the correct method is that elaborated by Yvor Winters in his crucial essay "The Audible Reading of Poetry" as a reading somewhere between sing-song and conversation.[1] Winter's essay, as well as his various recordings, should be required reading, and listening, for anyone who teaches poetry.

Only by hearing poems read constantly will the students ever hope to train their ears, as they must, if they are to understand poetry. Make no mistake: This is a skill, and it can be acquired only with hard work. However, I have found numerous students amenable to the discipline required. Furthermore, it suggests to them the various spiritual, intel-lectual, and moral struggles attendant on writing well. When I taught high school, I also coached the baseball team. It was a fact understood by all my players/students that a certain degree of skill (and skill that could, to some extent, be achieved by hard work) was necessary to make the team; an even greater degree of skill was necessary to make the starting team. Surely, poetry is a more serious discipline?

About my second tool, I shall have little to say. One must provide the student with basic terminology. This is easily accomplished with a few pages of terms and definitions. I have heard it argued that time spent mastering this material is "deadening" for the student. If true, that is too bad. One cannot talk about prosody or any other discipline without the language. (To return to my earlier example: it was certainly assumed by my players/students that they had at some point mastered the terminology of baseball. They understood bunts, pitch-outs, stolen bases, and so on; and they would have been scandalized by anyone who did not.) What I find equally interesting about my colleagues who argue that prosodic terminology is "deadening" is that they do not scruple about having students learn, for instance, the terminology of figurative language. Enough said.

Third, and finally, I use extensive handouts containing individual lines and brief passages for illustrative purposes. These generally concern "special problems," and I find them extremely useful for discussing everything from substitution to the pronunciation key in the dictionary. For example, one particular page contains some 35 lines of iambic pentameter by various poets ranging in time from George Gascoigne to Thom Gunn, arranged in chronological order. In some line or other, this page provides an example of most of the special problems I might wish to address. On the one hand, it covers the working of prosody and related subjects on a small scale, providing, as it does, substitutions, alliterations, caesural placements and so forth. On the other hand, it is set up in such a way that it suggests and therefore allows me to talk about larger issues, such as the evolution of the iambic pentameter line. Naturally, the progress and ability of the students help determine when particular issues are introduced.

Let me give a few examples from this sample page, to suggest how I use it. My first example is from George Gascoigne's "The Passion of a Lover."

> I smile sometimes, although my grief be great, . . .

This is a representative line of early sixteenth century plain style composition. Minimally, it can be used to illustrate these tendencies: the relatively equally and obviously unstressed quality of the unaccented syllables, along with the relatively equal and obviously stressed quality of the accented syllables; the use of alliteration, frequently to underline accented syllables; the use of the caesura after the fourth (sometimes the sixth) syllable; the end-stopped character of the poem's lines.

Next, consider the following line from John Donne's "The Dream":

> So, if I dream I have you, I have you, . . .

Here, I might discuss the nature of the line's rhythmic movement, contrasting it with Gascoigne's line. Donne's caesuras are more varied (even falling within the foot), the quantity (or variation) of syllables is less heavy, more subtle. Equally important, the line usefully points up how rhetoric and meter/rhythm reinforce each other. For some reason, students want to read the last part of this line thus: "Ĭ háve yŏu, Ĭ háve yŏu." In fact, this is the correct reading: "Ĭ háve yŏu, Í hăve yóu." Similarly, this line may lead back to a discussion of the syllables of a foot only being considered in relation to the syllables of the foot itself. Here, the repeated phrase falls across three different feet, and the arrangement of syllables is different in each foot. Obviously, this is an example of Donne's artistry, not accident.

Finally, consider the following line from Wallace Stevens's "Sunday Morning":

> Complacencies of the peignor, and late . . .

According to dictionary pronunciation, the word "peignor" can correctly be pronounced with the accent on either syllable. As this line (and poem) is written in iambic pentameter, it is much simpler to posit a pronunciation that does not disturb the rhythmic nature of the line. A substitution in the fourth foot here would be uncalled for, not to say inept. This line might be used as the starting point for a discussion of local pronunciations and idioms, along with their rhythmical effects on the poem. If the discussion lends itself to substitutions generally, one might point out that substitutions are not used only to point up something important in the poem; they might just as profitably be used for the sake of rhythmical variety.

These remarks have been brief. Still, I think my essential approach has been indicated. The subtleties and shadings that remain suggest themselves inevitably as the course progresses. I do not pretend the teaching of meter is easy; it is not. And yet, it is not a pedantic exercise, but an absolute requirement in any poetry course. And we might as well be honest with our students: reading poetry requires, demands, hard-won skills, though it can be enjoyed—if only, in the truest sense, when these skills have been developed. To turn it into a game is an exercise in intellectual dishonesty.

Reference

1. Yvor Winters, "The Audible Reading of Poetry," in *The Function of Criticism: Problems and Exercises* (Athens, OH: Swallow Press, 1957, pp. 81–100).

Poetry Theater: Integrating Drama and Poetry

by Rose M. Feinberg

The Poetry Theater approach integrates dramatic technique with various aspects of reading, writing, analyzing and reciting poetry. The development of Poetry Theater was prompted by my search for ways to help junior high school students become more positive and responsive when asked to read or write poetry. The approach has proved successful in classrooms from the fourth grade up through college.

As students become involved in Poetry Theater presentations in groups, they not only search for and read poems, but they also become excited about the selection of lines from poems, the effects these lines may have, what new lines may be created, and, ultimately, the effect that a unique poem that they have created can have through dramatic presentation. The following description of the Poetry Theater approach can be easily modified to meet the needs and abilities of almost any grade level beyond the primary grades. The Poetry Theater Activity Card (Figure 1) outlines the key features of the approach.

The explanation of Poetry Theater provided below follows the progression outlines in the Poetry Theater Activity Card. Approximate class period directions are provided, allowing 45 minutes per period. The introductory lesson would be best done in one period, with shorter amounts of time from class sessions allowed to complete the group work required. Most classes should be able to complete Poetry Theater presentations by the end of one week, if time is given daily for a portion of the period.

Figure 1. Poetry Theater Activity Card

Steps with the Class

1. Divide into groups of 5 or 6 to practice *choral reading* of the same poem. Focus on presenting the poem using different voices, different levels and dramatic interpretation.

2. Discuss possible *themes* for Poetry Theater presentations, looking through poetry books and other sources to find a topic (Examples: seasons, night, feelings, animals, holidays . . .).

POETRY THEATER PRESENTATION
Steps within Each Group

1. Select a theme for your group. Come to agreement about your theme, using poetry books to help determine a topic (Examples: people, colors, houses, love, fear, need, money . . .).

2. Skim through poetry books and other sources to find 5 or 6 poems (a minimum of one from each group member) relating in some way to your theme.

3. From poems found, select lines, phrases, or words to include in your presentation. You will integrate several poems and add *original lines,* creating an original group poem.

4. As you determine lines to be used from published poems, write the source. Include author, poem title, book and page. This will enable you to cite works used in the group poem.

5. Decide on the final order of the poem that the group is creating. Try several variations, listening to various arrangements before writing out the group poem for each member.

6. Assign specific lines to people in the group. Use various voices (solo, echo, group . . .) to determine which combinations sound best for your poem. People should have more than one turn during the presentation and should learn the entire poem.

7. Determine appropriate movements, gestures, voices and levels to give the presentation a dramatic quality. Try variations before making a final decision.

8. *Practice* until you feel confident about your Poetry Theater presentation. Each group will show its Poetry Theater to the class.

First Session (approximately 45 minutes)

I. Choral Reading with the Class

Pass out any short poem (or use a literature book) and practice choral reading, demonstrating variations of voices. The following are samples of possible directions to students.

- First row or group says the first line.
- Two or three voices say the first few words of the next line.
- Each person of the next group or row says one word each of the following line.
- The class says any repeating refrain or line.
- One voice says the beginning syllable of the word, and three voices complete the word.
- Two voices say the last few words and the next voice repeats (echoes) those words.

Make assignments of this type until the entire poem's reading has been designated.

Using the same poem, provide different directions for voice variations (such as whisper, draw out the word, clip syllables, shriek) and for movement (such as stand, reach out, look upward, hang head, some stand, some sit on floor). By directing the entire class, you provide models of various approaches for incorporating dramatic techniques into choral reading.

II. Choral Reading in Groups

Divide the class into groups of five or six, insisting that no group contain all males or all females. My rationale for this stipulation is to provide greater variety in voice and presentation of the poetry reading. Since the group formed for this choral reading activity will be the same group which will work together to create the Poetry Theater, I find it important to establish the cooperative nature of the task at this point.

Each group is instructed to take the same poem as used in the class choral reading and to create a presentation, incorporating movement, various voices, and use of different levels. Encourage groups to focus first on voice, then to incorporate movement and levels. (Consider the visual effect of some standing, others sitting, etc.) Movement for each phrase or word is not necessary and should not be encouraged.

Each group needs to reach consensus to determine the manner of its presentation. Students should be encouraged to try suggestions made by group members, experimenting with variations until consensus is reached. A time limit needs to be given, with a reminder when five minutes are left. I generally emphasize that this will not be a finished product since time is limited. The purpose of this activity, as explained to the groups, is to work on the process of preparing a Poetry Theater presentation.

One group at a time shows its presentation of the poem. After each presentation, ask audience groups to focus on the variations and approaches used in the observed presentation, pointing out effective techniques employed by the group. In some cases, groups have difficulty reaching consensus and working cooperatively. Their presentations may not be ready to show, and the alternative I've used is to have the group merely say the poem. Since the emphasis is on process, not on the product, time limits should be maintained.

Second Session (The following could be done in one period or parts of two periods.)

I. Distribution and Discussion of Poetry Theater Activity Card

Provide a copy of the Poetry Theater Activity Card for each student. Review the directions, beginning with "Steps with the Class," pointing out that step one was completed in the previous period.

Brainstorm theme possibilities with the class after clarifying the understanding of "theme." List suggestions on the board, providing topics at intervals during the brainstorming. Seasons; times of day; feelings (ranging from love to fear); necessities; specific holidays; machines; specific colors; weather (sun, rain, moon and other aspects relating to nature); specific animals (cats, dogs, birds, insects, tigers); the sea; mountains; windows . . . are only some of the many possibilities. Remind students that the first task of the group will be to select a theme. They will have some time during class to do this, using poetry books and anthologies.

II. Steps within Each Group

Review the directions with the class before they are again divided into their groups formed during the previous session. Those absent the previous session can be added to groups already formed.

1. Select a theme for your group.

Students are told that they will use references before making a group decision. Theme selection is often based on poems available on themes of interest. Consensus will be necessary; but teacher guidance will be available. Groups having problems deciding on a theme should have a theme assigned to them by the teacher.

2. Skim through poetry books to find poems relating to a theme.

Remind students that each group member will have to contribute at least one poem relating to the theme. They will have some time in the library or will use classroom poetry books. In addition, they should explore other sources for poems, including home and the public library. The poetry contribution should be written in a form ready to share with the group. Original contributions of students are encouraged, in addition to use of a reference.

3. From poems found, select lines, phrases, or words to include.

This step involves an important sharing process where group members will read poems and lines selected. As they listen, group members will determine which lines, phrases, and words should be included. An important step will be to create original lines or find a basic refrain which will tie together the different poems into one poem.

4. As you determine lines, write the source.

Review the need to write the reference used, both in terms of giving credit and for again finding the reference. You may decide to provide specific guidelines for writing references or merely stipulate the information which should be included. The samples on the following pages include references used and suggest different formats.

5. Decide on the final order of the poem.

Encourage students to try many variations of line order and to experiment with different original lines created by group members. When some consensus has been reached, a copy of the completed group poem should be made for each group member, with an extra copy given to the teacher. Each group member could write out the poem, or one person could copy the poem on a master to be run off for everyone in the group.

6. Assign specific lines to people in the group.

Refer to the poetry presentations done the previous session. Encourage the group to practice many variations and to select the most interesting one. The group should use many voice variations for the presentation, making sure that line assignments are equitable.

7. Determine appropriate movements, gestures, voices and levels to give the presentation a dramatic quality.

Once lines are learned, group members will be ready to work on other aspects of the presentation. They can add movement, arrange themselves in various formations using different levels (e.g., heights, chairs, floor), and add props (e.g., paper moons, snowflakes, costumes), if appropriate. The final product sought is a Poetry Theater—a dramatic presentation of a group poem which would be viewed by an audience of peers and, perhaps, by other teachers.

8. Practice. Show to Class.

Students will need some time in class each day for work in groups on the Poetry Theater. The refinement of the presentation does take practice and time. With practice, groups can create Poetry Theaters which can be shown with confidence and pride.

If time permits following the review of directions, allow groups to use references and select a theme.

Third Session and Fourth Session

During these sessions, groups follow the steps outlined on the Poetry Theater Activity Card. While the groups are working, the teacher rotates, assisting in decision making and in guiding groups toward consensus. If appropriate, groups could, at this early stage, show trial runs of presentations, seeking feedback and suggestions for improvement from their peers or from the teacher. I have used videotaping to show student presentations for self-evaluation and to share final productions with other classes.

Fifth Session (If more time were given for allowing groups to refine presentations, this would be a later session.)

The presentation of the Poetry Theaters could be scheduled for a particular day in advance or be informally conducted when groups are ready. When groups are particularly proud of their presentations, they often wish to show them to other classes. This could be handled by students becoming "traveling players," where a particular group makes arrangements to visit a class to present its Poetry Theater; or, other classes could be invited to see all the Poetry Theater presentations. Videotaping of the presentations can be used for viewing by other classes and for critical viewing by the performers, particularly if they wish to further refine presentations or to create new Poetry Theaters in the future.

Conclusion

The obvious purpose of Poetry Theater is to involve students in reading, writing, creating, and performing poetry. As I developed Poetry Theater and implemented it with students, I consciously tried to incorporate additional learning aspects within the framework of the approach. Based on teacher feedback and my own observations of students who have participated in Poetry Theater, I believe that, in addition to experiences with poetry, students gain positive group experiences, learn to be more open to variations and alternatives and become more creative in their thinking. With guidance and time for practice, groups do create Poetry Theaters which they are proud to perform and to publish.

The following poem was written by a group in grade eight and represents a Poetry Theater presentation created in my school system in the fall of the school year.

THUNDERSTORMS
(Grade Eight)

The wind began to rock the grass   "Thunderstorms" by William Cole

    (steps kneeling in front of
     audience, hands raised—one voice)

With threatening tunes and low!
     (steps in front of audience, speaking powerfully—one voice)

He flung a menace at the earth/A menace at the sky!
     (standing on chairs, hands upraised, speaking loudly—3 voices)

Deep into the darkness peering   "The Raven" by Edgar Allan Poe
     (speaking loudly and mysteriously—one voice)

Long I stood there wondering (softer, kneeling on chairs—2 voices)

Fearing! (pretending to be afraid—6 voices)

And rained its life as though it bled

"Red, Gold Rain"

     (kneeling on chair—one voice)

by Sacheverell Sitwell

In the long days full of fire
     (spoken softly—2 voices)

We wake to hear the storm come down

"So Ghostly Then, The Girl
Came In" by Sacheverell Sitwell

     Sudden on roof and pane

(spoken strongly—3 voices-repeat sudden, sudden, sudden)

The thunder's loud, and the hasty wind
     hurries the beating rain (shouted in front of people—4 voices)

And, in the windless hour between (spoken softly—one voice)

The last of daylight and night (same tone standing on chairs—2 voices)

When fields give up their ebbing green
(3 voices and 2 for ebbing green)

And two bats interweave their flight (arms outstretched-all voices)

Poetry Theater contains elements of Readers Theater, Story Theater and Chamber Theater, other approaches for dramatizing readings. Excellent descriptions of these "Theater" techniques for readings are contained in *Student-Centered Language Arts and Reading, K-13* by James Moffett and Betty Jane Wagner (Houghton Mifflin, 1976). Any reading or English program would be enriched by the inclusion of these approaches that integrate drama with reading and writing.

Testing an Understanding of Poetry*

by David C. Schiller

How to test high school students' understanding of poetry? Any high school teacher knows how to avoid the question: give your students a hundred or so short-answer questions on poetic terms and the poems they've read. Have the students answer on computer cards, feed the tests into the grading machine, record the grades, and hand back, for a pre-fab, fast-food cultural "experience." You get my point: "objective" tests on poetry are like using a sledgehammer to kill a butterfly instead of nurturing it. Not all tests on poetry, let's hope, are destined to consume their subject in anomaly (Yeats, meet Mr. Gradgrind) or act as vulture or worse (Frost, I'd like you to meet School Superintendent Dracula, we have come to ask you a few questions . . .). For my twelfth graders, I wanted a test that would involve them in poetry and help them sum up their experience of it. I came up with an essay test that took my students three or four class periods to complete.

> Critical Analysis of Literature
> Mr. Schiller
>
> GENERAL INSTRUCTIONS
>
> I. Below there are eight poems. Read them carefully, keeping in mind what you have learned about how to read and interpret poems this quarter. The eight poems were written by four poets; each poet wrote two poems. Indicate which poems you think were written by the same poet. [Then the eight poems were listed: two sonnets by Milton, two by Shakespeare, two poems by Poe; two poems by Gerard Manley Hopkins. To pair the poems correctly required some close reading. Students had to be able, in differentiating the Milton poems from those by Shakespeare—the four could be

*This essay is unedited and is reprinted here from *Exercise Exchange* (Fall 1979) by permission. Copyright © 1979 by *Exercise Exchange*.

set aside easily because they were all sonnets—to distinguish between rhyme schemes, not just count lines and syllables. The two poems by Poe were the worst in the lot and to pair them required sensitivity to tones of egotism, self-pity, and sentimentality. The two poems by Hopkins were distinguished from the others by their common—or uncommon—delicacy of metaphor and their unusual meter.]

II. Now indicate *why* you paired the poems as you did, by writing a paragraph or two on each of your choices. Did you distinguish your pairs because of their rhyme schemes, their meter, their subject, their overall form? I will give you credit for good answers even if you have mistaken which poems belong together.

III. Now choose any one of the poems in the test and write a five paragraph essay about it. Be sure to use whatever you have learned about poetry in your answer. Apply the following terms to your analysis of the poem where relevant: rhyme, meter, alliteration, metaphor and synecdoche. You may use any notes you have taken in class.

The students relaxed, knowing that they would be given as long as they needed to complete the test. They even enjoyed reading the poems they had never seen before, and applying their knowledge. "Hard," was the consensus, "but interesting. It made us think." The test got a high mark; so did the students, because the test involved them. And nurtured them.

Poetry in the English Class*

by Thomas G. Devine

The place of poetry in the classroom, as indeed in our society generally, is paradoxical. In America, at least for the past few years, poetry is not a public matter: few, if any, poets can actually earn a livelihood as poets pure-and-simple; the media rarely, if ever, devote precious space to it; publishers avoid it; dinner table conversation hardly rings with talk of poets and their doings. Yet, one finds almost daily reference to ''two roads diverged in a woods'' or ''miles to go before I sleep,'' everyone seems to know who murdered sleep and what it means when ladies do protest too much, the humblest paperback bookstore regularly stocks a set of shelves marked ''Poetry'' and piles Rod McKuen books in eye-catching displays. And, surprisingly, a number of friends and acquaintances can be discovered who know, from memory (and not necessarily childhood), lines and verses from Longfellow to Yeats to Auden. Most surprisingly of all, a number of the same can be discovered (if the searcher penetrates a little) to have actually written ''something of their own.''

The same paradoxical situation, as almost every teacher knows, is to be found in the classroom. Students regularly, insistently, agonizingly groan when a poetry lesson is announced. When asked, they usually rank poetry with sentence diagramming as one of the least attractive aspects of the English program. And yet, as more than a few teachers can testify, these are the same students who show delight in certain classroom moments when poetry does touch some naked nerve, does cut through the protecting calluses students have developed around their psyches, does furnish the stuff of memories. And it is these same students, surely, who, like their parents and older brothers and sisters, know about the diverging roads and Gertrude's protestations, and who buy those paperback books in the poetry section, who have hidden within them special lines and stanzas of great and not-so-great poets and, within notebooks and bureau drawers, keep some lines and stanzas of their own.

---

*This essay is unedited and is reprinted here from *Connecticut English Journal* (Spring 1979) by permission.

Recognizing, then, the paradox, can teachers treat the subject "Poetry" in such a way that they can strengthen and further develop the interest (and love) that is inherent in students while diminishing the negative coloration that seems too often to surround poetry in the English class? Can lessons and units be fashioned in a way that will not "turn kids off" but rather stimulate, pique, fertilize what seems to be within them? Can the English class be a place where young people have chances (which they will not necessarily have elsewhere) to explore their own "secret places," to measure their own deepest and least understood feelings and ideas against those of fellow human beings who happen to be poets, to sharpen and shape the anfractuous parts of themselves, to, perhaps, learn to shape language, feelings, and ideas in poetry themselves?

The suggestions presented here are derived from the collective experience of many successful teachers of poetry. They were developed in their present form over a period of years by teachers participating in the summer workshops in English at Boston University. They should provide some guidance for other teachers who want to make students begin to see that poetry, in one form or another, is an integral part of the human condition. The suggestions are hardly based on "scientific research" (for who, after all has the temerity to test and measure the workings of the soul?). They may give, nevertheless, some common-sensical bases for designing lessons, units, and courses that make poetry more significant in the lives of students.

- Suggestion 1. *Select poems for study carefully*. Most anthologists and compilers of literature textbooks are readers (presumably) of taste and discernment. There is, however, something about the "chemistry" of a class that deters complete and consistent success when poems for "teaching" are selected promiscuously from the standard classroom literature book. The chemistry involves the poem, the students (with all their varied backgrounds, individual experiences, predispositions, biases, and resulting singularities), and the teacher (with all his or her prejudices, experiential limitations, peculiarities). Students and teacher bring to the teaching moment differing expectations and predilections. For success, even comparative success, the chemistry has to be right. In planning for success, the teacher can do little to control what the students bring to the class within themselves on a given day and little but acknowledge what he or she brings to the confrontation. The teacher can, however, control the third element in this meeting—the poem itself.

It is somewhat disheartening to find teachers who do not exercise this control they have but who, uncritically, accept what their books give them for teaching. One recalls the teacher in a large, urban junior high school teaching "I wandered lonely as a cloud/That floats on high o'er vales and hills/When all at once I saw a crowd,/A host, of golden daffodils." The students, mostly boys, mostly Black, were barely able to discern flowers from non-flowers, much less daffodils from geraniums; their concept of "dale and hill" rested on the asphalt rise in their bleak neighborhood playground. The poem was, simply, completely inappropriate for that class of boys, in that environment, at that moment in their (and their teacher's) time. It was, unfortunately, the next poem to be "studied" in the anthology.

There are at least three dimensions to the problem of selection that need to be examined by teachers.

First, students must "enjoy" the poem. Admittedly, "enjoy" is a troublesome word. Can enjoyment go hand-in-hand with discomfort? With pain? With boredom? Probably, our understanding of enjoyment ought to include the troublesome realization that pleasure can be mingled (and often is) with fatigue, boredom, discomfort, anguish. Yet, some element of pleasure, however defined, seems necessary for the success of the teaching moment in the classroom. Certainly, within the comparatively structured environment of the classroom when students are meeting poetry at least somewhat formally for the first time, teachers should strive for poems that give immediate, or almost immediate, delight rather than poems which present unnecessary obscurities, unrelieved boredom, information that could easily be presented in prose.

Second, the teacher should probably enjoy the poem. It is possible that students may have some kind of literary experience with a poem the teacher finds in the school anthology but, the teaching-learning situation being what it is, it surely is better if the one who guides students through their first reading of the poem obviously thinks well of the poem. Considering the vast riches available to the teacher, it seems clear that he or she should select a poem that he or she cares about, is moved by, thinks significant.

Third, the teacher must recognize the maturity level of the students. Enough research has been done in the area of young adult reading interests for teachers to know that twelve-year-old boys and girls are more apt to read about animals (and the girls, about horses, in particular) than seventeen-year-olds; that high school juniors are more inclined to read about man-kind's search for ideals than seventh graders are. Yet, often a poem is chosen because it is a "great" poem (in the judgment of critics and anthologists) rather than because it seems appropriate for eighth graders, tenth graders, or advanced placement seniors.

Selection of poems for study in class is obviously crucial. Uncritical acceptance of material presented in someone else's anthology can lead to a bland classroom exercise; poems chosen carefully by an informed, sensitive teacher can stimulate classroom moments which are rich, satisfying, memorable, sometimes exciting.

- Suggestion 2. *Help students see the meaning of the poem.* Certainly, some poems seem to be meaningless; they are verbal music pure-and-simple. The delightful English nonsense poems of the nineteenth century and the deliberate verbal sonorities of poets like Swinburne ought to be in the curriculum, but, generally speaking, most poems introduced in school should have some kind of meaning, and it is the primary purpose of the teacher in the classroom environment to help students see what the poet is trying to say.

A direct approach to meaning may occur, and frequently does, in a traditional lecture or semi-Socratic question-and-answer discussion in which the teacher knows in advance the direction he or she wants the class to move and, often, the destination of the flow of discussion. Two examples of this direct approach to meaning are given here.

In teaching "My Last Duchess" by Robert Browning, the teacher asks such questions as: What is the significance of the poem's title? Who is the speaker? To whom is he speaking? What are they discussing? What is the purpose of the listener's visit? Once students have an idea of the setting and situation, the teacher tries to develop specific understandings about the poet's craft (in this case, recognizing the ways in which an author reveals character) by asking: What inferences do you draw about the Duchess? about her age? her personality? her beauty? What inferences do you draw about the Duke from his reference to his "gift of a nine-hundred-year-old name"? from his saying, "I choose never to stoop"? Why do you draw these inferences? What clues has the poet given to you?[1]

In helping students to get to the meaning of Yeats' "Sailing to Byzantium," Sauer sets out similar questions: What does the title suggest? *To* Byzantium implies sailing *from* somewhere. Where? What is the antecedent of "that" in the first line? What does the first stanza suggest about the climate and geography of the country which the speaker is leaving? What kind of place, on the other hand, was Byzantium? etc.[2]

Such an approach to meaning is, of course, valid and, in the hands of a skillful teacher, it can be enormously exciting. Students can have the pleasure of noting clues, significant word uses, the interplay of ideas, the fitting together of pieces; they can begin to see how a poet works, how language is fitted together for certain effects, how their own thoughts and feelings can be manipulated by the poet. The danger is that this approach, like all others, can be overdone and can lead to boredom and rejection of the poem and poetry in general.

- Suggestion 3. *Try a "brainstorming" approach to some poems.* Not always, certainly, but with certain poems, at certain times, a group problem-solving session is valuable. With a poem which looks attractive and sounds appealing but whose meaning is not readily apparent, divide the larger class into groups of four, five, or six, and ask the smaller groups to suggest meanings and interpretations. Too often, students have been led to believe that the poet and the teacher are in league somehow and that the poem's meaning is only to be obtained from one of them. In such a situation, the reader—certainly as important as the poet if the poem is to come alive—is passive, an observer on the sidelines, lucky to be allowed in the sharing.

In "brainstorming" each individual reader admits initially to some befuddlement. The task facing his group is to somehow pool the individual reading efforts to come up with a valid interpretation based on the members' combined insights, questioning ability, and interpretive judgments. Rather than have the teacher simply share his idea of what the poem means (an idea often derived, in turn, from his favorite teacher, professor, or critic), it makes for a more stimulating, if not exciting, class session to have the students bounce ideas off one another, try out fuzzy or daring opinions and hypotheses, gradually shape, in group give-and-take, a defensible interpretation. This approach, unlike that of the traditional take-it-from-me lecture or the all too often teacher-dominated, teacher-controlled Socratic question-and-answer session, tends to provide for maximum use of their own language in a setting that is anything but static.

- Suggestion 4. *Try "Acting Out."* Another approach to poetry which involves students in more than a passive reading situation is "acting out." Here the teacher selects a poem which has three or more characters and an inherent dramatic situation ("Hunchback in the Park" but not "Do Not Go Gentle into That Good Night"; "My Last Duchess" but better the medieval ballad "The Two Sisters of Binorrie"). Again, the class is divided into smaller groups, enough students in each for the various roles. Students are given a definite time budget (fifteen or twenty minutes) and a problem to be solved: How can you "show" your poem to the class in a few minutes? As in the brainstorming approach, acting out involves, or should involve, everyone. A narrator may be required, a sound-effects expert, the actors, a chorus; sometimes students are needed to "act out" walls, trees, or other objects in the poem.[3]

Teachers who regularly have students act out poems have noted three highly positive characteristics of this approach: students understand better (they are forced to think through the sequence of events, the motivation of characters, the setting, etc.); they remember more (months—years—later, individuals will recall playing a specific part in a poem that would otherwise have been forgotten); and they will enjoy more (better to stand up, move around, say something—anything, rather than sit passively ingesting the prepared lessons of the lecturer or waiting one's turn in the recitational round). As noted in relation to brainstorming, this approach to poetry is not for every poem, always, or for every class; it is a refreshing, and sometimes exciting, way to involve students in poetry.

- Suggestion 5. *Have students write.* Many teachers for many years have had students write haiku, simple ballads, limericks, etc.; some teachers, with able classes, have assigned sonnet writing. However, there is a wider variety of effective approaches to poetry writing in class that are now available.

Some of the most effective have been developed by the young Canadian poet and teacher, Brian Powell.[4] Powell calls his structures "triggers." Four are presented here.

1. *Sound-motion sequences.* Students are asked to choose an object in motion, an event they have recently noted or experienced, a happening that piques them (e.g., the lunch line in the school cafeteria, getting off the school bus, a driving lesson, etc.) and then string together a handful of words that seem to them to sum up the selected topic. Two or three examples are given to students as "triggers":

A bird taking off:	lumbering, leaping, bounding. skipping, hopping, off.
Roller coaster:	rolling, speeding, swerving, coasting, shuddering, stop.
Studying:	sharpening, sitting, shifting, sipping, sighing, slumping, sleeping.

Students are given no directions; the examples themselves, the only guides. When they ask: Do we have to have -ing words? or May we have more than five or six? or Does the last word have to be a short one? etc., they are told to write whatever they think sounds good and somehow captures the sight and feeling of the event. In a sharing session afterwards, the teacher accepts all contributions, avoiding, of course, negative criticisms.

2. *Dylan Thomas Portraits*. Here, again, the trigger is the set of examples the teacher provides, on the board or on ditto sheets. Students are asked to fill in the blank in the question: Did you ever see a _____?, and then write four lines of hyphenated description if they can. Two examples of this trigger are:

Did you ever see *an otter?*	Did you ever see *a school boy?*
Fierce-faced,	Shirt out-hanging,
Fish-fanged,	Sox half-masted,
Silvery-sided,	Messy-haired,
Mottled.	Homeworkless.

Again, there is no pressure for students to conform to the patterns given. They are merely "triggers" whose sole purpose is to get students to say something, possibly significant, in a more or less structured utterance. The results from the class are not analyzed, discussed, or criticized, simply read aloud and accepted.

3. *Form Poem*. Here students are given more structure than in other triggers. They are given the pattern below and asked to put words on each line which will present a more complete picture of whatever they decide to title their "poem." If possible, they are told, they should find words that rhyme at the end of each line as indicated. The form:

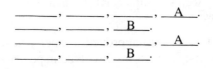

Powell gives an example of a "form poem" a sixth-grader did for him when he was an exchange teacher in Moscow:

INDUSTRY

Smoke, soot, smell, choke.
Flash, orange, black.
Steel, iron, coal, coke.
Truck, rails, track.

4. *"Completed image poem."* Students are told to write four sentences, each independent (with its own subject and predicate); the first three should treat one of the senses and the last be an "emotional response" to what has preceded. The form for the trigger, presented on the chalkboard to the class, might look this way:

> TITLE
>
> (line 1 - SIGHT) _____ .
> (line 2 - SOUND) _____ .
> (line 3 - SMELL) _____ .
> (line 4 - EMOTIONAL _____ .
>   RESPONSE)

An example, derived from classic Chinese poetry (where Powell first encountered this trigger) is:

> Cool perfume of bamboo pervades my room.
> Wild moonlight fills the whole courtyard.
> The waterfowl on the riverbank call to one another.
> I sit on my bed meditating through the long night.

(A "completed image poem" developed by a teacher working with Powell's ideas expresses his feelings on viewing Boston at night from the top of the Boston University Law-Education Building:

> Lights streak endlessly down the tiny highways.
> Distant and faint are the soundings of the horns
>   and brakes.
> The air feels cool and damp at this height.
> The city seems manipulatable from the top of the
>   tower.)

The values of this writing approach to poetry have been 'apparent to many teachers for years: students are involved in poetry in a far more direct and immediate way than they are when they simply sit in a classroom, passively, consuming the ideas of the teacher; they begin to appreciate the process of creating with words more because they are doers themselves; and they tend to look at poets and poetry somewhat differently—sometimes more appreciatively, certainly less disparagingly.

- Suggestion 6. *Teach technical matters as the need arises.* One still hears of teachers who present students with four-or-five (or more) page, single-spaced lists of poetic terms to be studied or memorized (or both). Possibly, some rare students may come to have a positive feeling for poetry by studying definitions of simile, onomatopoeia, mood, alliteration, etc., but it is doubtful. Certainly, knowledge of the English metric system enhances the (advanced) poetry lover's enjoyment of "Sailing to Byzantium" or, even, Eliot's "Macavity, the Mystery Cat." The danger is that the intellectualizing, coming too soon, *may* stunt the growth of love.

The issue of how much theory and how much terminology the student needs to know is a difficult one but one which must be faced by each teacher. "If I force too much technical information on the class," the teacher must ask himself or herself, "do I stifle all interest in the poem? If I neglect all attention to form, to metrics, to nomenclature, do I deprive students of the chance to enjoy and appreciate at higher and higher levels?" One way of treating the problem is suggested by Sauer: focus on meaning, ask what the poet seems to be saying, then, after arriving at some agreement (it does not have to be unanimous) the class can go on to consider the diction, figures of speech, versification, stanza form, rhyme scheme, and stanza arrangement:

> These matters should *not* be discussed in isolation from one another or from meaning. The teacher's first responsibility is to help the class see how each of these parts supports, and is actually an inextricable part of, the others, how meter and rhyme and diction are appropriate to what the poet is saying.[5]

- Suggestion 7. *Make use of all media approaches in introducing a poem.* With the exception of some 16th century and 20th century poems, poetry is meant to be sounded aloud. Some of the metaphysical poets and their followers in this century have relied on and exploited the subtle ambiguities that result from variant readings of certain phrases and lines; when the printed phrases can be sounded in two ways to result in two interpretations, tensions develop in the throat of the (silent) reader and these are planned for by the poet. Many of these same poets, in both centuries, also relied heavily on visual impact and arranged words in phrases, lines, and stanzas to deliberately form a picture, a symbol, or a structure of some sort. Most poetry, however, does not fall into this small category; the greatest number of poems—especially those one would knowingly choose for a secondary school class—are meant to be read aloud, to be heard. So, of all possible media approaches, certainly sound is essential in the poetry class.

How to let the sound ring out? The first recommendation must be, of course, the actual human voice, the most direct and immediate instrument for transforming that cold, black print into verbal music. Often classes are fortunate enough to have students who can read well, sensitively and knowingly, and, when such students are available, they should read aloud and read frequently. Even in classes where few or no individuals seem competent to treat language orally, teachers can make use of small and large choruses of voices—insuring maximum student participation while turning those graphemes into phonemes. The most available—and most trusted—instrument on a day-to-day basis, however, is the teacher's voice, and no teacher should shun the responsibility of learning to use it. For the tyro, this may mean a few hours of home preparation with a cassette recorder, but the reward, in terms of a career of successful teaching of poetry, is worth the time spent in practice. All can improve, with time and effort, their own reading of poems for their own classes.

As an adjunct to the teacher's frequent reading aloud of poetry—but never as a substitute—there is, of course, a galaxy of fine phonograph recordings. Fortunately, school and public libraries today can furnish teachers with a rich array of recordings by actors and poets, recordings which can make the walls of any classroom vibrate to the magnificent sounds of English and American poets.

A whole arsenal of media instruments is available now to teachers to supplement and enrich their own readings. It is sad to imagine a class studying Yeats without experiencing the fine (and readily available) film "Yeats Country," made and distributed by the Irish Tourist Bureau. So much formal study of poets and poetry can be enlivened and enhanced by commercially-prepared films obtainable through local public and university film libraries. Teacher-made films and slide-tapes are harder to come by but still available to teachers who watch for them. (One excellent slide-tape circulated informally for years in the Boston area: a teacher had juxtaposed Frost's reading of "Death of the Hired Man" with the teacher's own slides of Vermont and New Hampshire barns, apple trees, birches, porches, and people to make an exciting oral-visual experience of the poem for students). Even television is exploitable—in the best way—by the alert English teacher: Julie Harris' portrayal of Emily Dickinson as "The Belle of Amherst" has recently been shown on public TV.

- Suggestion 8. *Have poetry permeate the entire curriculum*. Poetry is, at the one extreme, delicate and elusive, subtle and almost impossible to pin-down, at the other extreme, forceful and overwhelming, terrifying and awesome. To expect anyone, even the most experienced, committed poetry lover to live on poetry alone for a lengthy period of time is asking much, perhaps too much. Yet, one finds poetry units of two weeks, four weeks, or more. Most sensitive, caring readers of poetry would agree that it is probably better to have students meet poems under a variety of conditions, having class attention focused occasionally on one poem, sometimes on a few related poems, once in a while on one type of poem or one period in the history of the art but having the riches spread throughout the year's work. Individual poems or poets can be related to other poems, to stories, to novels, to film, to other aspects of the total English curriculum. Certainly the brainstorming approach, acting out, and poetry writing should be spread throughout the year so that no single approach bores or confuses students, causes resistance or even antagonism to poetry.

An ideal climate for the development of appreciation and love would be one in which poetry is a living part of the daily-doings of the English class, in which poems are introduced through the teacher's reading, through films and records and choral readings, each day or week, in which students have frequent opportunities, spread over the entire year, to brainstorm, act out, write, and experience poetry in a variety of ways. If present practices seem to be edging out a neat rut, perhaps it is time to think of a diverging road.

References

1. Thomas G. Devine, *Achievement through Reading,* Boston: Ginn and Company, 1968.

2. Edwin Sauer, *English in the Secondary School,* New York: Holt, Rinehart and Winston, 1961.

3. Marilyn McCaffrey, *The Development and Evaluation of an Oral-Dramatic Approach for the Teaching of Poetry,* Doctoral Dissertation, Boston University, 1973.

4. Brian Powell, *English through Poetry Writing,* Itasca, Illinois: Peacock Press, 1968.

5. Edwin Sauer, *op. cit.*

RESOURCES

Introduction

The conventional resource for teaching poetry is the basic textbook, most often a literature anthology containing a representative selection of poetry from various periods and countries. Few of these anthologies offer any suggestions about the rich potential which might lie beyond the two covers of the book. As a result, many instructors fail to see the resources that lie close at hand. These resources include bringing practicing poets into the classroom to work with students; identifying and studying ethnic poetry; exploring the relationships among poetry, music, film, and art; publishing student poetry; and building classroom libraries of poetry.

Although poetry and poets do not receive a great deal of recognition in our culture, some efforts have been made to overcome that problem. The most notable of these efforts has been the ''Poets-in-the-Schools'' program, initially funded by the National Endowment for the Arts, and now supported by many states' art organizations. As R. Baird Shuman, a poet who works in the schools frequently, suggests, these visits take many forms and may be for the duration of one day or several weeks. He describes how the poets spend their time: writing with students, discussing poetry, sharing each other's efforts. The result of such a program is a better understanding on the part of students as to what kind of people poets are and how they go about their work; the visiting poets learn much about young people, their views on life, their interests, and their ways of responding to the language of their time.

The traditional literature anthology tends not to provide much information or representation concerning ethnic poetry. Few teachers have had courses or done extensive reading in ethnic literature. As a result, students and teachers often remain unaware of some important aspects of our literary heritage and culture. The Native American, for example, frequently appears only as a stereotype in literature and in the minds of many Americans. Yet ample resources—collections and explanations of Native American poetry—exist. Anna Lee Stensland offers suggestions about what resources may be most appropriate and how instructors may want to view Native American poets and their work. Black poets also are inadequately represented in many anthologies. Here again, the busy teacher may remain unaware of the appropriate resources. Sally A. Jacobsen's suggestions of representative Black poets and collections of their work provide a starting point for broadening the perspectives on Black poetry in the classroom.

Poetry has always had many similarities to other art forms and media, yet these similarities remain unexplored with students. If that were not the case, students might have a better appreciation of how symbols and images from their own world relate to the worlds of the poet, the musician, the artist, and the filmmaker. Students, for example, are in constant touch with the music scene; with the abundance of radios, record players, and tape players, the poetry of music surrounds them. Patricia Holler suggests bringing such a rich resource, already accessible to students, into the classroom as a complement to the study of poetry. Her suggestions of how to do this, along with a rationale for the use of popular music in poetry classes, should provide some ideal starting points for instructors who are sensitive to how important it is to make connections for students between their world and the world of the classroom.

But one need not stop with music. In a world that abounds with technology, Harry MacCormack urges us to capitalize on this technology to expand students' views of poetry. His suggestions for the use of tape recorders, slide projectors, and videotape to enhance students' sensitivity to language and to increase their awareness of environment should open new areas for teachers and students to explore in their study of poetry. Even for those teachers who view themselves as impossible ''media klutzes,'' the background information can be passed on to students who demonstrate an interest and skill in using technology.

Still another way of bringing together various media with the study of poetry is suggested by Michael Cohen; the joining of the visual, in this case art, and poetry can be done through carefully prepared audiovisual presentations. Cohen's sample script that combines the art of Picasso with the poetry of Keats and Wallace Stevens demonstrates how this may be done. The script may be used as a model that students can follow in setting up their own audiovisual presentations and interpretations of poetry to supplement their classroom study.

Film represents still another dimension of the students' world that should be capitalized on in the classroom. There are many ways that filmmakers use poetry and poetic images in their work, and the enterprising instructor need not be a film buff to bring these connections to students' attention. With the abundance of fine short films now available at reasonable cost to schools, the forms of poetry and film can be brought together in the classroom as a means of expanding students' aural and visual perceptions. Robert A. Armour's listing of films appropriate for this purpose provides an excellent starting point.

But with all the emphasis upon the reading and responding to poetry, we should not ignore the fact that one of the best ways to help students become involved with poetry is through the experience of writing it. Too often, however, these efforts go unnoticed except by a few classmates and a teacher. Diane P. Shugert suggests that this need not be the case. Her practical ideas for publishing student writing show how another valuable resource can be added to the classroom. Poetry readers, designed and written by students, are a welcome addition to any classroom poetry library and bring well-deserved attention to students' efforts.

Finally, for those instructors who want to reach beyond the traditional literature anthology and select poems reflecting a variety of subjects, cultures, and student interests, Charles R. Duke offers an annotated listing of inexpensive paperback poetry collections. These collections, selected because of their potential for use with students, suggest the wide range of choices available to the instructor who wants to develop a relatively inexpensive classroom or personal library of poems suitable for young people.

Poets-in-the-Schools: Builders of Language Sensitivity

by R. Baird Shuman

It has long been common practice to bring writers to college campuses for periods varying from a single evening to a year or more to work with students and faculty interested in writing and in literature. However, it has been only during the past 10 to 15 years that public school districts, spurred by the availability of federal funds through Title III, the National Endowment for the Humanities, and other such sources, have been able on any widespread and continuing basis to bring such artists into the classrooms of their districts. Since 1970, literally hundreds of writers have visited public schools and have worked with millions of students, K through 12, throughout the nation.

Most recently, however, as federal funds have evaporated, and as many school teachers and administrators have joined the frenzied hordes rushing with a vigor and enthusiasm suggestive of the 49ers in the Yukon to get back to the basics, programs aimed at bringing poets into the schools have in many places undergone a decline in popularity. This decline is foreclosing for many students the best opportunity they may have to learn how to work most effectively with language and with writing. If language learning begins with exposure to and writing of poetry—as it does, for example, in Japan, where school children are constantly expected to compose haiku, a practice which continues consistently from the earliest school years through all preuniversity training—students will ultimately come to use language more effectively and to write it more easily than they otherwise might have.

Resource Materials for Teachers

Teachers and administrators interested in poet-in-the-schools programs will find useful suggestions and insights in the following materials, some of which deal specifically with how to set up poet-in-the-schools programs and others of which deal with more general areas of poetry instruction which will help teachers to provide background for their students prior to the arrival on the scene of a visiting poet.

Berger, Art. "Poet as Teacher, Teacher as Poet." *English Journal* 62 (December 1973): 1238–44.

Holbrook, David. *Children's Writing*. Cambridge: Cambridge University Press, 1967. (See particularly Chapters 1 and 2, "Symbolism in Children's Writing" and " 'Sincerity' and 'Realism.' ")

Jordan, June and Bush, Teri. *The Voice of the Children*. New York: Washington Square Press, 1974.

Koch, Kenneth. *Wishes, Lies, and Dreams*. New York: Chelsea House, 1970.

Kimzey, Ardis. *To Defend a Form: The Romance of Administration and Teaching in a Poetry-in-the-Schools Program*. Urbana, IL: National Council of Teachers of English, 1979.

National Endowment for the Humanities. *Artists in Schools*. Washington, DC: US Office of Education, [1973]. (See particularly pp. 89–117, which deal with poetry.)

Nebraska Curriculum Development Center. *Poetry for the Elementary Grades*. Lincoln, NE: University of Nebraska Press, 1966.

Petitt, Dorothy, ed. *Poetry in the Classroom*. Urbana, IL. National Council of Teachers of English, 1966.

Shuman, R. Baird. "A Poetry Workshop for the Upper Elementary Grades." *Elementary English* 50 (November/December 1973): 1199–1204.

————. "Teasing Writing out of High School Students." *English Journal* 62 (December 1973): 1267–71.

Terry, Ann. *Children's Poetry Preferences: A National Survey of Upper Elementary Grades*. Urbana, IL: National Council of Teachers of English, 1974.

True, Michael. *Poets in the Schools: A Handbook*. Urbana, IL: National Council of Teachers of English, 1976.

Whitman, Ruth and Feinberg, Harriet, eds. *Poemmaking: Poets in Classrooms*. Massachusetts Council of Teachers of English, 1975.

What Poets-in-the-Schools Cannot Do

Poets-in-the-schools will not and should not try to transform students into accomplished poets with publishing potential. The educational purposes of getting youngsters to write poetry are not in any way connected with ultimate commercial publication, although it is rewarding to students to see their best work printed in inexpensively produced school magazines or other such local publications.

For the most part, poets-in-the-schools will not encourage students to deluge the editors of poetry magazines with their work, although on occasion a truly gifted student may be found among those with little or no publishing potential and may be encouraged to make judicious submissions to appropriate magazines. Poets-in-the-schools will not allow students to persist in the oft-held misconception that writing a publishable poem immediately makes a person rich and famous. Rather they will probably feel the need to point out that of all the creative artists who write for publication in the United States today, fewer than 100 support themselves solely from their writing, and of this select group, almost none is primarily a poet.

Poets-in-the-schools, if they are worth their salt, will refrain from making critical judgments about the work that students are producing but rather will set up situations which will encourage writing, revision, and self-evaluation, and which will make it possible for regular classroom teachers to continue worthwhile writing activities after the poet has departed. A visiting poet who tells youngsters that they are writing immaturely or poorly leaves students with little impetus to go on writing and creates problems for regular classroom teachers, rather than paving the way toward future writing experiences.

What Poets-in-the-Schools Can Do

Poets-in-the-schools can build in students an enthusiasm for words and for language structure which will increase their eagerness to experiment with language, to play in the future with style, sound, and structure. They can also give gentle nurture to students' self-confidence in working with words and interpersonal ideas and feelings, encouraging students to develop a heightened ability to observe and react to their surroundings and to their inmost feelings. They can help each student to define his/her personal space and to function with it, ever seeking simultaneously to expand it. Their work with a poet should make students eager to try out the possibilities of their language, to test these possibilities in imaginative ways, and to invent with words.

Visiting poets who are to be with students for short periods, let us say for periods of from three to five days, which is their usual tenure in a given school district, need to provide students with a structure which will make it possible for them to produce a substantial quantity of writing in a brief time span; and then they must allow, within the structure they provide, the freedom that students will require in order to write freely, authentically, and with conviction. Finding the balance between freedom and discipline is challenging; the visiting poet is the fulcrum upon which the balance rests and by which it is achieved.

First Assumptions

Most poets-in-the-schools are working in districts where they do not live. It is useful to them to arrive a day before their teaching stints begin so that they can look around the town and get some feeling for the environment from which their students come. By doing this, they can make local allusions in their presentations which will quickly build rapport between them and their audiences. It is also useful for visiting poets to receive in advance a substantial sampling of writing from students in the district in which they are serving. I always read through this writing carefully and generally read some of the work into a cassette that I play during the initial sessions with students.

When I am going to work with combined classes of over 100 students in a given hour, I must assume that not all of them come to me with an enthusiasm for poetry, particularly for poetry writing, which *is* hard work. I must anticipate that even those who like poetry might not come to me in a mood conducive to writing it; the child still sweaty from gym class, the girl who has fought with her boyfriend in the previous hour, the boy whose parents were drunk the night before and physically abused him—all of these students approach a poetry workshop with substantial static from other sources, and it is my job as a visiting poet to clear the static. I will discuss my specific means of doing this below.

Even when I am dealing with single sections of 25–35 students, I must assume that not everyone is well-motivated to function productively in a workshop situation, and my first duty is to build motivation. I also usually assume that some students will come to class without paper and writing equipment. Therefore, I hand out mimeographed work packets on the pages of which students write directly, and I keep a goodly supply of sharpened pencils at hand which I lend to students for a 5¢ returnable deposit.

Building Motivation

As the workshop is beginning, I usually play either music or a cassette on which I have read poetry written by students in the school where I am working. The music or poetry is playing as the students enter the room; this usually quiets them down. Once the group has assembled, the cassette still playing, I hand out poetry packets which are stapled shut. The front page simply says, "Poetry Packet: Do Not Open Until You Are Directed To Do So."

Setting the Mood for Writing

Once the packets have been handed out, I lower the music or turn off the poetry which is being read on the cassette and in a very quiet, almost monotonous voice say:

> Today we have to work on getting in the mood to write. We do not always feel like writing, but if we wait for an inspiration, we might have a long wait. It is not difficult to find excuses for not writing; however, if we are serious about wanting to learn how to write, we have to write as much as possible. Constant practice makes writing easier and more natural for us.
>
> Sometimes we have to force ourselves to get words down on paper even if we have trouble in thinking of something to say. We must begin first by getting in a mood for writing. To do this today, when I say "Go," relax as completely as you can, open your packet, and stare at the figure on it until I tell you to stop. Do not take your eyes from the figure. Make no sound. Have a pen or a pencil ready, because you will be asked to write something after I call time. GO.

I have used the figure below with considerable success. It is simple to draw on a stencil. It should be as dark as possible, centered on a white sheet.

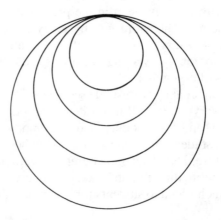

Normally, I allow classes a full two minutes to stare at the figure, a very long time indeed to sit completely still with eyes fixed on something. However, this exercise wipes from every student's mind all of the clutter which was there at the beginning of class. By the end of two minutes, an atmosphere has been built in which writing can take place. At the end of the two minutes, I say, "Turn to the next page of your booklet," which is a blank page, "and write as much as you can in one minute, telling what you saw as you stared at the figure." This exercise, which demands that the students make comparisons, also serves to encourage fluency.

The responses vary greatly from student to student, from grade level to grade level, and range from "four circles joined at the top" or "rings within rings" to "an earring" or "a petrified oyster shell" or "a bald fat man looking down" to my very favorite, "Buddha from above."

The next step is to turn to the next page, which I introduce by saying:

Now you should be in a more relaxed state than you were before we began. Your mind should be freer than it was at the beginning of the period, so you will want to take advantage of that freedom to let your mind wander. Look at the words on the sheet before you, and in the empty spaces, write whatever comes into your mind—single words, sentences, phrases, or anything else that you like—when you look at and think about each word. You may even wish to draw a picture for some of them. You may work alone or in pairs.

rObIN

oTTo

miRRor   Shadow   T
                                                                H
presidentcarterusa   E

                                                                E
                                                                N
BOB DYLAN   A   D
                                   V   L
                                O   T   OF
     HUMPE   E   I
ENGLEBERT R DINCK   N   F
                                                                e
                                                                b
                                                                r
                                                                u
   IIIIIIIIIIII   ary
IIII AIR FORCE IIII
   IIIIIIIIIIII

When the time has elapsed for this exercise, I ask, "Does it matter how something is written on a page?" This generates considerable discussion, after which I ask each student to write his or her name in at least three different ways. This leads the students to devise ingenious configurations. It is important to note at this point that the students have been writing almost continuously since they stopped looking at the figure, but that no student in all my experience has been unable to do any of the writing activities here outlined—nor, indeed, has any student complained about having to write. It is vital that visiting poets realize that they must ease students into imaginative writing, moving slowly along, step by step, from one short easy exercise to the next. It is in this way that students build self-confidence.

Encouraging Productive Moving About

I try to devise situations in which students can move about during poetry workshops, because productive physical movement will aid in building motivation. To encourage this, I write on the chalkboard statements to be completed. Statements that will work well are "Happiness is," "School is," "Contentment is," and "Trust is." When students have finished what they are working on at their desks, I urge them to go to the board and write completions for these statements. We use the completions later in writing group poetry.

The Cinquain

I then introduce students to the *cinquain,* an easily manageable poetic form for beginning writers. The worksheet on this is as follows:

CAN YOU WRITE A POEM IN FIVE MINUTES? TRY IT.

1. In the space below, write your first name.
2. On line 2, write two words which describe you.
3. On line 3, write three words which tell something you do.
4. On line 4, write a thought about yourself—just a short phrase.
5. On line 5, write your first name again.

EXAMPLE:

1. Janice
2. Tall, sun-tanned,
3. Laughing, singing, caring;
4. Seeing beauty in everything
5. Janice

YOUR POEM:

1.
2.
3.
4.
5.

Making Fresh Comparisons

We move from this exercise to one that is more taxing, because it demands that students make fresh comparisons. Students are encouraged to work in pairs. Their worksheet reads:

Most people make comparisons all the time, usually without giving a second thought to what they are doing. We say that we were "as sick as a dog," "as stubborn as a mule," or "sleepier than Rip Van Winkle," seldom giving much attention to the comparisons we have made. Similarly, we talk constantly in *metaphors* (comparisons not using the words *like, as,* or *than*), saying without a second thought that chairs have arms and legs, that corn stalks have ears, and that pitchers have lips. We are so used to hearing terms like these that few of us stop to think that in each of the instances above, we are comparing non-human things to parts of the human body.

Working separately or in pairs, try to find at least five fresh comparisons for the following:

1. She was angrier than _____.
2. The sky was as dark as _____.
3. The house was quieter than _____.
4. My roller skates are faster than _____.

Writing Haiku

Working on this exercise leads directly to the final exercise of a three- or four-day workshop, the writing of haiku. The worksheet reads:

Sometimes it is satisfying to describe as briefly and clearly as possible just one simple thing. The Japanese have long done this in a very brief poem called the haiku. Recently people from many countries have been writing haiku in many languages. The haiku is usually three lines and always seventeen syllables in length. It may not be sixteen or eighteen syllables, for then it will not be a haiku. The following are some haiku:

I. The birds of autumn
Fly south in V-shaped squadrons
Escape from winter.

(Does this haiku leave you with a sharp image? Can you
draw what it makes you imagine?)

> II. Flowers on the stem
>   Heavy-headed, bending
>   To thank the fertile earth.

(How is the image different from that in number I?)

> III. Happiness to me
>   Is walking barefoot
>   On a beach in moonlight.

(Why don't you try to write a haiku, using the first line
of this one?)

> IV. Death took the old man
>   Set all the deep lines
>   Time had etched upon his face.

(How does this poem make you feel? Does it bring an image to your
mind?)

Occasionally, the visiting poet needs to be able to improvise. During
the haiku part of one of my presentations, a student asked, "Is it OK if my
haiku has 18 syllables?" My haiku response was,

> It's OK, but it is not haiku,
> Seventeen can't be
> Eighteen, too.

Afterword to Visiting Poets

It is essential for visiting poets to have sufficiently varied activities to
enable them to move easily and quickly from one thing to another. Timing
is the *sine qua non* of a successful workshop. Good presenters learn to intuit
approaching boredom and to move quickly into a new activity before it hits.
Like good teachers, they must think on their feet and respond quickly. They
must make sure that their materials are specific and clear. Materials should
be sequential, but not so much so that students who miss a day are unable to
follow what is going on when they return to school.

There always exists in poetry workshops, particularly in those which
are run for combined classes of 100 or more students, the potential for

disciplinary problems. Fast thinking can prevent most such problems as can exercises which set the mood for writing.

On one occasion, as about 200 students were filing into a library for the first day of a poetry workshop with me, a brawny student punched an already seated student on his arm with such force that I cringed. The assaulted student sprang to his feet, fists up, face flushed. I screamed, "Freeze! OK, now we're going to do it over in slow motion, and everyone needs to watch what happens." The astounded contestants in this combat said, "Whaddaya mean, man?" "Just what I said," I told them. "Do it over in slow motion. You sit down, and you get back there and start walking toward him. Reenact it, but don't touch."

The two combatants did as I bid them, and when they had, I said urgently, "OK, poets, let's start to write about it!" And I sat down and wrote along with the 200 kids, gaining my somewhat shattered composure as I went along.

Resources for Teaching the Traditional Poetry of the Native American

by Anna Lee Stensland

"If you would seek to know a people, look to their poetry."[1] So wrote Thomas Sanders and Walter Peek, two modern American Indian collectors of the works of American Indian authors. The serious teacher of poetry to junior and senior high school students who wants to help them understand traditional Native American verse must first try to understand the place and the uses of poetry in American Indian life and then try to help students understand it. Natalie Curtis, who recorded American Indian music around the beginning of this century, when it was against the law for American Indians to sing their native songs in government schools, wrote, "Indian thought presents material absolutely unique. . . ."[2]

Few examples of American Indian poetry exist which were not originally songs, many of them religious. Such songs were neither entertainment nor the innermost expression of individual feelings, and they were not valued for their aesthetic qualities. The words of poetry were first and foremost the Native American's desire for power, the need to tap the supernatural forces in every phase of his life. Medicine men used the songs for healing, and other Indians used them to help with the hunt, with planting, in war, at the birth of a child, or at the death of an elderly person. Anything an Indian did might call on supernatural power, and this was tapped through a song. The following, for example, is a Zuñi invocation to the dawn, in which the singer calls upon the supernatural to make his crops grow.

> Now this day.
> My sun father,
> Now that you have come out standing to your sacred place,
> That from which we draw the water of life,
> Prayer meal,

> Here I give to you.
> Your long life,
> Your old age,
> Your waters,
> Your seeds,
> Your riches,
> Your power,
> Your strong spirit,
> All these to me may you grant.[3]

Songs were usually accompanied by gestures and sometimes by dances. The music and gestures expressed meaning as much as the words did. One type of poem, which was inspired by visions and accompanied by dancing, was the Ghost Dance poem. A whole series of these songs and dances, begun at the time of the vision of Wovoka, a Paiute medicine man in 1889, were ended with the tragic massacre of Chief Big Foot's band at Wounded Knee Creek in South Dakota in December, 1890. The Indians, following Wovoka's advice, wore a particular kind of shirt, which was believed to be bullet-proof, and they danced and sang for days. Nowhere is there more powerful evidence of the belief in the power of the word, music, and dance. If the people followed the ritual, it was believed, the buffalo herds would return, people who had died would return to earth, and together, with those who danced, they would drive out the hated White man. As the following example demonstrates, what the words said was not so important as was the repetition of the words as a ritual which was to accomplish the miracle.

> The whirlwind! The whirlwind!
> The whirlwind! The whirlwind!
> The snowy earth comes gliding,
> The snowy earth comes gliding,
> The snowy earth comes gliding,
> The snowy earth comes gliding.[4]

Every Native American male could create his own song. To do so was not the province only of especially talented individuals in the tribe. Each individual sang in order to bring himself into harmony with the tribe, Nature, and the Supernatural. The singer usually did not consider himself the author, but rather the messenger from the Great Spirit, who was the author. Most cherished of an individual's songs were those the male member of the tribe received when vision-seeking. After preparing himself ceremoniously, the young Indian went out, often to a mountain top, where for days he would fast, without food or water, until he received a vision or dream which would determine his future. Some of these songs could not be shared lest their power be lost, so they could never be recorded. One song, which *was* recorded, is from the Teton Sioux.

> Where the wind is blowing
> The wind is roaring
> I stand.
>
> Westward the wind is blowing
> The wind is roaring
> I stand.[5]

Some of the most lyric, and perhaps understandable, songs for modern students are the love lyrics, which were believed to act as charms to bring back the loved one. Such a lyric was recorded from the Chippewa by Francis Densmore.

> A loon
> I thought it was
> But it was
> My love's splashing oar.
>
> To Sault Ste. Marie
> He has departed.
> My love
> Has gone on before me
> Never again
> Can I see him.[6]

Native American songs are usually very short, free verse forms, filled with strong sense imagery. Meter and rhyme are often absent, except that syllables are added in order to complete the Indian drum beat. Some of the very short translations are as fine as some of the best imagist poetry.

> As my eyes search the prairie
> I feel the summer in the spring.[7]

Other poems are short because a simple image represents an entire myth which the tribe shares. A Papago woman once told anthropologist Ruth Underhill, ''The song is very short because we understand so much.''[8] The Navajo ''Song of the Rain Chant'' is an example.

> Far as man can see
>   Comes the rain,
>   Comes the rain with me.[9]

The non-Indian reader needs to understand that the poem is talking about the Rain-Youth, a Navajo deity who comes from the Rain Mountain with the rain and who sings as he journeys. A storm with thunder and lightning is the Male-Rain and a gentle shower is the Female-Rain. The two rendezvous and from this union comes all vegetation.

Traditional Indian poetry might best be understood by junior and senior high school students if it is taught in connection with mythology rather than with other poetry. Out of the study of myth must come some understanding of Indian life and values. Much Indian art of the past and present grows out of the myths of the tribes. Jamake Highwater's history of Indian art, *Song from the Earth: American Indian Painting,* published by the New York Graphic Society of Boston in 1976, contains both black and white and color illustrations of the works of artists from 1870 to modern times. Many of the works show tribal members in ceremonials as well as everyday tasks where they are dancing, singing or praying. Other publications of beautiful Indian art and photographs, which are available in school libraries, will bring Indian life of the past to modern students.

Perhaps most important for students to understand is the power of the word in Indian poetry. N. Scott Momaday writes, "A word has power in and of itself. It comes from nothing into sound and meaning; it gives origin to all things. By means of words can a man deal with the world on equal terms. The word is sacred."[10] Modern young people might be reminded of word magic in their lives. It is almost compulsive for many of us that when someone sneezes we must respond, "God bless you," "Gesundheit," "Salud," or some other such expression. Somehow that is supposed to keep away a cold or other illness. Even quite young children learn that when two people walk, one on each side of a post, the friendship can be saved only by saying, "bread and butter." When two people say exactly the same words in answer to a question in a conversation, the two must hook their little fingers in order to avoid bad luck. Many will remember how necessary it was to repeat after stepping on a sidewalk crack, "Step on a crack; break your mother's back," in order to avoid its happening. Students and teacher can come up with even more serious, and less superstition-related, examples. Some may even remember, "In the beginning was the Word, and the Word was with God and the Word was God."

To complicate the teaching, teachers and students need to recognize that there are two types of Indian verse in translation: (1) that which has been translated directly from Indian originals, usually by ethnologists—poetry which may not impress modern readers of poetry as great verse; and (2) that which employs Indian subjects and rhythms drawn from Native life and song to make interpretations of the spirit of Indian poetry. The latter may impress the teacher as better poetry, but she or he must also recognize that such poetry may be less truly Indian. Some of the most accessible collections of works from many tribes are the following, all in paperback:

Astrov, Margot. *American Indian Prose and Poetry: An Anthology.* Berkeley, CA: Capricorn Press, 1962. (Originally published in 1946 under the title *The Winged Serpent.*)
Although it contains both prose and poetry and has been criticized by some as being mainly the work of anthropologists, the translations are quite literal and close to the original Indian. The book is divided into 10 geographical, cultural sections. It also has a good introduction about American Indian poetry.

Bierhorst, John. *In the Trail of the Wind: American Indian Poems and Ritual Orations.* New York: Farrar, Straus, and Giroux, 1972.
The arrangement here is thematic rather than geographical. Translations are chosen from well-known American Indian specialists, using mainly literal translations. The beauty of the book is enhanced by carefully chosen engravings.

Brandon, William. *The Magic World: American Indian Songs and Poems.* New York: William Morrow, 1971.
The editor says that his only criterion for inclusion of a poem was, "Do the lines feel good, moving?" The result is some very free translations taken from the original, more literal translations. (See the William Bevis article, listed in the Bibliography, for the kinds of changes Brandon has made.) The book is organized geographically by tribes.

Cronyn, George W. *American Indian Poetry: An Anthology of Songs and Chants.* New York: Liveright, 1970. (Originally published in 1918 under the title *The Path on the Rainbow.*)
This is the earliest of collections. It has been much criticized because of certain errors: The author assumes that the Ojibwa and Chippewa are different tribes; the writer of the introduction praises an alleged Indian poem, which had years before proved to be a fraud; and the section of 'Interpretations'' turns out to be quite non-Indian. For its time, however, the work is important.

Day, A. Grove. *The Sky Clears: Poetry of the American Indians.* Lincoln, NE: University of Nebraska Press, 1964.
This is a book *about* American Indian poetry more than an anthology of poems, but it does contain more than 200 poems from approximately 40 Indian tribes as examples of points the author is making. The book is organized geographically by tribes. It is a useful reference book for teachers to have.

Rothenburg, Jerome. *Shaking the Pumpkin: Traditional Poetry of the Indian North Americas.* Garden City, NY: Doubleday, 1972.
The editor of this book has been quite free in his translations. He sees the translator as one who "attempts to restore what has been torn apart." The

vulgarity and lust which were part of Indian life are found in these translations.

Traditional American Indian poetry is difficult, because it is so unlike poetry we know. The personal ownership of it, the oral tradition with its background in nature, and the singing and body movements which went with the verse are all missing for the modern reader. Poetry in print was alien to the traditional Indian. But any effort the teacher makes to help students understand will give them a different perspective on their own lives and help correct erroneous ideas about the First Americans.

References

1. Thomas E. Sanders and Walter W. Peek, *Literature of the American Indian* (Beverly Hills, CA: Glencoe Press, 1973), p. 103.

2. Natalie Curtis, *The Indians' Book* (New York: Dover, 1968), p. XXIX.

3. Ruth L. Bunzel, "Zuni Ritual Poetry," in *Forty-Seventh Annual Report*, Bureau of American Ethnology, Part 2 (Washington, DC: Government Printing Office, 1930), p. 635.

4. James Mooney, "The Ghost Dance Religion," in *Fourteenth Annual Report*, Bureau of American Ethnology, Part 2 (Washington, DC: Government Printing Office, 1896), p. 1054.

5. Francis Densmore, *Teton Sioux Music*. Bureau of American Ethnology, Bulletin 61 (Washington, DC: Government Printing Office, 1918), p. 186.

6. ———, *Chippewa Music*, Bureau of American Ethnology, Bulletin 45 (Washington, DC: Government Printing Office, 1910), p. 150–51.

7. ———, *Chippewa Music II*, Bureau of American Ethnology, Bulletin 53 (Washington, DC: Government Printing Office, 1913), p. 254.

8. Ruth Underhill, *The Autobiography of a Papago Woman* (Menasha, WI: American Anthropological Association, 1936), p. 11.

9. Curtis, p. 365.

10. N. Scott Momaday, *The Way to Rainy Mountain*. (New York: Ballantine, 1969), p. 42.

Bibliography

Astrov, Margot. *American Indian Prose and Poetry: An Anthology*. New York: Capricorn, 1962.

Bevis, William. "American Indian Verse Translations." *College English* (35) (March 1974): 693–703.

Bunzel, Ruth L. "Zuni Ritual Poetry," *Forty-Seventh Annual Report*. Part 2. Bureau of American Ethnology. Washington, DC: Government Printing Office, 1930.

Curtis, Natalie. *The Indians' Book*. New York: Dover, 1968.

Day, A. Grove. *The Sky Clears: Poetry of the American Indians*. Lincoln, NE: University of Nebraska Press, 1964.

Densmore, Francis. *Chippewa Music*. Bureau of American Ethnology, Bulletin 45. Washington, DC: Government Printing Office, 1910.

———. *Chippewa Music II*. Bureau of American Ethnology, Bulletin 53. Washington, DC: Government Printing Office, 1913.

———. *Teton Sioux Music*. Bureau of American Ethnology, Bulletin 61. Washington, DC: Government Printing Office, 1918.

Highwater, Jamake. *Song from the Earth: American Indian Painting*. Boston: New York Graphic Society, 1976.

Howard, Helen Addison. *American Indian Poetry*. Boston: Twayne, 1979.

Momaday, N. Scott. *The Way to Rainy Mountain*. New York: Ballantine, 1969.

Mooney, James. "The Ghost Dance Religion," in *Fourteenth Annual Report*. Bureau of American Ethnology, Part 2. Washington, DC: Government Printing Office, 1896.

Rothenburg, Jerome. *Shaking the Pumpkin: Traditional Poetry of the Indian North Americas*. Garden City, NY: Doubleday, 1972.

Sanders, Thomas E. and Walter W. Peek. *Literature of the American Indian*. Beverly Hills, CA: Glencoe Press, 1972.

Underhill, Ruth. *The Autobiography of a Papago Woman*. Menasha, WI: American Anthropological Association, 1936.

Resources for Teaching Black Poetry

by Sally A. Jacobsen

Black poetry is part of every American student's cultural heritage. At last, Black poets are beginning to be appreciated for their individual distinction as poets, rather than primarily for their expression of Black community values. Poems by Black poets should be included in the regular literature curriculum, since not all students will take a "Black Literature" elective. Some of the resources described here would also be useful in a specialized course, but their use should not be limited to that. Of first consideration for us, then, are general literature textbooks that integrate Black poetry into the mainstream, and resources for poems and poets too recent to be included in standard textbooks. Black literature anthologies and secondary sources follow, with a note on recordings and film resources. These are valuable aids to teachers in planning and presenting their coursework, but they would also interest students whose curiosity has been sparked in the classroom. Finally, a book and articles are described that are primarily useful as resources for teachers.

Textbooks

Many of the Black poets who appeal most vividly to students are modern writers, and their work is beginning to be included beyond a token one or two poems in the standard literature series, particularly those published since 1975. McGraw-Hill's "Themes in Literature" series (revised, 1979) is perhaps the most impressive, with poems by Langston Hughes, Lucille Clifton, Nikki Giovanni, Margaret Walker, June Jordan, Richard Wright, and Gordon Parks being included in the ninth-grade *Insights* volume alone. Harcourt Brace Jovanovich, Inc.'s "Adventures" series (revised, 1980) and Ginn's Literature Series (Xerox Corp., 1981) follow close behind, with Ginn outdoing McGraw-Hill in its basic sequence for the middle school, particularly in *Responding: One* (for seventh grade, 1973), edited by Robert S. Johnson and James N. Britton.

D. C. Heath's *American Voices* volume (1981) for the 11th grade has an entire chapter on "The Literature of Emancipation," with multiple poems by Langston Hughes, Arna Bontemps, and Robert Hayden—and poems by Lucille Clifton, Countee Cullen, Gwendolyn Brooks, I. Amiri Baraka (LeRoi Jones), James Emanuel, and Nikki Giovanni appearing in three other chapters. Giovanni's matter-of-fact "Legacies," for example, describes a grandmother's attempt to teach her grandaughter her way of "making rolls" and the girl's refusal to learn—because she is unwilling to acknowledge that her grandmother may be approaching death. The grandmother's Black dialect is so sensitively presented that no student, regardless of race, could fail to recognize her dignity. The representation in *American Voices* makes up somewhat for Heath's scanty offerings in other volumes in its "Living Literature" series (1981). (That Houghton-Mifflin's offerings are skimpy, too, probably owes something to the fact that their series was last revised in 1975.)

The general 11th-grade *American Literature* by Ginn and *Adventures in American Literature* by Harcourt Brace Jovanovich both go back as far as Phyllis Wheatley in the era of the Revolutionary War. Ginn offers more lively contemporary poets (Claude McKay, Baraka/Jones, Mari Evans, and Alice Walker, better known for her fiction), while a sound/filmstrip series from Guidance Associates is available for the Harcourt Brace Jovanovich chapter on the "Harlem Renaissance" of the 20s and 30s.

Recent Individual Poets

1920s–50s poets Langston Hughes, Arna Bontemps, Countee Cullen, Margaret Walker, Claude McKay, Robert Hayden, Gwendolyn Brooks, and Richard Wright, and more recent poets Lucille Clifton, Nikki Giovanni, Mari Evans—even revolutionary poets June Jordan ("I Am," in McGraw-Hill's ninth-grade volume) and I. Amiri Baraka—are represented in the general literature textbooks being published today. Several contemporary Black poets whose vibrant language would unfailingly hook students on poetry are too new to be represented yet in the standard textbooks. Five who must be mentioned—so that teachers can at least refer students to them—are Don L. Lee (Haki R. Madhubuti), Ishmael Reed, Sonia Sanchez, Michael Harper, and Ntozake Shange.

My favorites by Don Lee (Haki Makhubuti), born in 1942, are "But He Was Cool/ or: he even stopped for green lights" and "The Self-Hatred of Don L. Lee.'' More experimental in form, ''A Poem to Complement Other Poems'' rings an insistence on ''change'' through social outrages that Blacks endure, culminating in a powerful rage wrought through word combinations—and a surprise ending. These poems are found in *The Black Poets*, a paperback anthology edited by Dudley Randall (New York: Bantam, 1971), as are other poems mentioned below, unless otherwise noted.

Students should know of Berkeley, California, poet Ishmael Reed, also a fiction writer, who, believing that poetry ''should be accessible to all people, of all ages, without footnotes'' (University of Cincinnati Fiction Festival, April 1, 1980), produces wild juxtapositions of myth, film, Black identity, and childhood games and nursery rhymes. ''I Am a Cowboy in the Boat of Ra'' is widely anthologized (e.g., in *The New Black Poets*, edited by Clarence Major, New York: International Pubs., 1969). Reed's whimsical ''black power poem'' and ''Beware: Do Not Read This Poem'' appear in *The Black Poets* (the latter is also found in James M. McCrimmon's *Writing with a Purpose*, Boston: Houghton-Mifflin, a widely used college rhetoric).

A contemporary poet whose experimental forms students might want to try themselves is Sonia Sanchez (born in 1935); her work is difficult to find in textbooks because of her frank, powerful language—very effective in conveying her agony for friends who have become hooked on heroin, or her indignation when an acquaintance's actions are not consistent with Black Power values. Like Nikki Giovanni and Ntozake Shange, Sanchez is superb at capturing the flavor, the vividness, of jive talk. ''Nigger'' and ''Black Magic'' in *The Black Poets* could be presented in class, while students could enjoy others on their own.

Michael Harper (born in 1938, Director of the Writing Program at Brown University) has two moving poems about tragic deaths of young Blacks at White hands in *The Black Poets:* ''American History,'' about the Alabama church explosion in the mid-60s which killed four children, and ''A Mother Speaks: The Algier Motel Incident, Detroit.'' Students would also enjoy Harper's later poems, in many of which he explores Black versus White identity with imagery from photography, identifying with the negative image. Some of these, along with Robert Stepto's excellent article discussing the poems and Harper's literary antecedent in poet Robert Hayden, may be found in *Chant of Saints* (edited by Michael S. Harper and Robert B. Stepto, Champaign, IL: University of Illinois, 1979).

Finally, Ntozake Shange is too new to appear in 70s anthologies and too good not to be mentioned. Students will delight in her rebellious disregard for spelling and punctuation. (Her jaunty tone is conveyed effectively without it.) In her work poetry pervades even prose forms. Luckily, some of her work is available in cheap paperbacks: *Nappy Edges* (New York: Bantam, 1980) which contains not only wonderful poems like "What Do You Believe a Poem Shd Do?" (in an interview with herself), but also verse essays, like her argument that the styles of Black poets are as distinctive as those of jazz musicians, in "takin a solo/ a poetic possibility/ a poetic imperative." *Sassafrass, Cypress and Indigo*, a delightful novel in verse, has just been published (New York: St. Martin's Press, 1982). Students would enjoy listening to selections from Shange's choreopoem, *for colored girls who have considered suicide/ when the rainbow is enuf*, like "graduation night" or "somebody almost walked off wid alla my stuff" (recording available from Better Duck Productions, Box 3092, Berkeley, CA 94703). *Colored girls* enjoyed a long theatrical run in New York, like her more recent poetic drama, *Spell #7* (in *three pieces*, New York: St. Martin's, 1981).

Black Literature Anthologies

If a school system is not ready to replace a pre-1976 textbook series, the best alternative is to purchase a classroom set of a paperback anthology to be passed from room to room as needed. For grades 9–12, *The Black Poets*, edited by Dudley Randall (New York: Bantam, 1971), covering the period from slavery to the 1970s, is probably a better choice than some published a few years later, since it includes at least six or seven poems by each poet with whom students should be familiar. The fatter *Black Voices* (New York: Mentor, New American Library, 1968) would also be a good choice, since it includes fiction, autobiography, and criticism, as well as poetry. Both have first-rate introductions to help teachers and students alike get their bearings. Arnold Adoff's award-winning *I Am the Darker Brother* (New York: Macmillan, 1968), containing just modern poems, would be a good alternative.

For the middle school, Adoff's *Black Out Loud* (New York: Dell, 1970) is an excellent supplementary Black poetry anthology. (Actually, at least single copies of all these collections should be in the school library, whether or not classroom sets are offered.)

Dark Symphony: Negro Literature in America, edited by James A. Emanuel and Theodore L. Gross (New York: Free Press, 1968) is a standard anthology with well-selected poems and short stories from early literature, the "Negro Awakening" of the 20s and 30s, and contemporary literature, concluding with four articles on recent literature that help students place writers in the American literary tradition. "Early Literature" contains handy selections from Frederick Douglass and W.E.B. Du Bois which can be consulted when a poem or story refers to one of them.

Black Fire: An Anthology of Afro-American Writing, edited by LeRoi Jones (I. Amiri Baraka) and Larry Neal (New York: William Morrow, 1968), is an "alternative" anthology containing many more writers of the Black Power movement than any of the standard volumes and is thus a good resource for finding pieces by modern authors not included elsewhere. A huge poetry section, with fiction, drama, and essays, including "African Responses to Malcolm X" and activist perspectives—one by Stokely Carmichael, for example—provides useful references for students whose reading has aroused their curiosity about Black militancy.

Chant of Saints: A Gathering of Afro-American Literature, Art, and Scholarship, edited by Michael S. Harper and Robert B. Stepto (Champaign, IL: University of Illinois, 1979), is an exciting contemporary anthology interweaving stories and poems of consummate craft with photographs of paintings and sculpture by Black artists, interviews, and critical essays—sometimes by the authors (e.g., Sherley A. Williams' "The Blues Roots of Contemporary Afro-American Poetry"). *Chant of Saints* is a "must" for the school library because of the literary and cultural roots it establishes for some of today's most accomplished Black writers; it is fascinating reading.

The New Black Poetry, edited by Clarence Major (New York: International Pubs., 1969), contains contemporary poetry since the 40s, but only one poem per poet. It is a good paperback to supplement other books, including poems appropriate for high school students by poets too young to appear yet in other collections: Elton Hill/Abu Ishak's "Theme Brown Girl," capturing an element of Black identity in each of six places—Dakar, the Congo, Haiti, Harlem, Watts, and Detroit; Michael Nicholas' "Today: The Idea Market" on a school theme; and Quincy Troupe's accessible juxtaposition of rioting scenes with White indifference in "White Weekend" are good examples.

Black Identity: A Thematic Reader, edited by Francis Kearns (New York: Holt, Rinehart and Winston, 1970), interweaves poems, biographical essays, stories, and opinion, on the themes, for instance, of "Heritage," "Brutality," and modern racism, each section ending with a prose perspective. *Black Insights,* edited by Nick Aaron Ford (Lexington, MA: Ginn-Xerox, 1971), another thematic paperback, contains more early writing (beginning with Phyllis Wheatley) than any of the anthologies mentioned above and, in addition to a generous selection of poems by each figure, stories, criticism, biographical accounts, opinion, and drama. Biographical notes and suggested further reading helpfully appear just before and after each author's selections. Musical notation is included for some of the spirituals and blues songs.

Voices from the Black Experience: Afro-American and African Literature, edited by Darwin Turner, Jean Bright, and Richard Wright (Lexington, MA: Ginn-Xerox, 1972, paper), is designed as a text for high school Black Literature courses but would also be a useful library resource for students wishing to compare African and American poetry.

The work of most of the poets mentioned above is available in individual paperback editions; just by browsing through some of these one can find poems the class would enjoy. To be convinced of I. Amiri Baraka's full power and range, for example, one needs to leaf through *The Selected Poetry of Amiri Baraka/LeRoi Jones* (New York: William Morrow, 1979), perhaps finding a poem like "Look For You Yesterday/ Here You Come Today"—the Lone Ranger poem ("My Silver bullets all gone/ . . . & Tonto way off in the hills/ Moaning like Bessie Smith"—pp. 10–13). One could capitalize on students' enthusiasm for poets in their textbooks by sending them to the library to see if single volumes by their favorites are in the school collection; if they are not, teams could take on the project of delving into public and college library collections to find poetry volumes to recommend adding to the school library, and perhaps even involve their parents and the business community in their enthusiasm by publicizing the library's need.

Secondary Sources

Backgrounds to Blackamerican Literature, edited by Ruth Miller (New York: Chandler, 1971, paper), is divided into two large sections: (1) "Historical Backgrounds," containing accounts of the slave ships, Negro insurrections, classes in the South, the Ku Klux Klan (by W.E.B. Du Bois), the Black Muslims, and the Black Panthers; and (2) "Literary Backgrounds," containing critical articles by and about Black writers, including Arna Bontemps on "The Negro Renaissance" and Arthur P. Davis on Gwendolyn Brooks. The chronology of significant events in Black American history and literature, 1501–1968, is a handy reference.

C.W.E. Bigsby in *The Second Black Renaissance: Essays in Black Literature* (Westport, CT: Greenwood Press, 1980; "Contributions in Afro-American and African Studies," No. 50) devotes two of his nine critical-historical chapters to Black poetry—an excellent guide to contemporary writers.

Interviews with Black Writers, edited by John O'Brien (New York: Liveright, 1973), contains interviews with Arna Bontemps, Owen Dodson,

Michael Harper, Clarence Major, Ann Petry, Ishmael Reed, and Al Young, as well as with numerous novelists. Each interview is preceded by a photograph of the subject.

Recordings and Film Resources

Barbara Stanford and Karima Amin's *Black Literature for High School Students* (Urbana, IL: National Council of Teachers of English, 1978) and Randall's *The Black Poets* offer ample lists of phonograph records of both collections of Black poetry and single poets' work. *The Black Poets* also lists tape recordings, videotapes, and films—for example, *Gwendolyn Brooks,* 16mm, 30 minutes, showing scenes in Brooks's Chicago neighborhood as she reads her poems (produced by WTTW, Chicago; order from Indiana University Audio-Visual Center, Blooming-ton, IN 47401; rental, $6.75), and *Ridn and Stridn, Reachn and Teachn,* 16 mm, 30 minutes, showing Brooks in action in the classroom (Roy Lewis, 206 N. La Porte Ave., South Bend, IN 46616; rental).

Holt, Rinehart, and Winston's "Impact" series of recordings is appropriate for specific mention here, since the records embody the principle of integrating Black poetry with White. The *Cities* album contains the most Black poetry of any in this series, including Langston Hughes's "A Dream Deferred" and "The City," Bontemps' "A Note of Humility," and a spiritual, "Go Tell It On the Mountain," but the *I've Got a Name, Search for America,* and *Conflict* albums carry two poems each by Black poets.

Resources for Teachers

Probably the single most important secondary resource which teachers should have available to them is *Black Literature for High School Students* (containing information explicitly for middle school), by Barbara D. Stan-ford and Karima Amin (Urbana, IL: National Council of Teachers of English, 1978, paper). This immensely useful book includes a historical survey of Black writers, with handy biographical information about the achievement of every writer included in the new standard literature texts, a chapter on adolescent literature, and comprehensive bibliographies. The second half of the volume is devoted to Black literature units appropriate for several secondary grade and ability levels and a wealth of stimulating supplemental activities—games, for example. The book opens with a frank discussion of problems which might confront the unsuspecting teacher teaching Black works for the first time and how to forestall them.

The September 1981 issue of *Ms*. carries a similarly valuable article, Mary Helen Washington's account of teaching Black and White literature to racially mixed college literature classes. Washington's students resented being expected to act as spokespersons for the values of their respective races, yet, through open discussion, much mutual understanding was achieved. Washington describes how she reexamined her goals and restructured the class to prevent resentful confrontation the next time she offered it.

For teachers wishing to design units containing Black poetry along thematic lines, Jean Dubois' "An Introduction to Black American Poetry" would be useful (*English Journal*, May 1973, pp. 718–23). The article prints a sample poem each for the themes of slavery (Hayden's "Runagate, Runagate," in Heath's *American Voices* text for 11th grade); acquiescence, integration (Naomi Long Madgett's "Alabama Centennial"); separatism (Dudley Randall's "The Melting Pot"); and militancy (Hughes's "Epilogue" and Margaret Walker's "For My People").

One's style, however, may be to select poems so good one cannot resist presenting them to students, rather than selecting according to themes in Black literature. Also, most of the poets mentioned above are of such worth that the use of their poems should not be restricted to units on Black literature. A Gwendolyn Brooks sonnet, for example, can allow students to discover for themselves the natural connection between content or outcome of a situation and the sonnet form, rather than forcing them to learn the mechanics of form first. This approach works with virtually all of Brooks's sonnets found in "The Children of the Poor" series in *Annie Allen* (1949), e.g., the understated and moving "Children of the Poor" itself (sometimes entitled from the first line, "What Shall I Give My Children?"). Several of these sonnets are represented in the various school anthologies, and *Adventures in Appreciation* for the tenth grade (San Diego, CA: Harcourt Brace Jovanovich, Inc., 1980) implies this use of them to teach form by including Brooks's "Sonnet/Ballad" with a Cullen sonnet.

In fact, Black poetry (or any poetry) should not be limited to "literature" units in the classroom. Poetry is a very effective stimulus for student writing. The nine "dream" poems by Langston Hughes in the tenth grade *Encounters* text in McGraw-Hill's "Themes in Literature" series, or his dream poems in textbooks from other publishers, could be used to prompt journal writing on the students' own dreams, leading to class discussion of the writing and, in turn, to more polished writing. The poems by teenage writers, some of them Black students, published by Millicent Lenz in "The Poetry of Today's Teenage Feminists, or How to Survive as Young, Gifted, and Female" (*Arizona English Bulletin*, February 1979, pp. 41–49) suggest other subjects besides dreams one might use to spark student writing. (For this journal-to-publication method, see Tom Liners' article in the Applications section of this book.) For a Black poet's perspective (beyond several by Shange in *Nappy Edges*, New York: Bantam, 1980) richly evocative of the permanent value of poetry throughout life, one should read Naomi Long Madgett's ''By Fools Like Me'' in *Goal Making for English Teaching* (edited by Henry B. Maloney, Urbana, IL: National Council of Teachers of English, 1973), pp. 99–104.

Rhythm and Rime: Resources in Popular Music

by Patricia Holler

The average student talks, walks, breathes, and sleeps to popular music; yet this most obvious and easily accessible media form is sadly neglected in the classroom, particularly in conjunction with the study of poetry. Like poetry, music involves a process through which creative minds seek to express emotions, ideas, and concerns. Creativity, whether it comes in the form of a rock song or a poem, is something to be admired and encouraged. Critics may argue incessantly about the quality of an art form; they cannot, however, argue that writing a song does not require many of the same skills found in writing a poem: an ear for words, a delight in a metaphor, an understanding of the power of images, a sense of rhythm.

It is not particularly difficult to justify the use of popular music in the classroom, for through the study of such music, students may experience vicariously many of the universal concerns of humanity. While many popular song lyrics do not explore life experiences in depth, the lyrics do present situations that are real for both adolescents and adults. In fact, many young people first become aware of the commonality of their experiences through listening to music. Love, war, death, joy, and alienation—nearly any human emotion—as well as many life experiences, show up in the lyrics of popular music.

In the usual classroom, we find advanced, average, and reluctant readers. Although the advanced or average reader is usually able to read and understand many of the poems in the usual literature anthology, reluctant readers often are not so fortunate. They must struggle to read most traditional lyric poems and ballads. Frustrated by words beyond their reading level and numerous historical notes that try the patience of even good readers, the reluctant reader often becomes convinced that poetry is an indecipherable language.

One of the most important reasons for considering the use of song lyrics and poetry together is the interest or motivation that one can provide for the other. Oddly enough, the reluctant readers will thumb eagerly through the pages of an issue of *Hit Parader,* looking for their favorite songs; once they find the lyrics, students will read avidly, and perhaps even copy down the words. The reluctant reader may be interested enough to read a three-page article about a popular singer. Why this strange transformation? Simple. Students are interested in what they're reading, and, more importantly, they enjoy what they read.

One reason for the enjoyment is that the words to most popular songs are within most students' vocabulary range. For once in their reading experience, they do not have to struggle to read nor do they have to feel ashamed because they fail to understand what many of their classmates seem to comprehend easily. In addition, because the slow reader has previously enjoyed listening to a song, he or she experiences, perhaps for the first time in school, the "expectation" of reading pleasure. For most reluctant readers, reading enjoyment, much less the expectation of that enjoyment, is a rare experience. Too rare. For only when readers are able to expect and then experience reading pleasure will they read willingly both in and out of the classroom.

We need not worry that by letting popular music into the classroom we are somehow ignoring some of the basic skills and knowledge about poetry which students are expected to gain. For example, popular music, like poetry, employs many of the same literary devices. Although rime and repetition may be the most common elements, alliteration, metaphor, personification, imagery, symbolism and theme are not unknown to writers of popular songs. While little is to be gained by having students memorize the definitions of such elements in isolation, increasing students' awareness of them in contemporary culture can lead to a greater appreciation of their use by both poet and song writer down through the years.

There are additional advantages. Song magazines such as *Hit Parader,* and *Song Hits,* accessible on practically any newsstand, not only provide high interest reading activities but also may stimulate student writing. Such magazines contain interviews with singers, biographies, commentaries on the music scene, "mail bag" sections, and critical reviews. For many students, the chance to send in a personal opinion or brief comment about the latest recording of a favorite singer is hard to resist. Other students may want to write their own commentaries; still others may wish to take on the challenge of writing a critical review. Some students even may be encouraged to write songs or poems of their own and perform them.

Writing skills are not the only skills enhanced by the use of popular music. Listening skills should receive as much attention in the classroom as writing and speaking skills, but often this does not occur. For example, many times students will have memorized the words to a favorite song, but seldom do they discuss the ''experience'' of listening to a song. Since each listener responds differently to a song, such an experience may well be compared to responding to poetry because poetry is intended to be an aural experience as well. By encouraging students to discuss what happens as they listen to a song or poem, teachers may discover ways to heighten both listening and interpretation skills.

With all these possibilities, then, the classroom teacher would be foolish indeed to overlook popular music as a welcome resource in teaching poetry. There are many ways the teacher may use such music, but using popular music means keeping up with the changes and using contemporary sources such as magazines and recordings. Although few teachers probably will have a collection of song magazines (the best source for lyrics), now might be a good time to start one, and students can be encouraged to bring in back issues. In addition to reading and discussing song lyrics, students may wish to listen to the original recordings of older popular songs. A search through the bibles of the music industry—Schwann or Phonolog catalogs available in most music stores—often uncovers numerous recordings which could be useful. But the most important and most accessible source of all is students. It is a rare adolescent who does not have a substantial record or tape collection and who would not be proud to share his or her holdings with others. There is another reason for seeking assistance from students; the nature of the music industry is such that popular songs change almost weekly and certainly annually; students keep up with these changes and will, again, need little encouragement to indicate what songs are currently available and appropriate for various aspects of study.

With all the material so close at hand, where does the teacher begin? The choices are limited only by the teacher's imagination. Here are some samples of what might be done.

Organization by Theme

Two samples of thematic focus might include romantic love and alienation. The instructor will have little difficulty locating examples of love poems written at different times in literary history. Ask students to locate the lyrics for a popular love song. Have the students reduce the love situation or comment to a one sentence description of what the song says about love. Then ask students to read several love poems and discuss the differences and similarities with the ideas expressed in the popular song. An excellent starting choice for this activity is William Shakespeare's "My Mistress' Eyes Are Nothing Like the Sun." In focusing on alienation, the teacher might ask students to compare the first paragraph of John Donne's "No Man Is an Island" with the song "I Am a Rock" by Paul Simon ("Simon and Garfunkel's Greatest Hits," Columbia Records) or students might listen to "The Sounds of Silence" by Paul Simon (same recording) and compare the lyrics to "Preface to a Twenty Volume Suicide Note" by Leroi Jones, found in *Sounds and Silences* (edited by Richard Peck, New York: Dell, 1970). Other thematic focuses might include war, death, poverty, and growing up.

Focus on Literary Devices

Most popular songs show an awareness of some of the basic poetic devices. With a minimum of explanation and introduction, teachers will discover that students quickly are able to locate songs that have powerful images (see "Lucy in the Sky with Diamonds" by the Beatles—lyrics found in *Sounds and Silences* with the actual song available on several Beatles collections). Most popular songs also employ a considerable amount of alliteration: "Back in Black" by AC/DC; "Maxwell's Silver Hammer" by the Beatles; "Double Dutch Bus" by Frankie Smith. Again, ask students to provide their favorite samples and then match them with poems. For examples of repetition, select a blues song from a source such as *The Poetry of the Blues* (edited by Samuel Charters, New York: Avon Books) and see if students can explain how repetition is used in conjunction with the blues beat. This may be done by simply singing the lyrics to a blues song and tapping out the rhythm or having students listen to a blues recording and mark the repetition and rhythm as they follow the song. Another way to make the students aware of repetition is to have them select a popular ballad and compare it with a literary ballad. When students are ready to consider form and pattern in poetry, introduce them to some selections from May Swenson's *More Poems to Solve* (New York: Scribner's, 1970); and then ask students to seek popular songs which have unusual forms or patterns and bring them to class for comparison and discussion. Once the teacher introduces popular music into the classroom, there will be little difficulty in finding fresh material, for students will volunteer eagerly each new discovery that they make and will begin to talk knowledgeably about the various literary devices that they hear and see in their music.

Teachers and students need not stop with just the few ideas suggested above. Here are a few others.

1. Ask students to select a poem and then find a musical selection which seems to represent best the mood of the poem; students can record their own readings of the poem to the music and then answer questions from the class about the interpretation and the selection. Such an activity can be enhanced further if students are able to find pictures to go along with the music and poem.

2. Some music composers have written what are called "tone poems." Students interested in classical and contemporary music may find it interesting to seek out some of these selections and introduce them to the class for discussion.

3. Suggest to students that they find a poet and a singer or song writer who seem to explore certain ideas or themes in similar or different ways; the result could be a paper, an oral presentation, or even a taped collection of readings and songs to illustrate the points of similarity or difference.

4. Suggest that students explore the poetry and music of American minority groups; e.g., Black, Mexican, and Native American. A panel discussion might develop from such research.

5. Encourage students to explore songs and poems which seem to celebrate or explain various heroes and villains; compare and contrast the versions and the accuracy of facts and historical context.

6. Select a song and remove all adjectives from the lyrics; have students attempt to replace the adjectives; do the same thing with a poem. After comparing rewritten versions, discuss the appropriateness or lack of it in their choices of words.

7. Select the lyrics of a popular song and present them without music. Ask students to "free write" about their impressions based just on the lyrics; then play the song and ask students to free write their impressions again. Discuss the results and ask students to explain what effect music may or may not have on certain lyrics. This should lead to a discussion of the difference between poetry written for music and poetry which is not and what difference there may be between lyrics to a song and words to a poem.

8. Introduce students to choral reading; provide opportunities for them to experiment with different arrangements of words, voices, rhythms, and volume. This might lead to a class presentation.

9. Introduce students to popular songs from different periods in history; discuss the lyrics and the effect they might have had then as compared to the present; present poetry of the same periods and discuss how the poems do or do not reflect the concerns of the period.

10. Suggest that students attend a poetry reading (many colleges and public libraries sponsor these) and compare it with a rock concert.

11. Invite a song writer and a poet to discuss their work with the class; tape the session for later use.

Resources

The following books, magazines, and articles should help the teacher who is interested in becoming more familiar with the relationships between popular music and poetry.

BOOKS

Anderson, Douglas. *My Sister Looks Like a Pear*. New York: Hart Publishing Co., 1974.

Charters, Samuel, ed. *The Poetry of the Blues*. New York: Avon Books, 1970.

Chipman, Bruce L., ed. *Hardening Rock: An Organic Anthology of the Adolescence of Rock n' Roll*. Boston: Little, Brown and Company, 1972.

Goldstein, Richard, ed. *The Poetry of Rock*. New York: Bantam, 1968.

Mitchell, George. *Blow My Blues Away*. Baton Rouge, LA: Louisiana State University Press, 1971.

Morse, David, ed. *Grandfather Rock: The New Poetry*. New York: Dell, 1973.

Nicolas, A.X., ed. *The Poetry of Soul*. New York: Bantam, 1971.

Peck, Richard, ed. *Sounds and Silences*. New York: Dell, 1970.

Ryan, Betsy, ed. *Sounds of Silence*. New York: Scholastic Services, 1975.

MAGAZINES

Country Hits. Derby, CT: Charlton Publications, Inc.
Country Song Roundup. Derby, CT: Charlton Publications, Inc.
Hit Parader. Derby, CT: Charlton Publications, Inc.
Rock and Roll. New York: Lorelei Publishing Company.
Song Hits. Derby, CT: Charlton Publications, Inc.
Super Song Hits. Derby, CT: Charlton Publications, Inc.

ARTICLES

Ashby-Davis, Claire, and Robinson, Denise. "Teaching Poetry through Music and Dance." *Connecticut English Journal* (Spring 1979): 47–53.

Jackson, Dan, and Wirth, Debbie. "Confrontational Aesthetics: The Shotgun Wedding of Music and Poetry." *Media and Methods* (September 1979): 49–52.

Ruth, Leo. "The Scene." *English Journal* (February 1973): 293–304.

Wetherell, Nancy B. "Leonard Cohen: Poems Set to Music." *English Journal* (April 1973): 551–55.

Widoe, Russ, "Getting Enthused over Pop Music." *Media and Methods* (March 1980): 36–38.

Tease Teaching with Technology

by Harry MacCormack

The task of teaching involves excitement and enthusiasm as necessary elements. These forces often are lacking in classrooms, for teachers are in quiet competition with informational overloading as it is presented by television, movies, advertising, and the accompanying seductions of the high-speed, technological realities of the Space Age. Faced with this condition, yet charged with teaching poetry as a subject and as technique for communication, is it little wonder that teachers tend to question where poetic language fits into the scheme of things?

In a sense, though, the poet is a specialist in control communications, measuring with extreme care how words in context can kindle forgotten memories and force the recall of patterns perhaps more ancient than human consciousness. Poets probe the realms of subtlety and nuance, the undercurrent of languages. From these realms come bubbles of insight into the possibility of a more brilliant and precise usage of ordinary language. In this sense, poetic language becomes a sensing tool. There appear to be three major areas of concentration where these bubbles of insight can be developed: *perception, hearing,* and *context awareness.* All of these areas can be made accessible to students using technology already available.

When we enter the realm of *perception,* we enter the realm of the visual arts. Many of the techniques associated with classes in painting, technical lighting, symbology, etc., can be used effectively with poetry. For instance, the use of color wheels, available commercially from theater crafts houses, along with simple experiments in prismatic reflections and distortions, can stimulate students to become involved in the world of color. Slide shows organized to present the color intensities of such things as insects, birds, the galaxy, stones, costumes, and human architecture are a means for involving students in close observation. Once the involvement is achieved, then exercises in ''word painting'' can occur. These exercises are not merely descriptions of what has been seen. Rather, they rely on students' imaginations, with the emphasis on the creation of language color, using words to create in readers intense pictures, powerful enough to have impact in our visually oriented world.

One such exercise is to list ways in which a scene could be expressed; for instance, a confrontation between riot police and students: What colors might be involved? How many ways could those colors be achieved in word images? Another whole element in this training should expose the student to simple symbols: the circle (riot helmets encircling protestors), the square, the human body as a five-pointed star, the four directions, and colors as they are used for orientation in various cultures. Correct and intentionally misused colors offer still another whole area for exploration.

A second concern in perception training is that of object discrimination. Again, slides, movies, microscopes, or any visual-technological aid can be the teacher's tools for involving students in a familiar process, familiar only because in our time we are trained to believe that such hardware is a proper crutch for learning. Teachers might again develop competitive word-defining games to see how many different ways an object or a group of objects can be expressed. The point here is to help students see, in fresh, imaginative ways, the immediate "table and chairs world" which surrounds them daily, for it is through these material, physical considerations that poets develop their metaphysical considerations.

A third area of perception training has to do with the recognition of motions and/or actions. Within poems, poets make choices as to how objects will move in their particular work of art, usually through careful choices of verbs. There are ways to interest students in this process, to loosen their mind sets. Here one might want to make use of videotape techniques, taking a scene or situation and looking at each moving part—a cat walking, a rocket launching. With videotapes of such scenes, there can be reversals of actions of simultaneous showings of two different sorts of actions, creating a basis for surreality. With videotape loops, the element of visual repetition can be introduced. The teacher's responsibility is to continually relate this kind of technological exploration to intensity in poetic language building.

Even if one is charged with teaching poetry in a historical sense, some of these same techniques are useful. Whole environments can be created by selecting pictures, paintings, and maps from, say, Shelley's or Wordsworth's era. The same student exercises can be created, only concentrating upon what particular poets have chosen to use as they attempted to express the reality of their world.

A second major area of emphasis when teaching poetry concerns alerting the sense of *hearing*. It is in this area, usually taught as an introduction to the various metrical forms making up measured language or poetry, where many students seem to experience the most difficulty. But a teacher can alleviate at least some of the difficulty by turning once again to technological devices; in this case, the tape recorder becomes a simple tool for doing rhythmical experimentation.

Descriptive language of a heightened visual content can be placed on several tracks of tape. Using either a four-track system or four separate recorders which have been synchronized through a single starting switch, the language can be moved around a room space, through that space, starting in one part of the room and ending in another. A set of microphones placed on a disc suspended from the ceiling and whirled at various speeds can function as a mixing or switching station, creating extremely complicated verbal rhythms moving within a space. By using tape loops, reverberators, echo chambers, and other simple tape recorder techniques, students can explore the exciting possibilities of language manipulation through rhythmic and tonal control. And in the more traditional sense, tape recorders can alert students to the power in measured iambic feet, syllabics, or in the repetitive chants of other cultures as well as the rhyming techniques and other sound devices used by well-known poets. These all become more easily understood once the student has heard how the language can be modified, heightened, and made more intense by manipulation of rhythmic patterns within ordinary language.

From this point, it is just another step to the teaching of the forms, the couplets, tercets, and quatrains which are the foundations poured by each poet and poem. The trick is to allow the technology to act as the "tease factor" in teaching, for in our time, students are attracted to digital everythings as well as computer derived, coded, cataloged, and sorted materials. We must never forget that students we encounter in today's classrooms were raised collectively on the high energy teachings of 'Sesame Street" and "The Electric Company."

If you are fortunate enough to have a computer available, you can go still another step in introducing poetic languages. Computer-derived intensity in language can be very unusual and often very insightful. Coupled with tape loops, it can produce an awareness of heightened language which is often ceremonial or ritualistic in scope.

The third major area of concentration is that of *context awareness*. Putting together what is perceived and what is heard by a poet focuses a particular poem in a particular territory or locale—its context. An Allen Ginsberg poem is quite different in context from a piece by Elizabeth Barrett Browning. Often we rely upon classroom discussions to develop the context, but such discussions often become boring for both students and teachers if too much emphasis is placed on historical footnoting. Wouldn't it be more fun and create more understanding of a poem if it were recreated by bringing to life the environment of the poem?

This can be done simply by taking advantage of slide machines and tape recorders once again. Slides relevant to the poetic material would, of course, have to be carefully selected. Usually two to four slide projectors are enough to create the necessary effect. These projections are then "cross-fired" within a circular or elliptical environment of white muslin or some other white material. At the same time, the language of the poem is played on two to four simultaneous tape recorders, with the language being moved creatively throughout the visual environment. The participant within this sound and light environment gets to experience something like what was happening to the poet during the creative process. In this way the context of the poem becomes an intense human experience, even surpassing the powerful environments of television, movies, or sports events. Taking the poem from the page and placing it back into a total environment which establishes an appropriate context brings many poems to life for students and comes close to providing the total experience which every poet hopes to achieve.

"Tease teaching" of the type described here has the effect in the classroom of placing an equally shared amount of resource responsibility upon students and teachers. The teacher becomes the knowledgeable resource person, directing students to books, materials, paintings, etc. relevant to a particular day's or week's work. The teacher is also the one who does the structuring, carefully choosing what students' exposure to poetry will achieve, for in the end, it is not the passing of tests on poetic content or form which generates a poet to write or a student to appreciate what has been written. Instead, it is the shared excitement in being better able to express meaning with the world drama. As Mallarme put it, "to purify the dialect of the tribe" is the poet's task. It may also be that the poet is the most precise speaker of human history as it evolves on Earth. To transfer an appreciation of the poetic process is vitally important. If that transfer can be made continually new and fun, directly involving students, all the better. The technology is available to us. Like other poetic tools, it is loaded with tricks, but tricks that we as teachers should learn to use to our advantage and that of our students.

Keats, Stevens, and Picasso: Designing Audiovisual Poetry Presentations

by Michael Cohen

Audiovisual displays using poetry and other art forms can be useful in poetry courses and general humanities courses, for they help to show the ways in which poems connect with the rest of experience. Since such displays are intended for out-of-class use, they do not need to be stringently tied to unit objectives, and they can have rather modest aims. They are also surprisingly easy to design. The two scripts below are offered as models for such displays, and they show the variation that is possible in poem selection, treatment, and goals. One display uses a poem from the traditional canon of favorites (Keats' "Ode on a Grecian Urn") while the other's subject is a more modern poem some might consider less accessible: Wallace Stevens's "The Man with the Blue Guitar." The Keats selection is treated in a fairly basic exposition approaching a complete gloss of the poem, while the Stevens exhibit uses a freer, more heuristic and interdisciplinary approach. The Keats display asks the students to write a statement of the poem's theme once they have finished viewing; the Stevens asks for a statement connecting the display with the themes of the course. These are only two of many ways of eliciting student response, and more specific testing questions could be used with either kind of display.

Each presentation requires a small display area for printed materials (approximately 2½ by 2 feet), a recorded audio cassette, and several 35mm slides (a descriptive list follows each script below). Prominently marked directions are needed to tell the students what to do first; after the tape player is switched on, recorded directions can tell them what to do next. Slides and cassettes can be conveniently handled together in carousel-type projectors, but any small cassette player and separate magnifying slide viewer will serve instead. The printed display materials for these scripts include the complete text of Keats's "Ode on a Grecian Urn," but only six representative cantos from Stevens's "The Man with the Blue Guitar." After the students have read the materials, switched on the tape and listened to the script, and simultaneously viewed the slides, they are asked to write a response in notebooks provided within the display area.

Script for an Audiovisual Display of Keats's "Ode on a Grecian Urn"

TURN ON THE SLIDE VIEWER AND LOOK AT THE FIRST SLIDE FOR A MINUTE OR TWO. THEN TURN ON THE TAPE PLAYER. [These directions must be displayed prominently, along with the complete text of the "Ode on a Grecian Urn."]

The vase you are looking at is a Greek design and is called an *urn*. The poet John Keats was so impressed with the sculptured figures on such an urn that he wrote the following poem. In it he speaks directly *to* the urn and later in the poem, to some of the figures carved upon it.

[READING OF "ODE ON A GRECIAN URN"]

Some of the vocabulary of the poem may be unfamiliar to you. Look at the printed poem and notice its line numbers on the right side. Keats calls the urn a *sylvan* historian in line 3; *sylvan* means forest or woods. He talks about the scene being in *Tempe* or the *dales of Arcady* in line 7—these are rural places in Greece considered to be ideal for their beauty. The pipes and timbrels at the end of the first stanza (line 10) are small wind instruments like flutes and small percussion instruments like tambourines. In the second stanza, in line 13, Keats tells the pipes to play on, not to the *sensual* ear—that is, the physical ear—but to pipe to the spirit, and to play "ditties of no tone" (line 14)—that is, simple songs which, since they are only depicted on the silent vase and not real, are soundless, with no tone. In the third stanza, near the end, the word *cloyed* appears in line 29, when Keats says that ordinary human passion leaves the heart *cloyed*, or oversatisfied, having had too much. And finally, in the last stanza, Keats calls the urn an *Attic* shape in line 41; this means a shape from Attica, or Athens, where the style of objects like this was very simple and graceful. He also says in lines 41 and 42 that the urn is "with *brede* of marble men and maidens *over-wrought*," or in other words, worked over with a pattern or design of marble men and maidens.

It has long been common practice for poets to write about a work of art that has impressed them. Keats might have seen this vase in books of engravings which were available at the time he wrote the poem, but, whether he saw it or not, it is a typical and elaborate example of the type. There are leaf decorations along the top, a figure with pipes and another with a timbrel, and in the center of the part of the vase you can see a "bold lover" and a "maiden loth," that is, unwilling or reluctant.

ADVANCE THE NEXT SLIDE [pause for at least 5 seconds]

We know of Keats's interest in Greek urns not only from this poem, but also from a drawing of another vase in the Louvre museum (and again, one that had been depicted in engravings for sale in England). The Sosibios vase is also "leaf-fringed," and almost out of the picture to one side is a young man with pipes. The Sosibios vase seems to depict some sort of religious procession, but it is nothing like that described by Keats in his fourth stanza.

ADVANCE THE NEXT SLIDE [pause for at least 5 seconds]

There are urns which have scenes of sacrifice on them, and an example is this vase which was in Holland House in London and also depicted in books of engravings. This vase shows a group of people preparing for a traditional sacrifice of a pig, a sheep, and a bull.

[pause 5 seconds]

Although Keats may have had a specific urn in mind when he wrote the poem, it is more likely that what impressed him was what the urn accomplished in recording such scenes. For this reason, you should pay special attention not only to Keats's descriptions of scenes in stanzas one and four, but in what he says about art and time in stanzas two, three and five.

TURN OFF THE TAPE RECORDER AND FOLLOW THE INSTRUCTIONS PRINTED BELOW THE POEM.

YOU MAY LISTEN TO THE TAPE AND LOOK AT THE SLIDES MORE THAN ONCE IF YOU WISH. BEFORE YOU LEAVE:

Find the notebook for your section and after signing your name:

1. In a paragraph state what you think is the main point of Keats's poem. Don't just copy the last two lines; think about the whole poem.
2. If you have already seen the other poetry display, tell which one you prefer and why.

Approximate time 9:00 minutes.

Slides:
1. A photograph of the Borghese Vase (Louvre).
2. A line drawing of the Sosibios Vase (Louvre) attributed to Keats.
3. A Piranesi engraving of the Holland House Urn.

Script for an Audio-Visual Display of Stevens's "The Man with the Blue Guitar"*

TURN ON THE SLIDE VIEWER AND LOOK AT THE FIRST SLIDE FOR A FEW MINUTES. THEN TURN ON THE TAPE PLAYER. [These directions must be displayed prominently, along with an open copy of *The Collected Poems of Wallace Stevens,* Alfred A. Knopf, Inc., 1954, in which cantos 1, 2, 5, 6, 15 and 25 of "The Man with the Blue Guitar" have been marked.]

The painting you are looking at is Picasso's *The Old Guitarist,* painted in 1903. It was part of an exhibition Wallace Stevens attended the year before he wrote the poem in front of you, "The Man with the Blue Guitar." The poem is a long one . . . in fact, it has 33 of these numbered stanzas, which are called *cantos.* We've only included six of these cantos here. Turn off the tape player and read through Canto One slowly and carefully. Then turn the player back on.

[pause for 10 seconds]

Wallace Stevens begins his poem with a line that indicates he might be describing the painting: "The man bent over his guitar." But then things get complicated. He says the guitar player is a *shearsman,* and he also says that the day was *green.* Let's come back to these statements after we look at the rest of the canto.

People talk to the guitarist and ask him to play a tune of things exactly as they are . . . they also say he has a blue guitar and doesn't play things as

---

*Excerpts from Canto VI and Canto XXV are reprinted by permission of Alfred A. Knopf, Inc., from *The Collected Poems of Wallace Stevens.* Copyright © 1954 by Wallace Stevens.

they are. This may be puzzling at first, because we don't ordinarily ask a *musician* to describe the world for us—to *play* things as they are—though we may very well make such a request or demand of a photographer, a painter, a story writer . . . or a poet: "Show us the world as it is." At the same time, we seem to want a little more from our artists: we want "things as they are," but we also want some inspiration, some view of things we hadn't seen before or things as they might be with a bit of imagination. Stevens's way of saying all this is, "we want a tune" (he might have said a picture or a poem) "Beyond us, yet ourselves."

And now we can come back to the line describing the guitarist as a shearsman and the day as green. We can't understand these lines if they are just talking about a man with a guitar. But Stevens is talking about other kinds of art too—especially painting and poetry. Days aren't ordinarily green . . . or guitars blue, for that matter. But *pictures* have colored backgrounds . . . occasionally even green backgrounds . . . so that in a picture it might make sense to say the day was green. But what if we tried to photograph such a picture with a camera which had a blue lens? Wouldn't it come out blue? Wouldn't things be changed on the blue camera? In Picasso's picture, everything *is blue*, except for the guitar. Everything has been made blue by the artist's vision . . . except for the guitar itself. Both Picasso and Stevens use musical instruments to represent the way artists look at the world.

But what does Stevens mean when he says the guitarist is a *shearsman*? Well, *shears* or scissors cut . . . they cut away the unnecessary, and they also cut to refashion things into other shapes, as a tailor does. Stevens talks about "patching" things in the next canto, and in one of his letters he says that a tailor was what he had in mind when he used this word.

Let's stop for a moment to consider a question which might have occurred to you during the previous discussion—namely, "Why would an artist want to look at things through something so distorting as a blue lens?" Why, to put it another way, doesn't Picasso show us things and people as we ordinarily see them, instead of in strange shapes and colors?

First it might be a good idea to point out that Picasso does not paint the pictures he does because he isn't able to draw well; as the next slide shows, he is very capable of giving us the kind of art we may be more used to.

ADVANCE THE NEXT SLIDE [pause for 5 seconds]

But many of his paintings are even odder than *The Blue Guitarist*. Look, for example, at the next slide, which is a picture of Picasso's daughter with a doll.

ADVANCE THE NEXT SLIDE [pause for 5 seconds]

It is a disturbing picture, certainly not showing us "things as they are" in any usual sense. The face is especially strange; it is as if we saw the face through a prism, or from several different views at once, and there is a very unlifelike green cast to it as well. Why did Picasso paint this picture this way?

Picasso said that at a certain point in his life he realized "that painting had an intrinsic value, detached from any actual portrayal of objects. I asked myself," he said, "if one shouldn't rather portray things as one knows them than as one sees them." The difference between these two— things as one knows them and things as one sees them—may not be clear to you right away, but perhaps a child's drawing will help to make the difference clearer.

ADVANCE THE NEXT SLIDE [pause for 5 seconds]

What the child has done in his drawing is to show us both ends of the house at once. We know that we cannot see both ends at once, but the child *knows both ends are there* and has drawn them. He has also drawn the fence all the way around the house, even though we could not see part of that fence if we had the view of the front of the house which he shows us. He has drawn, not what he *sees* in one view of the house, but what *he knows about it*. To go back to Picasso's picture of his daughter, we know if we can't see both eyes of a face at the same time we are looking at a profile of it. But we also know that both views of the face are *there*. We even know that they are both necessary; that we can't really see what a person is like unless we have both views. That's what's behind the police photos of wanted criminals.

ADVANCE THE NEXT SLIDE [pause for 5 seconds]

One photo can't give us both views at once; we need two. Picasso is merely saying, "Why can't I give you both at once? After all, this isn't a photograph. It's my painting, and I can show you what I know about the subject, even if it's not what you would see standing in one spot." Another modern painter has expressed this idea: when a lady visiting his studio said, "But surely, the arm of this woman is much too long," the artist replied, "Madam, you are mistaken. This is not a woman; this is a picture."

In fact, people ask for more from their pictures, poems, songs, and other works of art then merely showing things "as they are." Stevens shows us this in cantos five and six. Turn off the tape player and read through these cantos slowly. Then turn the player back on.

Once again in these cantos we have the people speaking to the guitarist, although now Stevens does not conceal that he is talking about poetry as well as song, music, tunes. They say first that they don't wish to hear about the greatness of poetry, and then they describe their own world—there are no shadows, day is desire and night is sleep, the earth is flat and bare. Poetry, they say, must take the place of empty heaven and its hymns. Their world is plain and uninteresting; they want more, "A tune beyond us, yet ourselves," as they said in the first canto, but here things are more specific about what is wanted "beyond us."

> Ourselves in the tune as if in space,
> Yet nothing changed, except the place
> Of things as they are and only the place
> As you play them, on the blue guitar,
> Placed so, beyond the compass of change. . . .

These are difficult lines, but the last one is a little clearer than the others. The speakers want things in the poem or tune "beyond the compass of change"—one of the things that's wrong with their world is its *change*. Nothing lasts, people die too soon, nothing stays the same. It would be nice to have things a little more stable, and that's one of the things art does—it can create a world where things seem final and unchangeable:

> Placed so, beyond the compass of change,
> Perceived in a final atmosphere;
>
> For a moment final, in the way
> The thinking of art seems final when
>
> The thinking of god is smoky dew.

Art at least *seems* to be something more permanent than the world and people—that is, the thinking, or creation, of god. More than one poet or philosopher has said that life is short but art is long.

Perhaps we can summarize some of the things that have been said and hinted at in as much of the poem as we have read. What is "The Man with the Blue Guitar" about? Well, it's about poetry: "Poetry is the subject of the poem," Stevens says in Canto 22. But it's also about music and painting. It's about art.

It's about the world depicted by art—what the people talking to the guitarist call "things as they are." It's about what art *must* do—that is, change "things as they are" a little or a lot in order to depict them. And it's also about what art ought to be able to do, according to those who speak to the guitarist—depict a world which is somehow more interesting, different but not too different, and perhaps unchanging—they ask quite a lot from the guitarist.

Since we can't possibly include all of the poem's 33 cantos, it may be best to finish with one which shows something else about art—namely, that it's play. After all, we've been taking the rest of the poem horribly seriously. So this is Canto 25, where Stevens's guitarist becomes a kind of circus juggler, twirling the whole world like a ball on his nose. And while this is going on, what do the inhabitants of this world think about it? Nothing. They don't even know it's going on. The cats move in the grass, and have other cats, and the grass turns gray, and the guitarist plays his song:

> He held the world upon his nose
> And this-a-way he gave a fling.
>
> His robes and symbols, ai-yi-yi—
> And that-a-way he twirled the thing.
>
> Sombre as fir-trees, liquid cats
> Moved in the grass without a sound.
>
> They did not know the grass went round.
> The cats had cats and the grass turned gray
>
> And the world had worlds, ai, this-a-way:
> The grass turned green and the grass turned gray.
>
> And the nose is eternal, that-a-way.
> Things as they were, things as they are,
>
> Things as they will be by and by . . .
> A fat thumb beats out ai-yi-yi.

Turn off the tape recorder now and follow the directions outlined in front of you.

You may listen to the presentation more than once.

BEFORE YOU LEAVE:

Find the notebook for your class section and after signing you name:

1. Explain in a paragraph what you think this display has to do with the themes for this course which were outlined on the syllabus.

2. If you have already seen the other poetry display, tell which one you liked better and why.

Approximate time 13:00 minutes.

Slides:

1. Picasso, *The Old Guitarist* (1903), Art Institute of Chicago.
2. Picasso, *The Lovers* (neo-classical period), National Gallery of Art, Washington.
3. Picasso, *Maia* [the artist's daughter] *with Sailor Doll* (1938), Collection of the artist.
4. A child's drawing showing three sides of a house, after plate 10 in Miriam Lindstrom, *Children's Art* (Berkeley, Los Angeles, and London: University of California Press, 1957).
5. An FBI "Wanted" poster with full-face and profile photographs.

When these scripts were tested in an interdisciplinary humanities course, the students showed a slight preference for the Stevens display. They also demonstrated that even so brief an exposure to the poems enabled them to write a competent short statement of theme. A typical example: "In Keats's poem, 'Ode on a Grecian Urn,' he explains the everlasting impression on a Grecian Urn. In one passage two lovers are about to kiss. They are caught in time, never aging, never changing, beauty in its perfection. The main topic of the poem is that of everlasting beauty and truth." There were also perceptive comments which went beyond a simple statement of theme, as in the following: "Art defines eternal truth more precisely than science or religion. Stevens is trying to make a point about there being no absolute truth, and art is the most effective means for defining truth. Truth depends upon where you are at and what time it is. Without art we survive, with art we live."

The value of such audiovisual demonstrations depends on students, who need encouragement to use them thoughtfully and to repeat the presentations as often as necessary until they are understood. The presentations themselves need to be carefully planned so that they address the objectives of the course and unit. These models are presented in the hope they will prove adaptable to different courses and purposes.

Approaching Poetry through Film

by Robert A. Armour

One examination period a number of years ago when I was still a novice teacher, I included a question that asked the students to discuss the poetic qualities of a particular poem (I've long forgotten which one). In my innocence in the profession, I was surprised at their inability to describe what a poem was. After I had thought about it for a bit, however, I came to realize that this was a difficult question and ever since then I have been trying to devise methods for teaching the essence of poetry. The problem is complicated by the fact that we use the word *poetic* to characterize poetic qualities in objects that are not poems—a poetic painting, a poetic passage in a novel, a poetic movement in sports. Clearly poetry has qualities that are applicable to other media, but the literary problem is to isolate those qualities in poetry itself and by doing so to understand more of the poetic experience. One means of accomplishing this goal is to compare another poetic medium, such as film, with poetry to demonstrate that the poetic qualities of that other medium can identify the essence of poetry itself and help students appreciate those qualities that make it distinctive. Film is an especially appropriate medium for this exploration since in some ways, it is aesthetically close to poetry.

This article will discuss ways of using film to examine the essential qualities of poetry. It outlines a unit on poetry and film that can easily be shaped by individual teachers to class level and available time. The theory has been tested in classrooms from elementary schools through universities and has proven to be both effective and enjoyable. The elements of the unit are a good, basic definition of poetry and short films suitable for classroom use. A teacher may create a definition just for this exercise, but that found in any reliable dictionary of literary terms will do. Since *A Handbook to Literature* by William Flint Thrall, Addison Hibbard, and C. Hugh Holman (Darby, PA: Darby Books, 1980; hereafter referred to with all respect as THH) is both excellent and readily available, this essay is based on its definition of poetry; but of course no teacher need be slavish in adherence to anyone else's definition and will naturally take whatever liberties are necessary to reach an understanding of the essence of poetry. THH divide their discussion of poetry into four parts: content, form, classification, and effect—units that will serve to organize this essay. The films used here to illustrate the points are usually easily available to teachers. Most can be borrowed from local audiovisual centers or rented fairly cheaply from distributors. Most are based on poems, but all films need not have poetic sources in order for the unit to work. If the films do have poetic sources, however, the element of analysis is added to the exercise, in which case the teacher can use the filmmaker's interpretation of the poem as a means of discussing one person's view of what the poem means. The films mentioned in this essay are intended only to illustrate the methods proposed. I have found them useful in my own classrooms, but a teacher who spends a few hours in a local audiovisual center is likely to uncover other selections that will make the same points just as well.

THH first characterize the content of poetry to distingish it from the content of other types of creative literature. They write that poetry is emotional, which I translate into an effort to understand the emotional mood of a poem. Let us take two emotions to illustrate the point. *The New York Hat,* a short, silent film made in 1912 by D. W. Griffith, was not based on a poem, but on a screenplay by Anita Loos, and starred Mary Pickford in her first movie. It well illustrates the mood of sentiment, since it deals with a girl's attachment to a new hat and the trouble she and her benefactor get into when local denizens believe he bought her the hat for impure reasons. The film provides an excellent opportunity to define sentiment and to compare its usage with the sentiment in nineteenth-century poetry. As THH point out, sentiment is often coupled with passion, an emotion perhaps that need not be demonstrated for modern students, but they probably do need to have its literary use explained. An ironic view of passion can be found in *Naming of the Parts,* a short film based on a poem by Henry Reid in which a young soldier daydreams about nature, life, and sex while a drill instructor lectures him on the use of a rifle to kill the enemy. Both men are passionate about the things that are important to them, but those things vary greatly.

Next THH tell us that the content of poetry is imaginative, that the poet does not use "the language of science." It is the task of the poet to "tease us out of thought" through the use of images that inspire our imagination. The filmmaker has the same purpose. In the brief film presenting a haiku, *The Day Is Two Feet Long,* the filmmaker uses visual images to tickle our imagination into considering mortality. The poem

> The mud snail
> crawls two or three feet
> and the day is over

establishes the theme for the film while the visuals present both the passing of a day from morning to evening and the passing of the seasons. The imagination of the poet combines with the imagination of the filmmaker to stimulate the imagination of the viewer.

Poetry, according to THH, must also contain "elements of truth, thought, idea, meaning" and must significantly "contribute to the store of human knowledge or experience." This does not mean that poems, or films for that matter, must necessarily be didactic, but it does mean that they should contain insights into the nature of life and the essence of what it is to be human. *Jabberwocky*, a short film by Czechoslovakian Jan Svankmajer, is based on Lewis Carroll's poem and contains an exploration of one of the most basic human experiences—growing up. The poem, as we all remember, describes a boy's imaginative encounter with a monster, his victory over it, and his mother's celebration of his independence. The film presents this same theme but expands it to include not one, but several encounters with childhood monsters that must be overcome: birth, toys, school, the opposite sex. Its final statement seems to be that growing up is inevitable but not necessarily much fun.

According to THH, poetry is also marked with power, the power of passion which comes from the depth of feeling. This characteristic can be illustrated by a remarkable film, *The Hangman*, based on a poem by Maurice Ogden. The poem and film relate the anguish of a man who refuses to speak out when the hangman comes to his town and begins persecuting his fellow citizens. The Black, the foreigner, the Jew are taken away without the man's protest; finally when the hangman comes for the man, no one else is left to protest for him. The hangman laughs and tells him that all the earlier executions were simply practice for this, the most important one. The desperation and despair of the victim leave the viewer deeply moved, perhaps even shaken and touched with personal guilt.

The content of poetry is, of course, often marked by beauty; but the nature of beauty depends on the perceptions of the poet or the filmmaker. The aesthetics of both media can be illustrated through some comparisons. For instance, the film *Morning on the Lievre* is a visual version of a poem by the nineteenth-century Canadian poet Archibald Lampman. Both works describe the beauty of the coming day along a river, and students might be asked to consider the source of the beauty of the images in both media and to determine why they think certain images beautiful. They might speculate on ways their perceptions of beauty vary depending on the medium. Or the students might be shown more than one film and asked to contrast the beauty of the images in each; *Morning on the Lievre* can be contrasted with *Autumn: Frost Country*, which provides visual images of New England to complement the reading of two well-known Robert Frost poems.

While the content of films can ably be used to illustrate and explain the elements of the content of poetry, the most rewarding of all exercises is to compare the technique of poetry with the technique of film. In discussing the form of poetry, THH focus on three elements of technique that give poetry its distinctive form: rhythm, imagery, and language. All three have their cinematic analogies which can be used to teach their poetic counterparts. Rhythm in film results from the visual rhythm of the images photographed (for instance, a child toddling after its mother); the aural rhythm of the soundtrack (music, horse hooves, gunfire, and so on); and the rhythm of editing that places particular shots next to each other for effect (called montage in earlier film criticism). In 1936 Leni Riefenstahl made *Olympia*, a film about the Munich Olympics that included a now-famous diving sequence (available today for rent as an excerpt or as part of the complete film). The rhythm of the sequence is one of the most remarkable traits of the film. At the beginning of the sequence, Riefenstahl edited the shots to create a sense of quickness through fast music and brief dives off the lower diving board which toward the end change into a slower rhythm as the dives off the platform become longer and the music more sublime. The result is that the fast pace of the opening slows into a deliberate one that provides the audience the opportunity to contemplate the majesty of the athletes' feats.

Next THH discuss the importance of poetic images. Those looking for a useful explanation of imagery in poetry should turn to William Faulkner's *The Bear*. The boy, Ike, is asked by his cousin McCaslin what Keats meant when he wrote "Forever wilt thou love, and she be fair." When the boy tells him, "He's talking about a girl," McCaslin replies, "He had to talk about something." Poets have to talk about something concrete and specific to make whatever points they have in mind and that something is called an image. Filmmakers have the same problem: they have to photograph something. In the Odessa Steps sequence from *Potempkin* (also available in both an excerpted version and in the complete feature-length film), Sergi Eisenstein wanted to show the brutality of the Tzar's troops in dispersing the supporters of the rebellion. As the troops march down the steps firing, the camera gives the audience images of a woman's face as she screams, of a baby carriage rolling down the steps out of control, and of a man's face in agony. It shows us the rifles and the Cossack's horses, and finally the destruction of statues of lions representing the government as they are shelled by the rebels on board the ship in the nearby harbour. When edited together, the images leave the audience with the impression of the horror of war which indiscriminately butchers women, children, and old men. Students might be asked to consider the different effects rendered by the written images of poetry and the visual and aural images of cinema. The case might be made that the written images require more imagination on the part of the audience, but it should be shown that a good filmmaker does not reveal too much of his images and forces the viewers to finish the images for themselves.

The last determining element of poetry's form is language. Since the language of film is visual, it naturally works differently than the language of poetry, which is made up of words. The difference can be amusingly demonstrated by a film such as *Enter Hamlet,* which illustrates the spoken words of the "To be or not to be" soliloquy with visual drawings. The pop art paintings make visual puns on the words of the text: for example, when the narrator says that "Conscience doth make cowards of us all," a hand appears from out of a washing machine holding a box of detergent appropriately labeled ALL. Rarely, however, do filmmakers attempt to make such literal use of poetic language; most often the similarity between poetic and cinematic use of language lies in metaphors. The opening images of Leni Riefenstahl's *Triumph of the Will* (also available as an excerpt or as a complete film) show Adolf Hitler's plane descending through the clouds into the cheering crowds of Nuremberg. The effect of the images—both aural and visual—is to make it appear that another Norse god has descended to his people. This use of metaphor for propagandistic as well as cinematic purposes is an excellent introduction to the subject of figurative language in both media.

In addition to the form and content, THH also briefly treat the types of poetry, with an emphasis on the epic, the dramatic, and the lyric. Film can be used to illustrate the characteristics of these sub-genres, especially if we read "narrative poetry" for THH's "epic." Several of the films mentioned in the body of this essay contain elements of the narrative, but *The Hangman* and *The New York Hat* are the clearest examples of narrative techniques. *Jabberwocky* and *Naming of the Parts* are both based on dramatic poems and assume their characteristics. Lyric poetry forms the basis for such films as *The Day Is Two Feet Long, Morning on the Lievre,* and *Autumn: Frost Country.* When a film is taken from a literary source, the genre of that source helps determine the shape of the genre of the film: A lyric poem will make a different sort of film than will a dramatic one. This principle can be used in the classroom to explore the nature of both poetic and cinematic genres.

Finally, THH conclude their unit on poetry by discussing the effect of poetry: "Whatever the immediate appeal, the ultimate effect of poetry is giving pleasure." This classroom unit might well conclude with an examination of the effects of the two media in order to determine how pleasure is derived from each. What types of pleasure can each stimulate? Are there other worthy effects of either medium?

One obvious response to this teaching unit is to question the necessity for using films to teach poetry, which is usually a self-sufficient medium. A teacher might legitimately ask, "Why not use poetry to teach poetry?" And, of course, it should be used; this unit assumes that the students are reading poetry. Nevertheless, for the teacher of poetry, film is an auxiliary to be employed to provide a different approach to poetic characteristics. Sometimes it is necessary to explain difficult literary concepts in more than one way, and film offers a method for explanation that will be novel enough to hold student attention and pedagogically sound enough to provide fresh insights. One final unsolicited advantage of this unit is that students are likely to become more intelligent viewers of film while learning to understand poetry, a secondary goal that increases the appeal of the unit.

Filmography

Autumn: Frost Country. BFA, 9 minutes, color, 1969.

The Day Is Two Feet Long. Weston Woods, 9 minutes, color, 1965.

Enter Hamlet. Pyramid, 4 minutes, color, 1967.

The Hangman. Contemporary/McGraw Hill, 12 minutes, color, 1963.

Jabberwocky. Weston Woods, 14 minutes, color, 1973.

Morning on the Lievre. Encyclopedia Britannica Educational Corporation, 14 minutes, color, 1964.

Naming of the Parts. Contemporary/McGraw-Hill, 5 minutes, black and white, 1972.

The New York Hat. Museum of Modern Art, 12 minutes, black and white, 1912.

Olympia. Museum of Modern Art; Part 1, 119 minutes; Part II, 96 minutes; black and white, 1938.

Potempkin. Museum of Modern Art, 67 minutes, black and white, 1925.

Triumph of the Will. Museum of Modern Art, 110 minutes, black and white, 1934.

Poetry Readers: Publishing Student Writing*

by Diane P. Shugert

There is a sense in which a writer does not exist unless his work is published. Even Thomas Gray's "mute inglorious Milton" exists for us only because Gray took the time and trouble to think about him, to record the thought, and to publish what had been recorded. Anyone who writes or who has worked closely with a writer knows that sense of satisfaction, that sense of making the unreal and ephemeral into something real and permanent, which is associated with seeing one's writing printed and distributed to the world.

No matter what we study in our classes, we tend to have students do a lot of writing. If we ourselves are writers, we get students to write poems like the poems we are reading, to re-create the forms we study. If we are critics, we get students to write criticism, to analyze the forms. Why not, then, take these writings a step further? Why not shape the topics a bit more, keeping an audience in mind and aiming at some specific format for publication?

As students prepare their writings for publication, they learn some things that cannot, I think, be taught in any other way. They learn to care for what they write and to revise, edit, and proofread it. They experience (rather than merely imagine) audience response. Above all, they come into being as writers; a part of their identities is defined as "Me, writer." We know about the adolescent search for self-definition, for an identity. We can help young adults to find that identity as writers and thereby to connect what they do in English class with the deepest needs of their own personalities.

---

*This essay is unedited and is reprinted here from *Connecticut English Journal* (Spring 1979).

If publication is to serve those needs for all of our students, however, we must revise a few of our ideas about it. We have to get away from the limits of the school literary magazine or the school newspaper. Only a few students can publish there, and we want *all* the students to publish. Furthermore, school publications retain some slight flavor of officialdom, of the assignment, of doing the right thing. We want to emphasize real audiences who might actually be pleased to read what our students have written. By doing so we help students to move from satisfying the teacher to communicating with the reader.

Here are two outlines of publishing projects. The first would take several weeks to carry out and might serve as a culminating project for a poetry criticism unit. The second is much shorter, almost a casual project, but it still reaches an audience and can have many of the advantages of longer projects wthout requiring so much time to complete.

Critical Anthology of Poetry

Grades: 10–12

Topic: Make an anthology of eight or more poems—your own and others'—all on a single theme. (Maximum of two poems from records.) Write a foreword for the anthology explaining why you chose these poems and how each poem relates to the theme. Create a title for the anthology. You may illustrate it if you wish.

Audiences: The student himself. Or any person the student chooses. Or future classes. Save the anthologies to add to books kept in the classroom. (Student chooses which option.)

Publication format: Hand-bound book. Student chooses binding method appropriate to his interest and investment in project.

Procedures: Special lessons and materials will be needed on forewords, anthologies, and bindings. Class divided into editorial boards of five students. Each student's foreword, choices, format must be critiqued by the other four. Have a publishing day when all completed books can be read and shared by whole class.

Other comments: It is assumed that students have been reading and writing poems and that there are many appropriate, professional poetry collections available in the classroom.

One Liners

Grades: 7–9

Topic: What are some saying about money? (A fool and his money are soon
    parted, etc. Elicit from class.) Let's make up some crazy—or very
    true—sayings about money. Perhaps some of them will be variations
    on well-known sayings. (Money is the root of all evil, but trees without
    roots bear no fruit.)

Audience: Customers of the local bank.

Publication format: (1) Dittoed or mimeographed individually on small
    pieces of paper along with author's name (maybe a crazy pen name)
    and class. (2) Or collected onto a single sheet folded into thirds with
    title and class on cover. (3) To be distributed to bank customers along
    with receipts and cash *or* in bank statements.

Procedures: Editorial work aimed at honing the sayings, deciding
    on title (for the collection), and proofreading.

Other comments: Bank might well be talked into paying for nice looking
    printing.

The following are brief suggestions concerning formats, topics, potential audiences, and funding and a few tips on getting students to do the
necessary revisions. For more ideas see any of the materials published by
the Poets-in-the-Schools Programs (available from state Commissions on
the Arts and from the National Council of Teachers of English) or *The
Whole Word Catalog* (Teachers and Writers Collaborative, 186 West 4th
St., New York, NY 10014).

Formats

Short things:
Supermarket grocery bags
Small pieces of paper distributed
    1. with lunch in the cafeteria
    2. at the bank
    3. with report cards

    4. with office passes and tardy slips
    5. at the book fair
    6. under windshield wipers in the parking lot
    7. at sports events
    8. in unexpected places around the school
Bumper stickers
Post cards
Backs/fronts of envelopes
Book covers
Insert pages for looseleaf notebooks
Graffiti wall

Collections and longer things:
Slips of paper in decorated envelopes
Newsletter to class's parents (See David W. England, "Hearing from the
    Teacher When Nothing Is Wrong," *English Journal,* September
    1977, p. 45.)
Informal school or class newspaper (See Emily Strong, "Give Them a
    Reason To Write: Launching the Informal School Newspaper," *En-
    lish Journal,* May 1977, pp. 37–40.)
Index cards collected in boxes
Hand-bound books
Offset printed folders
Dittoed booklets, stapled with print-shop covers

Topics

Short things:
Original aphorisms
Crazy "facts"
Fortunes
"Clean" graffiti
Fictitious quotations
Cliché and metaphor exercises
Limericks
Wacky definitions
Short poems of all kinds
Imaginative school rules

Longer things:
Collections of any of the shorter things

Research reports on language in the community, folklore, etc. (See *Foxfire* series.)
Reviews of top 40 records, albums, movies, TV shows, books, magazines
Results of surveys to determine top 40, etc.
Reviews of school assignments
Biographies of community residents, family, school people, each other
Teen-age travel information
Reports and samples of any class activities
Single-copy anthologies with critical prefaces
Children's books

Potential Audiences

Members of the class
Relatives of class members
The whole school
Younger children
Customers of a particular business
Another class in same school
Another class in another school
Another school
Citizens of the community
Just one person

Money

Publishing is *not* very expensive. $25–$100 goes a very long way.
Mini-grants. Possible sources: the school, parents' organizations, local merchant(s), arts council, charitable organization.
Sales. Sell a few of the things for 25¢ or 50¢ a copy.
Patron. If your class has written something that a merchant or hospital or the town office can really use, ask the user for enough money to cover costs.

Revising Tips

Publish everyone's work, but insist that work be revised until it's suitable.
Create student editorial boards. Give the boards fancy names and real responsibilities.

Ask members of the potential audience to comment and criticize before
final printing.

Ask a variety of local experts (local printer, college teacher, teacher from
another school, bank officer) to assist as guest editors.

Finally, let me return to the format used in the Critical Anthology of
Poetry: the hand-bound, single copy book. This format is an especially
valuable one because it permits each student to publish very personal
materials. It requires an audience of only one person; therefore the student
can concentrate on communicating exactly what he or she wants to the one
person who is the student's best audience. Love poems can be collected for
lovers; poems on adolescent *angst* can be collected for parents; a whole
class's work can be assembled for the library. In the hand-bound book,
though, format is everything: the book when completed must look and feel
like a book, not a kindergarten construction paper project. The feel and look
of a real book are accomplished by using a true bookbinding stitch and by
adopting some of the techniques used by professional bookbinders.

Basic Bookbinding

All typing, writing and printing must be done in advance of binding.
This means that the whole book must be planned and "printed" before
assembling. To get some idea of spacing, "print" a dummy copy first.

Materials: sheets of paper (for text); 1 sheet of different paper—same size
as text paper (for endpapers); cloth strip (for hinge) 1.5"–3" wide; cardboard pieces (for boards); adhesive paper, wrapping paper, or cloth (for
covers); thread; needle; glue; waxed paper.

Preparing and sewing the signature: (Work with book open.)
1. Fold pages in half. Put one inside the other. End paper should be on
   outside. (This group of pages is called a *signature*.)
2. Crease pages to make a sharp, fine fold.
3. Cut strip of cloth for hinge 1"–1.5" shorter than fold of signature.
   Fold in half lengthwise, crease, and center on outside of signature
   fold.
4. Make holes (3 or 5 holes, depending on size of book) through signature
   and hinge at fold. Holes about 2" apart. First hole exactly in center.
   Second and third holes equidistant on either side of center hole.
5. Sewing *three* holes: 1st stitch: Insert needle with single thread through
   center hole from inside of signature to outside of hinge, leaving at least 4"

thread "tail." 2nd stitch: Sew from outside hinge to inside signature through next hole. 3rd stitch: Bring thread along inner fold to hole on other side of center hole. Sew from inside to outside. 4th stitch: Sew through center hole again, this time from outside to inside. (See figure 1)

6. Sewing *five* holes: (See figure 2)

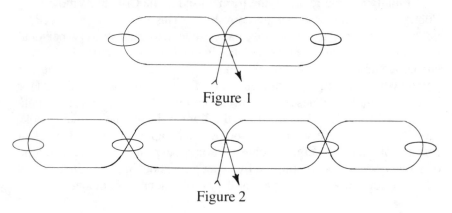

Figure 1

Figure 2

7. Firm up stitches. Tie ends so that long inner stitch is caught up and held in knot. Clip ends short.
8. Close book. Crease fold and press folded section under a weight for a bit.

Preparing and attaching the boards: (Work with book closed.)
1. Cut two pieces of cardboard. Each should be at least ¼" *longer* than signature fold and at least ⅛" *shorter* than signature width.
2. Spread paste along one side of hinge. (From now on place waxed paper between signature and cover to protect signature from paste. Change waxed paper each time book is moved around.)
3. Place one board along hinge so board extends ⅛"–½" beyond top, bottom, and open side of signature. Hinge piece stays on inside of board.
4. Turn book over and repeat for other board.
5. Close book. Protect with waxed paper above, below, and within and place under weight until paste dries.

Covering spine: (Work with book closed.)
1. Use strip of cloth several inches longer than spine and wide enough to partially cover boards.
2. Apply paste to one board, lay spine covering on board, straighten, and press.

3. Wrap cloth around spine and repeat for other side.
4. Weight folded book until glue dries.
5. Trim end of spine covering to ¾″–1″ longer than spine. Slit length-wise, and paste to inside of boards at top and bottom.

Covering boards:
1. Use wrapping paper, adhesive paper, or cloth.
2. Cut covering large enough to overlap spine covering and to extend ½″ at top, bottom, and front of each board.
3. Spread paste on outside of one board. Press covering onto board, overlapping spine covering slightly. (If cloth is used for covering, a selvage looks neater for overlap.) Smooth cover carefully.
4. Fold edges over board. Paste down on inside of board. (Miter corners.)
5. Repeat for other side.
6. Weight and dry.

Endpapers: Paste endpapers to inside of boards, covering everything up.

Simplifications

These result in a less attractive and less usable book.
1. Use attractive material for the boards. Stop after attaching boards. (A heavyweight greeting card could be used.)
2. Use staples rather than stitches in center fold.
3. For hinge use a piece of cloth large enough to serve as a cover.
4. Do not fold sheets. Use cloth or flexible plastic rather than boards. Punch holes along side of flat, full sheets and through covering material. Stitch with yarn or shoelaces, using the basic binding stitches. (This method looks particularly good for children's books, and it has the advantage of permitting the number of pages to be determined without much planning.)

Elaborations

1. When book is completed, cover may be lettered, pictures and designs added.
2. It is possible to sew several signatures to one hinge. This doesn't work very well, but it permits more text to be bound.
3. Cover may be extended to be much larger than pages.

Selecting Poetry: Resources

by Charles R. Duke

Time and again, when asked about what literary form they find most difficult to teach, English teachers usually identify poetry. The reasons for this may vary: lack of appropriate training on the part of teachers, student misconceptions about poetry, or, often as not, the inappropriateness of the selections used to introduce students to poetry.

Faced with the problem of finding appropriate poetry for young people, harassed teachers typically turn to the most immediate resource: the literature textbook. Here, teachers reason, one should find all the material necessary to spark students' interest. Several selections later, combined with several class periods later of muffled and not so muffled groans, sighs, and outright hostility, chastened teachers throw up their hands and come to the conclusion that nothing works. Here endeth the poetry unit.

Such experiences need not be the case. If we want to make any gains in helping students develop an appreciation and liking for poetry, we will need to expend much more effort in locating poems which students can respond to and find meaningful. To accomplish this, the teacher will need to spend a good deal of time becoming familiar with what is available in poetry—and that is no easy task, since poems appear in many places besides the traditional literary text: magazines, newspapers, gravestones, advertisements, television, songs, student writing, computers, and bathroom walls.

Many of the previously mentioned sources can be used only if the teacher remains alert to their existence and diligently collects samples as appropriate works appear. On the other hand, familiarity with a wide number of collections also can give the teacher a substantial body of poetry to draw upon and then supplement with selections from the other sources. In making selections from any source, however, the collector needs to keep several principles in mind.

1. *Select poems which deal with experiences that students can relate to.*

   Such selection does not mean that one must always choose contemporary works—although a good number of poems should come from modern times—but that the experience of the poem should be one accessible to students, either through their own experiences of a similar nature or through interest in the particular theme or concept.

2. *Select poems which can be grasped for their basic meaning in one reading.*

   Probably no greater damage has been done to the appreciation of poetry in students' eyes than forcing them to read poems which teachers wrestled with in undergraduate and graduate courses where line by line analysis and glossing were the principal activities, not the reader's response. Naturally, at some time in the students' experiences with poetry, they should encounter poems which stretch the mind and require considerable intellectual discipline in order to achieve understanding, but a steady diet of such works is the quickest route to apathy or outright hostility whenever poetry is mentioned. Selection should also mean that vocabulary is within reach of the student; an occasional unknown word is fine, but the student should not have to spend considerable time looking up unfamiliar words or consulting footnotes in order to achieve appreciation of the poem; the same may be said for images and symbols. The poem should not be overly long; shorter poems mean that more reading, oral and silent, can take place in one class period and a poem can be heard several times for several different reasons.

3. *Select poems which represent a variety of forms and language.*

   Traditionally, students seem to favor poems that rhyme and are somewhat humorous. Ann Terry in *Children's Poetry Preferences: A National Survey of Upper Elementary Grades* (National Council of Teachers of English, 1974) discovered that the 25 most popular poems among upper elementary students contained definite rhyming patterns. A review of collections of children's literature most frequently used in the early grades reveals that the majority of selections do, indeed, contain distinct rhyming patterns. Conditioned to believe this is the norm, students faced with unrhymed verse often reject it as not being "poetry." While acknowledging the existence of rhyme in poetry, teachers may want to introduce gradually poems which further the recognition of cadence and sounds and of the difference between prose and poetic utterance.

4. *Select only those poems for which the teacher can develop an enthusiasm.*

This advice may, at first glance, seem contradictory, since many teachers have been selecting works for which they have great interest and enthusiasm. However, it is primarily a case of using what you are most familiar with; for example, in the Terry study, of the 41 poems most frequently read by teachers to students, only four were written after 1928. Such information suggests that teachers need to become familiar with more contemporary works for which they may also engender some enthusiasm because it is these ''older'' poems which so many students seem to reject.

5. *Select poems that have been identified by students as favorites, or poems that they willingly want to read, study, and discuss, for use with future classes.*

Many teachers have found that their best lessons on poetry occur when the students themselves are allowed to select the works to be studied. Providing students with collections of poetry and encouraging them to consult some of the sources mentioned earlier, teachers will inevitably find poetry becoming a more natural part of classroom activity. This free selection is not without surprises for the teacher used to dealing with the ''old favorites.'' Rock lyrics, graffitti, and greeting card verse may all surface as student selections; but if teachers want to have equal time with their choices, then the same courtesy ought to be extended to students and their selections. Often such a mix produces a deeper appreciation for the strengths and weaknesses in all poetry.

Although placing grade level designations on types of poetry is not the most reliable means for arriving at a selection process—because it suggests a growth pattern that may not always reflect the true reading and interest levels of a class—the following general summaries may prove somewhat helpful:

Grades 5–8:
Students at this level tend to like story poems, folk ballads, humorous selections, and poems about animals and heroes; very short lyric

poems and selections with strong rhyme schemes and a definite meter seem to work well. Students at this level, however, should also have some introduction to poems without the strong rhyme.

Grades 9–10:
Students at this level can appreciate haiku and popular song lyrics as poetry; however, the liking for haiku may not be as widespread as once believed; students find it difficult to grasp the "frozen moment" of the traditional Japanese haiku although the simplicity of the form appeals to them. Concrete poetry for some students may stir strong interest; short lyric poems, dramatic poems, and free verse poems about modern life, adolescence, and nature meet with favorable response.

Grades 11–12:
Many students at this age can handle longer lyric poems, blank verse, and some of the traditional poetic forms such as the sonnet, literary ballad, and dramatic monologue. Poems exploring contemporary problems of love, death, human frailty, protest and identity remain popular with students.

The primary source for finding such poetry remains the anthology. A collection of poetry can be a quick and easy reference tool, simple to dip into for those few moments at the end of a class period when one wants to read a piece out loud just for the ideas or for the mood; or the anthology can be a source for sustained study. But simply having an anthology available does not solve the selection problem. Many poems which appear in anthologies do not work well when it comes to stimulating student interest in poetry. Therefore, a teacher must be quite familiar with the contents of many collections and select only those poems which will be appropriate for particular students. For the same reason, a particular anthology should not be kept too long as a prime resource. New collections appear frequently, and the teacher should attempt to become familiar with these, selecting those which seem to have the most appropriate selections to add to a desk or room collection.

The following list of anthologies, all available in paperback, suggests the richness of the field. No attempt has been made to deal with the myriad volumes of individual authors' works; the teacher seeking information on such materials should consult a reference such as *Granger's Index to Poetry* (New York: Columbia University Press, 7th ed., 1982) or the *Index to Children's Poetry* (New York: H. W. Wilson Company, 1965). Instead, an attempt has been made to offer a representative listing so that teachers may see what is available and start to compile a listing for themselves. In most cases, emphasis has been placed upon identifying collections of contemporary writers.

Representative Poetry Anthologies

Adoff, Arnold, ed. *Black Out Loud, An Anthology of Modern Poems by Black Americans*. New York: Dell, 1975.
> Selected as an ALA Notable Book and *New York Times* Outstanding Book, this collection offers an excellent sampling of modern Black poetry. The poems contain direct, vivid language which will appeal to young people.

Benedikt, Michael, ed. *The Prose Poem, An International Anthology*. New York: Dell, 1976.
> Although this collection is not poetry in the literal sense of the word, it is an anthology which shows a form of prose written with intense use of poetic devices. Arranged chronologically by country, the selections should offer the teacher some interesting material for comparison with recognized poems.

Bennett, George, and Malloy, Paul, eds. *Cavalcade of Poems*. New York: Scholastic, 1968.
> This anthology has proven useful with students; the poems are grouped under the following headings: poems of observation, narrative poems, heroic poems, poems of experience, poems in pairs for comparison, poems of the challenge of life, and a range beyond. The poems are short and accessible to average or above average readers.

Bettenbender, John, ed. *Poetry Festival*. New York: Dell, 1966.
> This book provides a mixture of poets from the past—Longfellow, Whittier, Keats and Poe—along with poets of more recent times such as Frost, Yeats and Joyce. A good collection for dipping into and as a resource for students.

Bich, Nguyen Ngoc, ed. *A Thousand Years of Vietnamese Poetry*. New York: Alfred A. Knopf, 1975.
> Although this anthology will not be for use in every class, the collection contains some poems which should pique student interest. It is arranged in four divisions: the scholarly tradition, the popular tradition, the rise of a national poetry, and modern times. Brief commentary provides an introduction to each section of the text and explains some of the special aspects of Vietnamese life.

Bierhorst, John, ed. *In the Trail of the Wind, American Indian Poems and Ritual Orations*. New York: Dell, 1971.
> American Indian literature is just beginning to be recognized for its proper place in our literary heritage; this collection provides a good introduction to the field. Students will be intrigued by the subject matter and the attitudes reflected in these poems.

Carruth, Hayden, ed. *The Voice that Is Great within Us: American Poetry of the Twentieth Century*. New York: Bantam, 1970.

The works of over 130 major American poets of the modern period are included in this collection; for a picture of the range of modern poetry, this volume should prove indispensable. It is not, however, a collection that one would want to use completely with a class.

Charge of the Light Brigade and Other Story Poems. New York: Scholastic, 1969.

This valuable collection of narrative poems is suitable for use with a wide range of students. It represents a variety of historical and literary story poems grouped under the following headings: patriotism and adventure ("The Charge of the Light Brigade," "Old Ironsides"); fun and fantasy ("Cremation of Sam McGee," "Casey at the Bat"); the famous and the infamous ("Gunga Din," "Jesse James"); ballads of yesterday and today ("Lord Randal," "Ode to Billy Joe"); poems of the heart ("The Creation," "Annabel Lee"); and the world today ("Mother to Son," "The Unknown").

Dunning, Stephen, ed. *Mad, Sad and Glad*. New York: Scholastic, 1972.

Poems in this collection were selected from those submitted for Scholastic's Creative Writing Awards. Many of the poems are certain to speak to young people because of the subject matter: love, fun, death, relationships. Students will be encouraged to write their own poems after seeing the work of other student poets.

Dunning, Stephen, and others, eds. *Reflections on a Gift of Watermelon Pickle. . . .* New York: Scholastic, 1966.

This anthology, originally published by Scott, Foresman, is one of the most popular collections with adolescents. Poems range from the serious to the humorous and span a number of years, although most of the authors are from the twentieth century. Appropriate photographs are interspersed throughout the book. A definite "must" for every poetry shelf.

Eaton, M. Joe, and Glass, Malcolm, eds. *Grab Me a Bus. . . .* New York: Scholastic, 1974.

Another collection of poems from the Scholastic Writing Awards, the poems are short and reflect adolescent concerns. Photographs, also by students, accompany many of the poems.

Field, Edward, ed. *A Geography of Poets*. New York: Bantam, 1979.

The more than 200 poets represented in this collection suggest the regional and cultural diversity of modern poetry. Poems in this anthology will probably have to be selected carefully for use with adolescents since much of the material is for mature readers.

Goldstein, Richard, ed. *The Poetry of Rock*. New York: Bantam, 1969.

This collection has been one of the most consistently popular anthologies of rock lyrics; Goldstein's informal and lively comments about the works of

Bob Dylan, Lennon-McCartney, Paul Simon, Donovan, and The Doors add value to the text. Somewhat dated now, it nevertheless remains popular with young people.

Haiku Poetry: A Children's Collection. New York: Bantam, n.d.

This anthology was created from the writings of four- to eight-year-old children in the Wilhelm School of Houston, Texas. The various haiku show a strong relationship to the traditional Japanese form and should prompt considerable interest and writing from students of various ages.

Halpern, Daniel, ed. *The American Poetry Anthology*. New York: Avon, 1975.

This anthology presents the works of poets whose poetry has been published since 1968. An excellent resource for becoming familiar with some of our most recent poets.

Joseph, Stephen M., ed. *The Me Nobody Knows*. New York: Avon, 1972.

Writers of the selections in this anthology are ghetto children. The poems touch upon family life, loneliness, neighborhoods, the world beyond, and fantasy. Seeing and reading these poems, students should be encouraged to produce some of their own.

Kenseth, Arnold, ed. *Poems of Protest Old and New*. New York: Macmillan Company, 1968.

This thematic collection draws on poems from a variety of cultures and time periods. Some of the poems may appear dated and may not be entirely accessible to some students upon first reading. However, the universality of this theme through the ages can be easily demonstrated through use of some of these selections.

Klonsky, Milton, ed. *The Best of Modern Poetry*. New York: Pocket Books, 1975.

This collection of over 300 British and American poems represents a good spectrum of modern poetry. Although it is an anthology of "adult" poetry, judicious use of the volume with older students should yield profitable moments. Of particular value are the inclusion of some lesser known poets, samples of concrete poetry, and less frequently anthologized pieces by well-known poets.

Knudson, R. R., and Ebert, P. K., eds. *Sports Poems*. New York: Dell, 1971.

A collection which ought to surprise a good number of students, particularly boys, it includes poems about football, baseball, basketball, and a number of minor sports. Poets include John Updike, May Swenson, James Dickey, Ogden Nash, and Carl Sandburg.

Larrick, Nancy, ed. *On City Streets*. New York: Bantam, 1968.

Short selections supported by black and white photographs focus on various aspects of city life. This is a popular anthology where poets such as Carl Sandburg, John Berryman, Langston Hughes, and Walt Whitman rub pages with lesser known writers like Gregory Corso, Joseph March, Tom Prideaux.

Lee, Al, ed. *The Major Young Poets*. New York: New American
Library, n.d.
This anthology contains the works of such poets as Marvin Bell, Michael
Benedikt, William Brown, Charles Simic, and others. It provides a view of
the directions some of our modern poets are going; selections are most
appropriate for mature readers.

Lewis, Richard, ed. *Miracles: Poems by Children of the English-Speaking
World*. New York: Bantam, 1977.
The value of this collection lies in its diversity; here are nearly 200 poems
written by children around the world, their ages ranging from 5 to 13. A
valuable stimulus for getting students to write their own poems.

Morse, David, ed. *Grandfather Rock*. New York: Dell, 1973.
This popular collection provides a comparison of rock lyrics and classical
poetry; the case is clearly made that both are based on the need to express
human thoughts and feelings. A valuable resource for dealing with the
popularity of modern song lyrics.

Niebling, Richard A. *A Journey of Poems*. New York: Dell, 1964.
Although this anthology has been available for some time, it remains a highly
popular one with students and teachers. The editor indicates that one of the
principles for including a selection was that it has worked with students for a
number of years. The collection is somewhat thematic and somewhat
chronological in organization; the text is one that fairly verbal students
should enjoy.

Palgrave, F. T. *The Golden Treasury*. New York: New American
Library, 1944.
Revised and updated, it contains 690 selections ranging from the sixteenth
century to the present. A valuable reference work.

Payne, Robert, ed. *The White Pony*. New York: New American
Library, n.d.
Few students will be aware of the traditions in Chinese poetry; this collection
offers examples of poetry spanning 3,000 years, from the Chou Dynasty in
1112 B.C. to the present. Certainly not for everyone, the collection still may
yield some interesting selections for better students.

Peck, Richard, ed. *Pictures that Storm Inside My Head: Poems for
the Inner You*. New York: Avon, 1976.
Designed to appeal to secondary school young people, this anthology addresses such themes as youth, life and death, role playing, and youth from
the perspectives of adulthood. Most students should be able to find a number
of selections that appeal to them.

―――. *Sounds and Silences*. New York: Dell, 1970.
Collected especially for adolescents, the selections in this anthology speak to
such concerns as family, childhood, isolation, identity, realities, illusion,
dissent, communication, love, war, pain, and recollections. A very useful
thematic collection.

Randall, Dudley, ed. *The Black Poets*. New York: Bantam, 1971.

> The anthology covers Black American poetry from the slave songs through the 1960s. Photographs and critical biographies of the poets are included. The range is sufficient so that the teacher should find a number of selections suitable for a variety of audiences.

Ryan, Betsy, ed. *Search the Silence: Poems of Self-Discovery*. New York: Scholastic, 1974.

> This collection contains mostly contemporary poems, a section of quotations, and a section of songs. The themes of loneliness and self-discovery form the organizational structure. Photographs accompany some of the selections.

Ryan, Betsy, ed. *Sounds of Silence*. New York: Scholastic, 1975.

> This slim volume—96 pages—contains both prose and poetry, but primarily the latter. Included as part of the poetry are lyrics from a number of popular songs. All selections key on the central theme of loneliness. Students will recognize easily a number of the sources, and the mixture of such poets as T. S. Eliot ("The Hollow Men") and Bob Dylan should provide a basis for interesting discussion.

Strand, Mark, ed. *The Contemporary American Poets*. New York: New American Library, 1969.

> A collection of poets who have written since 1940, it is useful as a reference and as a resource. Probably not appropriate as a class text.

Warren, Robert Penn, and Erskine, Albert, eds. *Six Centuries of Great Poetry*. New York: Dell, n.d.

> This anthology has been a popular one at both the secondary and college levels. It provides an extensive collection of English lyric poetry by more than 100 poets, ranging from Chaucer to Yeats. Excellent resource for the more traditional poetry.

Index

Compiled by Frederick Ramey